The Literature Student's Survival Kit

About the author:

Ian Littlewood has taught for many years at the University of Sussex as well as at universities in France, America, and Japan. He is the author of a number of books on literature, travel, and history, including *The Writings of Evelyn Waugh* (1983), literary guides to Paris and Venice (1987 and 1991), *The Idea of Japan* (1996), *Sultry Climates* (2001), and the Rough Guide *History of France* (2002).

Praise for *The Literature Student's Survival Kit*:

"What do Shadrach, Meshach, Abednego and the Private of the Buffs have in common? What are Tabitha or Hecuba for you? When did the Porteous riots begin, when was the hearth tax abandoned? Littlewood's *Survival Kit* provides all the answers to similar vexing questions, queries that students and teachers alike won't have time to "google" accurately. This is the best and most up-to-date compendium of essential facts drawn from biblical lore, universal history, literary chronologies, lists of tropes and poetic movements – a desperately needed survival kit for those who face our current mixture of information overload and short term memory."

J.-M. Rabaté, University of Pennsylvania

"*The Literature Student's Survival Kit* is a remarkably useful collection of information of sure value to many students of literature. Written in a measured way, it presents with both clarity and grace a wide but manageable range of knowledge – historical, political, cultural, biographical, mythological, theological – that will help open up the textures of literary texts, past and present, for readers without that information already at their fingertips. Littlewood's text offers the kind of knowledge – accessibly laid out, accessibly written – that a reader so often needs to know in order to enable informed and sensitive literary interpretation. A book not only valuable but enjoyable too."

Francis O'Gorman, University of Leeds

"This is exactly the kind of book I wish I'd had as a student. It introduces and explains the unfamiliar: the Bible, classics, history. A remarkable combination of explanation, encyclopedia, glossary and database – an indispensable *vade mecum*. It contains fascinating insights as well as useful facts. How can a reference work be so readable?"

Laurie Maguire, University of Oxford

The Literature Student's Survival Kit

What Every Reader Needs to Know

Ian Littlewood

Vincennes University
Shake Learning Resources Center
Vincennes, In 47591-9986

Blackwell
Publishing

BLACKWELL PUBLISHING
350 Main Street, Malden, MA 02148-5020, USA
9600 Garsington Road, Oxford OX4 2DQ, UK
550 Swanston Street, Carlton, Victoria 3053, Australia

First published 2006 by Blackwell Publishing Ltd

1   2006

Library of Congress Cataloging-in-Publication Data
Littlewood, Ian.
    The literature student's survival kit : what every reader needs to know
/ Ian Littlewood.
        p. cm.
    Includes bibliographical references and index.
    ISBN-13: 978-1-4051-2284-9 (hardcover : alk. paper)
    ISBN-10: 1-4051-2284-6 (hardcover : alk. paper)
    ISBN-13: 978-1-4051-2285-6 (pbk. : alk. paper)
    ISBN-10: 1-4051-2285-4 (pbk. : alk. paper)
    1. Allusions. 2. Literature. I. Title.
PN43.L585 2006
809′.891821—dc22

                                                                2005023309

A catalogue record for this title is available from the British Library.

Set in 9.5/14pt Bell Gothic
by Graphicraft Limited, Hong Kong
Printed and bound in the United Kingdom
by TJ International Ltd, Padstow, Cornwall

For further information on
Blackwell Publishing, visit our website:
www.blackwellpublishing.com

For Ayumi and Hanako

Contents

Foreword

Who was Absalom? What was Deism? When was the Industrial Revolution? How do you tell a strong rhyme from a weak? And why should Tiresias watch a small house agent's clerk having sex? If you already know the answers, then this book is probably not for you. If you don't . . . does it really matter?

At times, it matters in quite precise ways – when, for example, you read Dryden and turn to *Absalom and Achitophel*, when you read *Tom Jones* and find that one of Tom's tutors is a Deist, when you read *The Waste Land* and try to make sense of Eliot's claim that Tiresias is "the most important personage in the poem." Editorial notes will help, but they quickly turn reading into a chore: the more you have to rely on them, the more of an academic exercise it becomes. To some extent, this is inevitable. There will always be things you need to look up, just as there will always be words that send you back to a dictionary; but reading the literature of the past does not have to be like struggling with a foreign language. A relatively narrow range of knowledge can make a huge difference to how much you understand.

This is important because it's a kind of freedom, but there are less tangible considerations that are equally important. Writers of the Romantic period may not refer specifically to the French Revolution, but it was in the air they breathed; it had a vital effect on the way they thought and felt and wrote. Victorian novelists may not refer specifically to the Industrial Revolution, but it seeps into a thousand details of the world they create. To approach literary texts without some knowledge of their background is to impoverish the experience of reading them. And this applies to more than grand movements of history. John

McAdam was a civil engineer; he was also the main reason why coach journeys in Dickens are so different from those in Fielding. The Sermon on the Mount is a collection of religious precepts; it's also a recurring presence in every strand of English culture from Milton to Monty Python. But to be aware of this you need a basis from which to start. You have to know the event, the person, the passage, before you can recognize its influence.

Not surprisingly, students often find themselves at a loss. Until the middle of the last century there was a common culture that writers in English could expect most of their readers to share. It was drawn from the King James Bible, the classics, and a schoolroom version of British history. Between them these three provided a reservoir of stories and characters, themes and phrases that could be tapped at will. They reached into almost every kind of educated discourse. But what used to be common currency has now grown less familiar. As a result, the literature of past centuries seems more obscure, its cultural landscape more alien.

The answer, of course, is to return to the Bible and the classics, to study the cultural and social background, to learn the history of the period. But life is short and the required reading is long. Hence this book, whose first three parts are designed to offer a simple map of the territory. Read them, refer to them, and you should be able to cope. The fourth part is slightly different in that the background material is more academic than cultural. There are certain things you need to know in order to talk and write effectively about literature. Since some of them are less often taught in school than they used to be, I've tried to fill the more obvious gaps.

In a book of this kind, where the scope for further reading is endless, bibliographies tend to be decorative rather than practical – too short and too soon out of date. Ten minutes at a computer will give you a better idea of what's available in any particular field; specialist bibliographies will take you on from there. The low-tech option of browsing the library shelves may seem like an embarrassingly casual alternative, but it's still a useful way to turn up something unexpected. It's also one of the pleasures of studying literature.

Note on the text

Where it seemed helpful, I've put certain names in bold to signal their importance. Those with an asterisk have a separate entry elsewhere in the same section or on the page indicated in brackets. American spellings have been used in preference to British at the request of the publisher.

Acknowledgments

Several friends and colleagues have helped me with advice and suggestions. In particular, I'd like to thank Andrew Gibson, Duncan Fraser, Lyn Thomas, Ella Dzelzainis, Martin Dzelzainis, Rachel Bowlby, and Jonathan Dollimore. As always, the greatest debt by far is to my wife Ayumi.

The author and publisher wish to thank the following for permission to use copyright material:

"In a Station of the Metro" by Ezra Pound, from *Personae*, copyright © 1926 by Ezra Pound. Reprinted by permission of New Directions Publishing Corp.

"Leda and the Swan" by W. B. Yeats, from *The Collected Works of W. B. Yeats, Volume 1: The Poems, Revised*, edited by Richard J. Finneran. Copyright © 1928 by The Macmillan Company; copyright renewed © 1956 by Georgie Yeats. Reprinted by permission of Scribner, an imprint of Simon & Schuster Adult Publishing Group, and by A. P. Watt Ltd on behalf of Michael B. Yeats.

Map "The Retreat from Empire," from the *Oxford Companion to British History*, edited by John Cannon (Oxford: Oxford University Press, 1997). Reprinted by permission of Oxford University Press.

Maps "Coach Journey Times from London *c.* 1750," "Coach Journey Times from London in the 1830s," "The Railway System *c.* 1850," and "The Completed Railway Network *c.* 1890," from the *Atlas of British Social and Economic History since c. 1700*, by Rex Pope (London: Routledge, 1990).

Every effort has been made to trace copyright holders and to obtain their permission for the use of copyright material. The author and publisher will gladly receive any information enabling them to rectify any error or omission in subsequent editions.

Maps

Part 1

Surviving the Bible

The Bible (Greek *biblia* = books) is made up of a number of texts written at different times and later arranged into the **Old Testament**, the **New Testament**, and the **Apocrypha**. The aim of this part is to provide enough information for you to make sense of the biblical references, echoes, and quotations that permeate western art and literature. To give the dictionary some sort of context, I've prefaced it with a few details about the composition and historical framework of the Bible. Among general studies of the Bible's impact on literature, you'll find helpful material in *The Literary Guide to the Bible* (Collins, 1987) edited by Robert Alter and Frank Kermode and also in *The Bible and Literature: A Reader* by David Jasper and Stephen Prickett (Blackwell, 1999). For tracing sources and comparing texts, Alexander Cruden's *Complete Concordance to the Old and New Testaments*, first published in 1737, is a book that even now computer searches have not entirely replaced.

BOOKS OF THE BIBLE

Old Testament

Originally written in Hebrew, with a few passages of Aramaic, most of the Old Testament was composed between the tenth and third centuries BC. Some of its 24 books were further divided during the Reformation to make a total of 39. They are grouped into the Law, the Prophets, and the Writings.

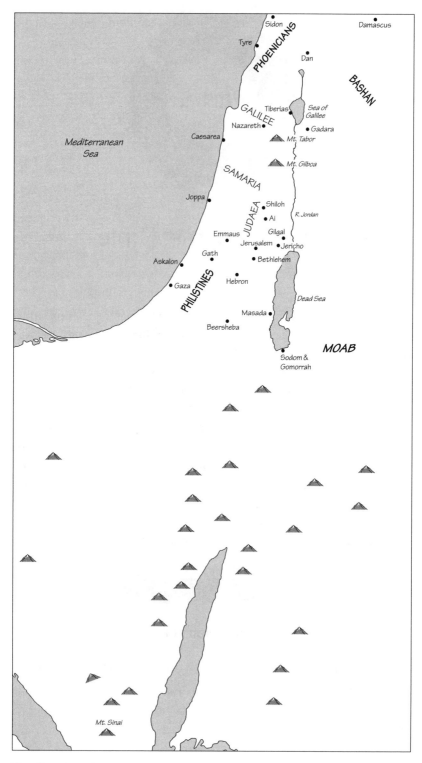

Map 1 The Biblical World

The Law (Torah): the first five books, known as the **Pentateuch** – Genesis, Exodus, Leviticus, Numbers, and Deuteronomy.

The Prophets: Joshua, Judges, Samuel, Kings, Isaiah, Jeremiah, Ezekiel; and the minor prophets: Hosea, Joel, Amos, Obadiah, Jonah, Micah, Nahum, Habakkuk, Zephaniah, Haggai, Zechariah, Malachi.

The Writings: Psalms, Proverbs, Job, Ruth, Song of Solomon, Lamentations, Ecclesiastes, Esther, Daniel, Ezra and Nehemiah, Chronicles.

Apocrypha

The texts which make up the Apocrypha (Greek = *hidden things*) were not part of the Hebrew Bible and are generally excluded from Protestant versions. They were, however, included in the **Septuagint** (see below) and are accepted as authoritative by the Roman Catholic Church. The Apocrypha consists of the following books: I and II Esdras, Tobit, Judith, additions to the Book of Esther, the Wisdom of Solomon, Ecclesiasticus, Baruch with the Epistle of Jeremy, the Song of the Three Holy Children, the History of Susanna, Bel and the Dragon, the Prayer of Manasses, I and II Maccabees.

New Testament

The **New Testament** is made up of 27 books: the four gospels, Acts, 21 epistles, and Revelation. They were all written in Greek, mainly in the second half of the first century AD. The authors of the gospels – St. Matthew, St. Mark, St. Luke, and St. John – are referred to as evangelists, the words *gospel* and *evangelist* coming respectively from the Old English and the Greek for "good news."

Books of the Bible: Old Testament

GENESIS The Creation and Fall; Noah and the Flood; the story of Abraham; Esau and Jacob; Joseph and his brothers; the establishment of Jacob and his family in Egypt.

EXODUS The story of Moses; Israel's slavery in Egypt; the ten plagues; the escape across the Red Sea; wanderings in the wilderness; the Golden Calf; the Ten Commandments.

LEVITICUS Instructions from God on issues concerning sacrifice, the priest-hood, clean and holy living. The book's name derives from its concern with the priestly functions carried out by members of the tribe of Levi.

NUMBERS Wanderings in the wilderness and early conquests; the approach to Canaan. The book's name refers to the census taken by Moses and Aaron on God's instructions.

DEUTERONOMY Laws, ordinances, exhortations, and prophecies. The book concludes with the death of Moses on the edge of the Promised Land.

JOSHUA Entry into the Promised Land; early conquests by the Israelites, includ-ing the capture of Jericho; allocation of land to the tribes; death of Joshua.

JUDGES The period between Joshua and the establishment of a monarchy, in-cluding the defeat of Sisera by Deborah and Barak, Gideon's victory over the Midianites, and the stories of Jephthah and Samson. By the end of the book, the Israelites are descending into anarchy.

RUTH The story of Ruth (see p. 52).

SAMUEL, 1 and 2 The calling of Samuel; the institution of the monarchy; the kingship of Saul; the rise of David; his reign over Israel; the rebellion of Absalom.

KINGS, 1 and 2 The period (over three and a half centuries) from Solomon to the beginning of the exile: the reign of Solomon; Elijah; Elisha; Ahab and Jezebel; the destruction of Jerusalem by Nebuchadnezzar.

CHRONICLES, 1 and 2 They cover more or less the same events as Samuel and Kings, supplying genealogies and sanitizing the behavior of David and Solomon.

EZRA and **NEHEMIAH** Originally one book, they cover the return from exile and the rebuilding of Jerusalem's Temple and walls.

ESTHER The story of Esther (see p. 23).

JOB The story of Job (see p. 33).

PSALMS The longest book in the Bible. The 150 Psalms (from the Greek word for a song accompanied on a stringed instrument) have been traditionally but implausibly attributed to David.

PROVERBS A collection of proverbial sayings and moral advice inaccurately attributed to Solomon. Their final form probably dates from about the fifth century BC.

ECCLESIASTES A collection of skeptical observations about the nature of life and the pursuit of satisfaction. Its composition may be as recent as the late third century BC.

SONG OF SOLOMON (also known as the **SONG OF SONGS)** A collection of love poems attributed to Solomon but actually written much later. They have been dubiously allegorized by commentators uneasy about their erotic content.

ISAIAH God's punishment of the kingdom of Judah (see p. 36), manifested in conquest by the Assyrians and Babylonians; prophecies of salvation from exile and sin.

JEREMIAH God's judgment on Jerusalem, manifested in the capture of the city by Nebuchadnezzar.

LAMENTATIONS Five poems of lament inspired by the destruction of Jerusalem. The tradition ascribing them to Jeremiah has been discredited.

EZEKIEL Visions and meditations inspired by Israel's captivity.

DANIEL Includes Daniel's interpretation of Nebuchadnezzar's dreams, the story of Shadrach, Meshach, and Abednego, Daniel in the lion's den, and Belshazzar's feast. The last part of the book is concerned with Daniel's visions.

HOSEA; JOEL; AMOS; OBADIAH Minor prophetic books.

JONAH The story of Jonah (see p. 34).

MICAH; NAHUM; HABBAKUK; ZEPHANIAH; HAGGAI; ZECHARIAH; MALACHI Minor prophetic books.

Books of the Bible: New Testament

MATTHEW; MARK; LUKE The synoptic gospels — so called because their accounts of the life of Jesus have a shared perspective. In contrast to John, they cover much the same ground in much the same way.

JOHN The fourth gospel. Like the other three, it deals with the life and ministry of Jesus, but there are significant differences in detail and theological emphasis.

ACTS The spread of the gospel following Jesus's resurrection: the ascension; Pentecost; Peter's deliverance from prison; Stephen's martyrdom; Paul's conversion, preaching, arrest, and journey to Rome.

ROMANS; 1 and 2 CORINTHIANS; GALATIANS; EPHESIANS; PHILIPPIANS; COLOSSIANS; 1 and 2 THESSALONIANS; 1 and 2 TIMOTHY; TITUS; PHILEMON; HEBREWS Epistles from Paul to a variety of groups and individuals in the early church concerning issues of spiritual health, theology, and conduct.

JAMES; 1 and 2 PETER; 1, 2, and 3 JOHN; JUDE General epistles from these figures, giving advice and exhortation to the faithful.

REVELATION The last book of the Bible, containing the apocalyptic vision of the seven seals and leading up to a vision of God's holy city in heaven, the new Jerusalem. Though ascribed to St. John, the book is no longer thought to have been written by him.

HISTORICAL FRAMEWORK

Old Testament

After the legendary time of Adam and Noah, the Old Testament enters a recognizable historical framework with the figure of Abraham. Dates remain highly speculative, but we can think of the period from Abraham to King David as stretching through the second millenium BC. This covers the settling of Abraham and his descendants in Canaan, the famine that drives Jacob and his sons to the protection of Joseph in Egypt, the period of enslavement under the

Egyptians, the Exodus and wanderings in the wilderness (perhaps occurring in the thirteenth century BC), and finally the reestablishment of the Israelites in the Promised Land of Canaan. The kingdoms of David and Solomon in the tenth century BC are the high point of Israel's Old Testament history. Afterwards came the division of the kingdom into Israel and Judah, and subjection successively to the empires of the Assyrians, the Babylonians and the Persians.

These are some relevant dates in the pre-Christian period:

BC

20C–17C	The time of the patriarchs – Abraham, Isaac, and Jacob.
17C–16C	Joseph in Egypt.
mid-13C	Exodus from Egypt, during the reign of Ramses II.
12C–11C	Period of the Judges, during which Israel is conquered by the Philistines.
ca. 1020	Saul becomes king of Israel and takes up arms against the Philistines.
ca. 1000	David succeeds Saul as king of Israel.
ca. 961	Solomon succeeds David as king of Israel.
mid-10C	Building of the Temple at Jerusalem.
922	Rehoboam succeeds Solomon as king of Israel, but a rebellion led by Jeroboam splits the kingdom, leaving Rehoboam in control of the southern kingdom of Judah and Jeroboam as king of the northern kingdom of Israel.
mid-9C	Jehu leads a rebellion against King Ahab's son and successor, Jehoram (or Joram), and founds a new dynasty.
722	The Assyrians capture Samaria, Israel's capital, and bring the kingdom to an end. The ten tribes who inhabited the kingdom are deported and disappear from history, becoming the "Lost Tribes."
late 7C	The Babylonians conquer the Assyrians.
late 6C	Darius I, king of Persia, authorizes the rebuilding the Temple.
586	Nebuchadnezzar II, the Babylonian king, sacks Jerusalem, destroying the Temple and bringing the kingdom of Judah to an end. Many of the inhabitants are deported to exile in Babylon.
539	The Persian king Cyrus the Great conquers Babylon.
538	The edict of Cyrus allows some of the captive Israelites to return from exile in Babylon.
mid-5C	Nehemiah, as governor of Judah, oversees the rebuilding of the walls of Jerusalem.

332	Alexander the Great defeats the Persians and conquers Palestine, which later comes under the control of the Seleucid dynasty established by one of his generals.
164	Judas Maccabeus leads a rebellion that ousts the Seleucid ruler Antiochus IV, who has desecrated the Temple by instituting the worship of Zeus. Palestine becomes an independent state under the Maccabees.
63	Pompey captures Jerusalem, putting an end to Maccabee rule and making Palestine part of the Roman empire.

New Testament

The New Testament is concerned with the first six decades of the Christian era. The period covers Jesus's life and also that of St. Paul, whose execution probably took place in AD 62 or 64.

THE BIBLE IN ENGLISH

It's worth having some basic information about translations of the Bible. The first milestone was the Greek version of the Old Testament known as the **Septuagint**, produced in Alexandria by 70 scholars (hence its name) in the third and second centuries BC. For medieval Europe, the most important translation was the Latin version by St. Jerome known as the **Vulgate**. Taken from the original Hebrew and Greek, it was completed in AD 405. This was the standard version of the Bible in the Middle Ages and the source used for the earliest, fragmentary, translations into English by **Bede*** and the Anglo-Saxon monk **Aelfric**. It was also the basis of **John Wycliffe's*** translation of the whole Bible in the late fourteenth century.

The central figure in the Renaissance is **William Tyndale**,* whose translations from the original languages in the early sixteenth century laid the groundwork for later versions. They also brought him to the stake for heresy. In 1535 **Miles Coverdale** was responsible for the first English translation of the whole Bible to be printed. This was followed by a number of other sixteenth-century versions, notably the 1560 Geneva Bible, which remained the most commonly used translation until the **Authorised Version**, or **King James Bible**, was published in 1611. Commissioned by the **Hampton Court Conference** in 1604 and produced from the earliest known Hebrew and Greek texts by six committees of translators, headed by **Lancelot Andrewes**, the Authorised

Version became the standard English Bible for the next three and a half centuries and one of the cornerstones of English literature. A **Revised Version** was issued in the late nineteenth century, but it was not until the publication of the **New English Bible** (New Testament in 1961, Old Testament and Apocrypha in 1970) that the position of the Authorised Version was seriously challenged.

DICTIONARY

All quotations are from the Authorised Version of the Bible.

AARON Brother of Moses, he helped to lead the Children of Israel out of Egypt. With his miraculous rod, which on one occasion was transformed into a serpent and on another blossomed and produced almonds, he initiated the first three of the ten **plagues**.* While Moses was on Mount Sinai, receiving the Ten Commandments, Aaron gave way to the disillusioned Israelites and made the **Golden Calf*** for them to worship. In spite of this, he was appointed chief priest, and his descendants took on important roles within the priesthood.

ABEL Second son of Adam and Eve. A shepherd, he was killed by his elder brother **Cain*** out of jealousy, when God accepted Abel's sacrifice from his flock but rejected the fruits of agriculture offered by his brother.

ABRAHAM Known as Abram in early life, he was the first of the patriarchs of Israel. At the age of 76, still childless, he took his wife's maidservant **Hagar*** as a concubine and fathered **Ishmael**.* His second son, **Isaac**,* was born to him and his aged wife Sarah (also called Sarai) when he was 100 years old. To test his faith, God ordered him to kill Isaac as a sacrifice, but just as Abraham was about to strike, the angel of the Lord stayed his hand: "*And he said, Lay not thine hand upon the lad, neither do thou any thing unto him: for now I know that thou fearest God, seeing thou hast not withheld thy son, thine only son from me*" (Genesis 22:12). In place of Isaac, a ram caught in a nearby thicket was sacrificed. Through his grandson **Jacob**,* Abraham became the ancestor of the Jewish people.

ABSALOM The favorite son of King **David**,* he led an unsuccessful rebellion against his father. While he was fleeing from the battle on a mule, his luxuriant hair caught in the branches of an oak and he was left hanging from the tree. In spite of David's prohibition against killing him – "*Deal gently for my* *sake with the young man"* – Joab, the commander of the king's army, stabbed him through the heart. His death was bitterly mourned by David: *"Oh my son Absalom, my son, my son Absalom! would God I had died for thee, O Absalom, my son, my son!"* (2 Samuel 18:33). See AHITHOPHEL.

ADAM (Hebrew = *man, humanity*) The first human being, created by God and placed in the Garden of Eden: *"And the Lord God formed man of the dust of the ground, and breathed into his nostrils the breath of life; and man became a living soul"* (Genesis 2:7). See EDEN, EVE, FALL.

AGAG A king of the Amalekites, defeated in battle by **Saul**.* For the sin of sparing his life, Saul lost God's favor. The error was rectified by the prophet **Samuel**:* *"And Agag came unto him delicately. And Agag said, Surely the bitterness of death is past. And Samuel said, As thy sword hath made women childless, so shall thy mother be childless among women. And Samuel hewed Agag in pieces before the LORD in Gilgal"* (1 Samuel 15:32–33).

AHAB A king of Israel in the ninth century BC. His marriage to **Jezebel**,* a worshipper of Baal, brought him into conflict with the prophet **Elijah**.* In consequence, he cuts a villainous figure in the Old Testament. He died in battle against Syria when *"a certain man drew a bow at a venture"* and shot him in his chariot (1 Kings 22:34). See ELIJAH, JEZEBEL, NABOTH.

AHASUERUS The name given in the Old Testament to the Persian King Xerxes I, husband of **Esther**.*

AHITHOPHEL A counselor of **David**,* Ahithophel sided with **Absalom*** against the king. When his advice was foolishly ignored, *"he saddled his ass, and arose, and gat him home to his house, to his city, and put his household in order, and hanged himself"* (2 Samuel 17:23).

AMALEKITES A nomadic people, supposedly descended from **Esau**,* who occupied part of the Promised Land until ejected by the Israelites.

ANAK, CHILDREN OF A race of giants who lived in Palestine. They terrified the first Israelites sent ahead to spy out the land: *"And there we saw the giants, the sons of Anak, which come of the giants: and we were in our own sight as grasshoppers, and so we were in their sight"* (Numbers 13:33).

ANANIAS (1) A disciple in Damascus who released **Paul*** from blindness. (2) A high priest in Jerusalem who urged bystanders to strike Paul on the mouth (Acts 23). (3) An early Christian who, with his wife Sapphira, sold some land so that the money could be distributed by the apostles but then kept back part of the proceeds. He was upbraided by Peter and fell down dead. A few hours later his wife attempted the same deception and suffered a similar fate (Acts 5).

ANNUNCIATION The angel Gabriel's announcement to **Mary*** that she would conceive a child by the Holy Ghost and that he would be the Son of God (Luke 1:26–38).

APOCALYPSE From the Greek word for "unveil," it refers to dramatic visions of the establishment of God's future kingdom, most notably in the Book of Revelation but also in parts of the Old Testament. When the first four of the seven seals are opened, the **Four Horsemen of the Apocalypse** emerge: a rider with a bow, on a white horse; a rider who is presented with a sword, on a red horse; a rider who holds a pair of scales, on a black horse; Death, on a pale horse.

The Four Horsemen of the Apocalypse (Revelation 6:1–8)

1: And I saw when the Lamb opened one of the seals, and I heard, as it were the noise of thunder, one of the four beasts saying, Come and see.

2: And I saw, and behold a white horse: and he that sat on him had a bow; and a crown was given unto him: and he went forth conquering, and to conquer.

3: And when he had opened the second seal, I heard the second beast say, Come and see.

4: And there went out another horse that was red: and power was given to him that sat thereon to take peace from the earth, and that they should kill one another: and there was given unto him a great sword.

5: And when he had opened the third seal, I heard the third beast say, Come and see. And I beheld, and lo a black horse; and he that sat on him had a pair of balances in his hand.

6: And I heard a voice in the midst of the four beasts say, A measure of wheat for a penny, and three measures of barley for a penny; and see thou hurt not the oil and the wine.

7: And when he had opened the fourth seal, I heard the voice of the fourth beast say, Come and see.

8: And I looked, and behold a pale horse: and his name that sat on him was Death, and Hell followed with him. And power was given unto them over the fourth part of the earth, to kill with sword, and with hunger, and with death, and with the beasts of the earth.

APOLLYON (Greek = *destroyer*) Identified in Revelation 9:11 as the angel of the bottomless pit.

APOSTLES The 12 disciples chosen by Jesus to spread his teaching after his death: Andrew, Bartholomew, James and John the sons of Zebedee, James the Less, Judas Iscariot, Jude (or Thaddeus), Matthew (or Levi), Philip, Simon Peter, Simon the Zealot, Thomas. Later, Matthias took the place of Judas, and Paul was also included among the apostles.

APPLES OF SODOM (also known as Dead Sea Fruit) Fruit that have the appearance of being ripe and ready to eat but contain only ashes beneath the skin. The reference may be to a fruit that grows near the Dead Sea and turns to dust inside when attacked by a particular insect. Mentioned by a number of ancient writers, including **Tacitus*** and the Jewish historian **Josephus**, the apples of Sodom came to be used as an image of bitter disappointment.

ARAMAIC A Semitic language in which a few parts of the Old Testament were written.

ARK OF THE COVENANT A shrine containing the tablets of the Law, on which were written the **Ten Commandments**.* It was regarded by the Israelites with extreme reverence as the seat of God on earth, symbolic of his covenant with them. After accompanying them on their wanderings in the wilderness, it was placed in the Temple of Jerusalem.

ARMAGEDDON Referred to in Revelation 16 as the scene of the last great battle between the forces of good and evil, it has been identified with Megiddo in Israel.

ASCENSION The occasion, 40 days after the resurrection, when Jesus was taken from the presence of the apostles and ascended into heaven: *"And when he had spoken these things, while they beheld, he was taken up; and a cloud received him out of their sight"* (Acts 1:9).

ASHTORETH A Canaanite fertility goddess sometimes favored by backsliding Israelites and later associated with **Aphrodite*** (see p. 72). **Solomon*** was guilty of worshipping her in his old age.

ASSYRIA The Assyrian empire, in what is now northern Iraq, reached its zenith in the second half of the eighth century BC under Tiglath-Pileser III, who over-ran Israel. Its last ruler, legendary for his extravagant lifestyle and sensual indul-gence, was **Sardanapalus**. Besieged in Nineveh by the Medes in the late seventh century BC, he set fire to his palace and burned himself to death. The Assyrian empire gave way to that of the Babylonians.

BAAL The name, meaning *lord* or *master*, given to the principal Canaanite fer-tility god. His worship, which had an erotic character particularly deplored by the Hebrew prophets, was a constant temptation to the Israelites.

BABEL (Hebrew for Babylon) The name of the tower intended to reach to heaven which was built by the descendants of **Noah**.* God punished their presumption by making them all speak different languages so that the work could not be continued.

BABYLON Capital of the Babylonian empire, in what is now Iraq. After the fall of Jerusalem to **Nebuchadnezzar II*** in 586 BC, many of the survivors were deported and endured half a century of exile, known as the **Babylonian cap-tivity**. A symbol of iniquity, later identified with Rome, the city appears in Revelation as a scarlet woman, the **whore of Babylon**: *"And the woman was arrayed in purple and scarlet colour, and decked with gold and precious stones and pearls, having a golden cup in her hand full of abominations and filthiness of her fornication: And upon her forehead was a name written, MYSTERY, BABYLON THE GREAT, THE MOTHER OF HARLOTS AND ABOMINATIONS OF THE EARTH"* (Revelation 17:4–5). On the basis of this descripton, early Puritans referred to the Roman Catholic Church as the whore of Babylon.

Psalm 137:1–6, from the Book of Common Prayer (1662)

1. By the waters of Babylon we sat down and wept : when we remembered thee, O Sion.
2. As for our harps, we hanged them up : upon the trees that are therein.
3. For they that led us away captive required of us then a song, and melody in our heaviness : Sing us one of the songs of Sion.
4. How shall we sing the Lord's song : in a strange land?
5. If I forget thee, O Jerusalem : let my right hand forget her cunning.
6. If I do not remember thee, let my tongue cleave to the roof of my mouth : yea, if I prefer not Jerusalem in my mirth . . .

BALAAM A seer hired by Balak, king of Moab, to curse the invading Israelites. While he was on his way to do the king's bidding, an angel, unseen by Balaam but visible to his ass, barred the road. When Balaam beat the ass for turning aside and crushing his foot against a wall, the animal broke into speech and reproached him for his unkindness. Balaam then became aware of the angel, who pointed out that the ass had saved his life by refusing to pass. Instructed by the angel, Balaam later blessed the Israelites rather than cursing them – to the fury of Balak: *"I called thee to curse mine enemies, and, behold, thou hast altogether blessed them these three times"* (Numbers 24:10).

BARABBAS A criminal charged with murder and insurrection. According to the custom that allowed the release of a prisoner at the feast of the Passover, **Pontius Pilate*** offered the crowd a choice between Jesus and Barabbas. They chose Barabbas.

BATHSHEBA The wife of **Uriah*** the Hittite. Walking on his palace roof, **David*** saw her washing herself. After seducing her and arranging the death of her husband, he married her. Their first child died as a punishment for David's sin; their second was **Solomon.*** See NATHAN, URIAH.

BEATITUDES The eight blessings with which Jesus begins the Sermon on the Mount.

The Beatitudes (Matthew 5:3–11)

3: Blessed are the poor in spirit: for theirs is the kingdom of heaven.

4: Blessed are they that mourn: for they shall be comforted.

5: Blessed are the meek: for they shall inherit the earth.

6: Blessed are they which do hunger and thirst after righteousness: for they shall be filled.

7: Blessed are the merciful: for they shall obtain mercy.

8: Blessed are the pure in heart: for they shall see God.

9: Blessed are the peacemakers: for they shall be called the children of God.

10: Blessed are they which are persecuted for righteousness' sake: for theirs is the kingdom of heaven.

11: Blessed are ye, when men shall revile you, and persecute you, and shall say all manner of evil against you falsely, for my sake.

BEELZEBUB (Hebrew = *Lord of the Flies*) A name for the Devil, or sometimes for his principal assistant. The name should probably be Beelzebul (Lord of the House), derived from Baal.

BEHEMOTH The great beast described in Job 40:15–24 – perhaps a hippopotamus.

BELIAL (Hebrew = *worthlessness, wickedness*) In the Old Testament the word remains an abstract term denoting wickedness. It is only in the New Testament that it becomes a name for the Devil. Milton, in *Paradise Lost*, lists him as one of Satan's principal lieutenants.

BELSHAZZAR Wrongly identified in the Bible as the son of Nebuchadnezzar II and the last king of Babylon, he is remembered primarily for the episode, recorded in Daniel 5, known as **Belshazzar's Feast**. In the middle of the royal banquet the fingers of a man's hand appeared and wrote a series of words on the palace wall. Their meaning defeated all the king's wise men and soothsayers until Daniel explained that they foretold the fall of Babylon (hence the ominous meaning of the phrase "the writing on the wall"):

> **John Milton, Paradise Lost, Book 1, lines 490–502**
>
> Belial came last, than whom a Spirit more lewd
> Fell not from Heaven, or more gross to love
> Vice for itself. To him no temple stood
> Or altar smoked; yet who more oft than he
> In temples and at altars, when the priest
> Turns atheist, as did Eli's sons, who filled
> With lust and violence the house of God?
> In courts and palaces he also reigns,
> And in luxurious cities, where the noise
> Of riot ascends above their loftiest towers,
> And injury and outrage; and, when night
> Darkens the streets, then wander forth the sons
> Of Belial, flown with insolence and wine.

ME-NE; God hath numbered thy kingdom, and finished it.
TE-KEL; Thou art weighed in the balances, and art found wanting.
PE-RES; Thy kingdom is divided, and given to the Medes and Persians.

(Daniel 5:26–28)

In the same night Belshazzar was killed.

BETHESDA It was at the pool of Bethesda in Jerusalem, supposed at the time to have curative properties, that Jesus healed the impotent (i.e., paralyzed) man, saying simply, *"Rise, take up thy bed, and walk"* (John 5.8). The fact that Jesus had done this on the sabbath day inflamed the orthodox Jews against him.

BETHLEHEM A town a few miles south of Jerusalem, referred to in the Bible as the birthplace of both David and Jesus.

BOAZ See RUTH.

BURNING BUSH While tending his father-in-law's flocks on Mount Horeb (Sinai), Moses saw a bush that was burning but not consumed by the flames. It was from the middle of this burning bush that God called him to lead the Israelites out of Egypt (Exodus 3).

CAIAPHAS High priest in Jerusalem at the time of the crucifixion. Jesus was questioned by him and held to be guilty of blasphemy.

CAIN The elder son of Adam and Eve. He killed **Abel*** after God had shown preference for his brother's sacrifice. "*And the Lord said unto Cain, Where is thy brother? And he said, I know not: Am I my brother's keeper?*" (Genesis 4:9). The world's first murderer, Cain was cursed by God and went to live in the land of Nod on the East of Eden, where he built a city. God's mark, the so-called mark of Cain, was set on him for his protection so that he would not be randomly killed as an outcast. See ABEL.

CALEB One of the men sent ahead by **Moses*** to spy out the Promised Land of Canaan. Of the adult Israelites who took part in the **Exodus*** only Caleb the son of Jephunneh and **Joshua*** the son of Nun were allowed by God to reach the Promised Land (Numbers 14:26–30).

CALVARY The hill outside the city wall of Jerusalem where Jesus was crucified. Its Hebrew name is Golgotha (= *skull*, or *place of the skull*).

CANA A village in Galilee where Jesus performed his first miracle. When the wine ran out at a wedding feast to which he and his disciples had been invited, his mother urged him to intervene. In spite of his irritation – "*Woman, what have I to do with thee? mine hour is not yet come*" – Jesus turned six pots of water into wine. The man in charge of the feast then rebuked the bridegroom for keeping the best wine until last instead of serving it at the beginning, according to custom (John 2:1–11).

CANAAN The Promised Land. This was the "*land flowing with milk and honey*" promised by God to the Israelites at the time of the **Exodus**.* It was roughly the area from the Mediterranean coast, between Sidon and Gaza, inland to the River Jordan.

CRUCIFIXION The manner in which Jesus was executed by the Romans. After refusing the mixture of wine and myrrh offered to dull the pain, he was nailed to the cross, and the soldiers shared out his clothing by lot. Two thieves were crucified with him, one on either side. According to Luke, one of the thieves reacted to Jesus with contempt, the other with reverence. Towards the end, a bystander put a vinegar-soaked sponge on a reed and held it to his mouth. This is the account of his death in Matthew 27:50–54:

> *50:* Jesus, when he had cried again with a loud voice, yielded up the ghost.
> *51:* And, behold, the veil of the temple was rent in twain from the top to the bottom; and the earth did quake, and the rocks rent;
> *52:* And the graves were opened; and many bodies of the saints which slept arose,
> *53:* And came out of the graves after his resurrection, and went into the holy city, and appeared unto many.
> *54:* Now when the centurion, and they that were with him, watching Jesus, saw the earthquake, and those things that were done, they feared greatly, saying, Truly this was the Son of God.

Bodies were not allowed to remain on the cross during the sabbath, so the Jews requested that their legs be broken to hasten death. Since Jesus was already dead, his legs were left unbroken, but one of the soldiers pierced his side with a spear, producing a stream of water and blood. Afterwards, a rich disciple, **Joseph of Arimathea**, was allowed by **Pilate*** to dispose of the body. (It was anointed with myrrh and aloes and wrapped in linen before being buried in a sepulcher hewn out of the rock.) Among the onlookers at the crucifixion were Mary the mother of Jesus, her sister Mary, Mary Magdalene, and John the apostle. The gospels record seven utterances by Jesus during the crucifixion, known as the **Seven Words from the Cross**:

1 Of the soldiers carrying out the crucifixion: "*Father, forgive them; for they know not what they do*" (Luke 23:34).
2 To the penitent thief: "*Verily I say unto thee, To day shalt thou be with me in paradise*" (Luke 23:43).
3 To his mother, while she and St. John stood by the cross: "*Woman, behold thy son!*", and to the disciple: "*Behold thy mother!*" (John 19:26 and 27).
4 "*Eli, Eli, lama sabachthani?*", which Matthew and Mark gloss as "My God, my God, why hast thou forsaken me?" (Matthew 27:46).

5 "I thirst" (John 19:28).

6 "It is finished" (John 19:30).

7 "Father, into thy hands I commend my spirit" (Luke 23:46).

See INRI, PASSION.

DAGON A Philistine deity, probably fish-shaped. It was at a festival for Dagon that **Samson*** killed himself and 3,000 Philistines.

DANIEL A Jewish prophet of the sixth century BC at the Babylonian court, where he was known as Belteshazzar. His doings are recorded in the Book of Daniel, probably written in the second century BC. He won high status as the interpreter of **Nebuchadnezzar's*** dreams but later fell victim to a conspiracy. King Darius, **Belshazzar's*** conqueror and successor, was persuaded by his counselors to sign a decree that had the effect of outlawing Daniel's religious observances. Unable to rescind the decree – "The thing is true, according to the law of the Medes and Persians, which altereth not" (Daniel 6:12) – Darius was forced to cast Daniel into the den of lions. In the morning he was found to be safe, preserved by God from harm. Daniel's enemies were in their turn thrown to the lions and Daniel himself was restored to prosperity.

DAVID Son of Jesse and great-grandson of **Ruth.*** Anointed by **Samuel*** when he was still a youth keeping his father's sheep, David became Israel's greatest king. As a boy he found favor with **Saul*** by his harp-playing and was a close friend of the king's son **Jonathan.*** His defeat of **Goliath*** was a turning point. Alarmed by David's popularity, Saul took against him, demanding a hundred foreskins of the Philistines as the bride-price for his daughter Michal in the hope that this would lead to his death. Instead, David brought 200 foreskins. Later, Michal foiled a plot by Saul to kill him: while David fled, she put a dummy in his bed to throw her father's men off the scent. In spite of a lingering bond between them, Saul pursued David with increasing hostility, though David twice spared his life in the ensuing period. After Saul's death, David reigned as king of Judah for seven years until he finally established himself as king of a united Israel, which he ruled for another 33 years, making the captured city of Jerusalem his new capital. His later years were troubled by the rebellion of his son **Absalom**,* and also by the devastating pestilence with which God punished him for taking a census of the Israelites. Before dying, he appointed Solomon his successor. See ABSALOM, GOLIATH, JONATHAN, SHIMEI, URIAH.

DEAD SEA SCROLLS A group of ancient manuscripts discovered between 1947 and the mid-1960s in caves at Qumran and the neighboring area, just north-west of the Dead Sea. Among them are copies of Old Testament books in Hebrew older than any that were previously known.

DEBORAH A prophetess and one of the judges who led Israel in the period before the monarchy was established. She inspired the fight against the Canaanite commander **Sisera** and celebrated his murder with a famous song of triumph. See JAEL.

DECALOGUE The Greek word for the **Ten Commandments**.*

DELILAH A Philistine mistress of **Samson*** who persuaded him to reveal that the secret of his immense strength lay in his long hair. While he slept, she had his head shaved so that he could be taken by the Philistines.

DIVES Although the rich man in the parable of **Lazarus*** is not given a name in the Bible, he is traditionally known as Dives (Latin = *wealthy*). Consigned to hell after his life of callous luxury, he begs Abraham that Lazarus be allowed to visit him and cool his tongue with a drop of water on the tip of his finger, but all contact is refused: "*between us and you there is a great gulf fixed*" (Luke 16:26).

From ECCLESIASTES

Chapter 3

1: To every thing there is a season, and a time to every purpose under the heaven:

2: A time to be born, and a time to die; a time to plant, and a time to pluck up that which is planted;

3: A time to kill, and a time to heal; a time to break down, and a time to build up;

4: A time to weep, and a time to laugh; a time to mourn, and a time to dance;

5: A time to cast away stones, and a time to gather stones together; a time to embrace, and a time to refrain from embracing;

6: A time to get, and a time to lose; a time to keep, and a time to cast away;

7: A time to rend, and a time to sew; a time to keep silence, and a time to speak;

8: A time to love, and a time to hate; a time of war, and a time of peace ...

Chapter 9

11: I returned, and saw under the sun, that the race is not to the swift, nor the battle to the strong, neither yet bread to the wise, nor yet riches to men of understanding, nor yet favour to men of skill; but time and chance happeneth to them all ...

Chapter 12

1: Remember now thy Creator in the days of thy youth, while the evil days come not, nor the years draw nigh, when thou shalt say, I have no pleasure in them;

2: While the sun, or the light, or the moon, or the stars, be not darkened, nor the clouds return after the rain:

3: In the day when the keepers of the house shall tremble, and the strong men shall bow themselves, and the grinders cease because they are few, and those that look out of the windows be darkened,

4: And the doors shall be shut in the streets, when the sound of the grinding is low, and he shall rise up at the voice of the bird, and all the daughters of musick shall be brought low;

5: Also when they shall be afraid of that which is high, and fears shall be in the way, and the almond tree shall flourish, and the grasshopper shall be a burden, and desire shall fail: because man goeth to his long home, and the mourners go about the streets:

6: Or ever the silver cord be loosed, or the golden bowl be broken, or the pitcher be broken at the fountain, or the wheel broken at the cistern.

7: Then shall the dust return to the earth as it was: and the spirit shall return unto God who gave it.

8: Vanity of vanities, saith the preacher; all is vanity ...

ECCLESIASTICUS The longest book of the Apocrypha. The following examples give an indication of its humane and worldly tone:

Forsake not an old friend; for the new is not comparable to him: a new friend is as new wine; when it is old, thou shalt drink it with pleasure. (9:10)

He that toucheth pitch shall be defiled therewith . . . (13:1)

Envy and wrath shorten the life, and carefulness bringeth age before the time. (30:24)

Wine is as good as life to a man, if it be drunk moderately: what life is then to a man that is without wine? for it was made to make men glad. (31:27)

Let thy speech be short, comprehending much in few words; be as one that knoweth and yet holdeth his tongue. (32:8)

There be of them, that have left a name behind them, that their praises might be reported. And some there be, which have no memorial; who are perished, as though they had never been; and are become as though they had never been born; and their children after them. But these were merciful men, whose righteousness hath not been forgotten. (44:8–10)

EDEN The Garden of Eden was the paradise provided by God for Adam and Eve, from which they were expelled after the **Fall***: *"And the Lord God planted a garden eastward in Eden; and there he put the man whom he had formed"* (Genesis 2:8).

EGLON A notably fat king of Moab who kept the Israelites in subjection for 18 years. His assassination by the left-handed Ehud is described in graphic detail by the author of the Book of Judges. Claiming to be on a secret errand, Ehud obtained a private audience with Eglon, telling him that he had a message from God:

And Ehud put forth his left hand, and took the dagger from his right thigh, and thrust it into his belly:
And the haft also went in after the blade, so that he could not draw the dagger out of his belly; and the dirt came out. (Judges 3:21–22)

ELI The priest in Shiloh who instructed **Samuel**.* An upright man himself, he failed to check the greed and lust of his sons, who were also priests. God cursed the whole family and called Samuel to take over the spiritual leadership of the Israelites.

ELIJAH One of the greatest of the Old Testament prophets, Elijah the Tishbite lived in the middle of the ninth century BC. His opposition to Baal worship set him at odds with King **Ahab*** and his wife **Jezebel**.* After announcing a drought that would only be ended at his command, he fled to the brook Cherith where God sent ravens to feed him bread and flesh in the morning and evening. Later he took refuge with a poor widow who had only a handful of meal and a cruse of oil, but through the prophet's intervention both were miraculously replenished until the end of the drought. When the woman's son died, Elijah restored him to life. He won his most impressive victory by staging a contest on Mount Carmel between himself, the sole priest of Jehovah, and the 450 priests of Baal. Each side was given a bullock which their god was then invited to consume with fire as a sacrifice. The priests of Baal were conspicuously unsuccessful: "*And it came to pass at noon, that Elijah mocked them, and said, Cry aloud: for he is a god; either he is talking, or he is pursuing, or he is in a journey, or peradventure he sleepeth, and must be awaked*" (1 Kings 18:27). By contrast, the fire of the Lord utterly consumed the sacrifice of Elijah, who called on the Israelites to slaughter all the priests of Baal. Although Elijah then brought the drought to an end, the episode of **Naboth's*** vineyard led to further confrontation with Ahab and Jezebel. On God's instructions Elijah anointed as his successor Elisha, whom he found plowing with a yoke of oxen: "*and Elijah passed by him, and cast his mantle upon him*" (1 Kings 19:19). Elijah did not suffer death but was carried off to heaven in a whirlwind by a chariot and horses of fire, an event witnessed by Elisha with the cry, "*My father, my father, the chariot of Israel, and the horsemen thereof*" (1 Kings 2:12).

ELISHA Elijah's successor. Having requested that a double portion of Elijah's spirit be conferred on him, he took up the prophet's mantle and struck the waters of the River Jordan, which parted for him to cross. He is remembered for curing **Naaman's*** leprosy and, less gloriously, for calling up bears to devour some children who followed him out of Bethlehem with mocking cries, "*Go up, thou bald head; go up, thou bald head*" (2 Kings 2:23).

EMMANUEL (Hebrew = *God with us*) Used as a name for Jesus (see Matthew 1:23).

EMMAUS The village near Jerusalem towards which **Cleopas** and another disciple were traveling when Jesus appeared to them after the resurrection. They did not recognize him until supper in Emmaus when he broke bread for them and blessed it, at which point he vanished (Luke 24).

ENDOR, WITCH OF In spite of his edict banishing witches, **Saul*** himself went in disguise to visit the witch of Endor when anxious about the threat posed by the Philistines. She raised **Samuel*** from the dead, who informed him that the

Philistines would be victorious on the next day, and that he and his sons would be killed.

ENOCH Mentioned in Genesis as a man who walked with God and lived 365 years, Enoch is the only figure in the Old Testament, apart from Elijah, who escapes physical death.

The Epistle of Paul the Apostle to the EPHESIANS, Chapter 6

11: Put on the whole armour of God, that ye may be able to stand against the wiles of the Devil.

12: For we wrestle not against flesh and blood, but against principalities, against powers, against the rulers of the darkness of this world, against spiritual wickedness in high places.

13: Wherefore take unto you the whole armour of God, that ye may be able to withstand in the evil day, and having done all, to stand.

EPIPHANY (Greek = *manifestation, revelation*) The feast that marks the coming of the **Magi*** to visit Jesus, celebrated on January 6.

ESAU Son of Isaac and Rebekah, elder twin brother of **Jacob**:* *"Esau was a cunning hunter, a man of the field; and Jacob was a plain man, dwelling in tents."* Esau came in from hunting one day, faint with hunger, and agreed to sell Jacob his birthright for some of the pottage he had made. (The traditional phrase "a mess of pottage" does not actually appear in the Bible.) Later, Jacob conspired with his mother Rebekah to steal the blessing which the ailing Isaac intended for Esau, whom he had sent to hunt venison for him. Rebekah and Jacob quickly substituted kid's meat for the venison. To disguise the physical difference between the two brothers – *"Behold, Esau my brother is a hairy man, and I am a smooth man"* (Genesis 27:11) – they then put the skins of the kids on Jacob's hands and neck and managed to fool Isaac into bestowing the blessing that meant future dominance and prosperity. Esau returned just too late: *"And Esau said unto his father, Hast thou but one blessing, my father? bless me, even me also, O my father"* (Genesis 27:38). Forced to make do with a lesser blessing, Esau determined to kill Jacob, but the younger brother fled and the two were later reconciled.

ESTHER Jewish queen of the Persian King Ahasuerus (Xerxes I). The Old Testament Book of Esther tells how she frustrated a plot by the king's wicked counselor Haman to exterminate the Jews in the kingdom and to have Esther's adoptive father **Mordecai** hanged. The delivery of the Jews is celebrated in the feast of Purim.

EUPHRATES Referred to in Genesis as *"the great river, the river Euphrates"*, it formed the northern boundary of the **Promised Land*** (Genesis 15:18).

EVE The first woman, formed from the rib of Adam:

> And the Lord God caused a deep sleep to fall upon Adam, and he slept: and he took one of his ribs, and closed up the flesh instead thereof.
> And the rib, which the Lord God had taken from man, made he a woman, and brought her unto the man. (Genesis 2:21–22)

See FALL.

EXODUS The departure of the Israelites from Egypt, perhaps sometime around the mid-thirteenth century BC. The sons of Jacob and their families had gone there to escape famine (see JOSEPH), but their descendants were later enslaved by the Egyptians. The first 14 chapters of the Book of Exodus tell the story of their flight, including the ten **plagues*** visited upon Egypt and the journey of the Israelites to the Red Sea, led by God in a pillar of cloud by day and a pillar of fire by night. The high point both for the Israelites and for later cinema-goers was the crossing of the Red Sea, whose waters Moses parted by stretching out his hand. After the Israelites had crossed into freedom over dry land, the waters surged back to drown the pursuing forces of Pharaoh. See PASSOVER, PHARAOH.

FALL The original act of disobedience that brought sin into the world. God had put just one constraint on Adam's freedom to eat the fruit of the trees in Eden: *"But of the tree of the knowledge of good and evil, thou shalt not eat of it: for in the day that thou eatest thereof thou shalt surely die"* (Genesis 2:17). Tempted by the serpent, Eve succumbed and then gave the fruit to Adam. Immediately their eyes were opened and they became guiltily conscious of their nakedness. God punished all three – the serpent by forcing it to go upon its belly and eat dust, Eve by inflicting on women the pains of childbirth, and Adam by making agriculture an arduous labor: *"In the sweat of thy face shalt thou eat bread, till thou return unto the ground; for out of it wast thou taken: for dust thou art, and unto dust shalt thou return"* (Genesis 3:19). To prevent Adam and Eve from tasting the tree of life and becoming immortal, God drove them out of Eden, "*and he placed at the east of the garden of Eden Cherubims, and a flaming sword which turned every way, to keep the way of the tree of life*" (Genesis 3:24).

The Fall (Genesis 3:1–13)

1: Now the serpent was more subtil than any beast of the field which the LORD God had made. And he said unto the woman, Yea, hath God said, Ye shall not eat of every tree of the garden?

2: And the woman said unto the serpent, We may eat of the fruit of the trees of the garden:

3: But of the fruit of the tree which is in the midst of the garden, God hath said, Ye shall not eat of it, neither shall ye touch it, lest ye die.

4: And the serpent said unto the woman, Ye shall not surely die:

5: For God doth know that in the day ye eat thereof, then your eyes shall be opened, and ye shall be as gods, knowing good and evil.

6: And when the woman saw that the tree was good for food, and that it was pleasant to the eyes, and a tree to be desired to make one wise, she took of the fruit thereof, and did eat, and gave also unto her husband with her; and he did eat.

7: And the eyes of them both were opened, and they knew that they were naked; and they sewed fig leaves together, and made themselves aprons.

8: And they heard the voice of the LORD God walking in the garden in the cool of the day: and Adam and his wife hid themselves from the presence of the LORD God amongst the trees of the garden.

9: And the LORD God called unto Adam, and said unto him, Where art thou?

10: And he said, I heard thy voice in the garden, and I was afraid, because I was naked; and I hid myself.

11: And he said, Who told thee that thou wast naked? Hast thou eaten of the tree, whereof I commanded thee that thou shouldest not eat?

12: And the man said, The woman whom thou gavest to be with me, she gave me of the tree, and I did eat.

13: And the LORD God said unto the woman, What is this that thou hast done? And the woman said, The serpent beguiled me, and I did eat.

FLIGHT INTO EGYPT Warned in a dream that King Herod of Judaea would try to kill Jesus, Joseph and Mary fled Bethlehem by night and went into Egypt, returning to Israel only after Herod's death.

GADARENE SWINE In the country around Gadara, just southeast of the Sea of Galilee, Jesus was approached by a man known as Legion on account of the numerous devils that possessed him. Jesus exorcised them into a nearby herd of swine, which immediately careered down a steep slope into the sea.

GALILEE The area of ancient Palestine in which Jesus grew up.

GAMALIEL Paul's* Jewish teacher, a liberal Pharisee who advised the **Sanhedrin*** to take a moderate line towards the early Christians.

GEHAZI The servant of the prophet **Elisha**.* After **Naaman*** had been cured of leprosy, Gehazi solicited a reward from him and was then himself punished with leprosy by Elisha. See NAAMAN.

GEHENNA A valley outside Jerusalem where children were sacrificed to **Moloch**.* It became a synonym for hell.

GENTILES A term for those not Jewish.

GETHSEMANE A garden on the Mount of Olives – its name means oil-press – east of Jerusalem. It was here that Jesus prayed before his arrest and crucifixion. During this episode, referred to as the **Agony in the Garden**, he asked God to spare him the ordeal to come: *"O my Father, if it be possible, let this cup pass from me: nevertheless not as I will, but as thou wilt"* (Matthew 26:39). The disciples meanwhile slept a short distance away, provoking Jesus's reproach, *"What, could ye not watch with me one hour?"* (Matthew 26:40).

GIDEON One of Israel's judges, famed for his defeat of a vastly superior force of Midianites. Anxious to confirm that he had divine support, Gideon tested God by putting out a fleece and asking on one night that the fleece alone should be wet with dew and the surrounding ground dry, on the next that the fleece be dry and the ground wet. Having satisfied Gideon's doubts, God was keen to make it clear that the victory was to be his own work and not that of the Israelites themselves. He therefore restricted the attacking force to a small group of 300 men. Gideon was instructed to bring his men down to the river and choose only those who drank the water out of their hands rather than lapping it like dogs. Dividing his force into three, Gideon launched his victorious night-attack with a celebrated battle-cry: *"When I blow with a trumpet, I and all that are with me, then blow ye the trumpets also on every side of all the camp, and say, The sword of the Lord, and of Gideon"* (Judges 7:18).

GNOSTICISM (Greek *gnosis* = knowledge) A religious movement in the early centuries of the Christian era that stressed the acquisition of esoteric spiritual knowledge as a condition of salvation. Its dualistic beliefs, which influenced later medieval heresies such as Catharism, were perceived as a threat by the early Christian Fathers.

GOG AND MAGOG Gog is referred to in Ezekiel as a prince hostile to the Israelites, but more generally Gog and Magog are used in Revelation to symbolize the enemies of God. (In English folklore Gog and Magog were the sole survivors of a monstrous race of giants killed by Brutus, the legendary founder of Britain.)

GOLDEN CALF While Moses was on Mount Sinai receiving the Ten Commandments, the Israelites despaired of his return and demanded new gods. **Aaron*** took their earrings, melted them down, and fashioned them into a golden calf, which the Israelites worshipped with naked dancing: "*and they said, These be thy gods, O Israel, which brought thee up out of the land of Egypt*" (Exodus 32:4). On his return, Moses ground their idol to powder, strewed it on the water, and made them drink it.

GOLGOTHA See CALVARY.

GOLIATH A Philistine giant killed by **David**.* Goliath, whose height is given as "six cubits and a span" (perhaps something over 9 feet) and whose spear was like a weaver's beam, paraded daily in front of the Israelite forces, challenging them to single combat. David, too young to be part of the army, was taking food to his elder brothers in the Israelite camp when he saw Goliath and offered to fight him. With his sling and five smooth stones picked from the brook, he went out to face the giant. A single stone brought Goliath down, sinking into his forehead. David then used the giant's own sword to cut off his head. The subsequent adulation of the Israelite women – "*Saul hath slain his thousands, and David his ten thousands*" (1 Samuel 18:7) – stirred the beginnings of the king's hostility to David.

HAGAR The Egyptian maidservant of **Abraham's*** wife Sarah. Believing that she herself was past childbearing, Sarah gave Hagar to Abraham to produce a child but then in jealousy drove her out of the household. See ISHMAEL.

HEROD THE GREAT King of Judaea from 37–4 BC. According to Matthew 2, he was responsible for the **Murder of the Innocents**.* He was the father of Herod Antipas, known as Herod the Tetrarch, who had **John the Baptist*** beheaded.

HERODIAS Mother of **Salome*** by her first marriage. Her second marriage, to her brother-in-law Herod Antipas, was condemned by John the Baptist. It was this that led her to contrive his execution.

HOLY SPIRIT The Holy Spirit, or Holy Ghost, is one part of the **Trinity*** and may be thought of as the invisible force of God as it operates in the world.

HOSANNA (Hebrew = *God save*) The cry of those who hailed Jesus as he rode into Jerusalem on an ass before his death.

INNOCENTS, MURDER OF THE The slaughter, ordered by Herod the Great, of all the children under three years old in the Bethlehem area. Troubled by rumors of a child born in Bethlehem to be King of the Jews, Herod tried to discover his whereabouts from the wise men (see MAGI): *"Go and search diligently for the young child; and when ye have found him, bring me word again, that I may come and worship him also"* (Matthew 2:8). It was after the failure of this stratagem that he ordered the mass murder of children, ful- filling Jeremiah's prophecy: *"In Rama was there a voice heard, lamentation, and weeping, and great mourning, Rachel weeping for her children, and would not be comforted, because they are not"* (Matthew 2:18).

INRI Initial letters of the Latin inscription IESUS NAZARENUS REX IUDAEORUM (JESUS OF NAZARETH THE KING OF THE JEWS), which, according to John 19:19, **Pontius Pilate*** set on Jesus's cross:

> Then said the chief priests of the Jews to Pilate, Write not, The King of the Jews; but that he said, I am King of the Jews.
> Pilate answered, What I have written I have written. (John 19:21–22)

ISAAC Son of Abraham and Sarah, father of **Esau*** and **Jacob**.* For the story of God's command that he be sacrificed by his father, see ABRAHAM.

ISAIAH A major prophet whose name was given to the greatest of the prophetic books of the Old Testament. Isaiah prophesied in Judah towards the end of the eighth century BC.

ISCARIOT See JUDAS.

ISHBOSHETH A son of **Saul**,* Ishbosheth was **David's*** rival for the throne. He was killed by two of his own captains, who "*smote him under the fifth rib*" while he was taking a siesta (2 Samuel 4:6). They brought his head to David but were disappointed in their hopes of a reward. Incensed by what they had done, David ordered them to be executed, their hands and feet chopped off, their bodies hung above a pool in Hebron.

> **Isaiah 2:4**
>
> And he shall judge among the nations, and shall rebuke many people: and they shall beat their swords into plowshares, and their spears into pruninghooks: nation shall not lift up sword against nation, neither shall they learn war any more.

ISHMAEL Son of **Abraham*** and his wife's Egyptian maidservant **Hagar**.* When Hagar was pregnant and fleeing from Sarah's jealousy, she was visited by an angel who predicted of Ishmael, "*And he will be a wild man; his hand will be against every man, and every man's hand against him*" (Genesis 16:12). Nonetheless, Ishmael received God's promise that he would be father of a great nation, and he is traditionally regarded as the ancestor of the Arab peoples.

ISRAEL, TWELVE TRIBES OF The tribes descended from the 12 sons of **Jacob*** (also called Israel): Reuben, Simeon, Levi, Judah, Zebulun, Issachar, Dan, Gad, Asher, Naphtali, Joseph (whose sons Ephraim and Manasseh also gave their names to separate tribes), and Benjamin. Each occupied a distinct territory, except for the Levites, who served as priests.

JACOB Son of Isaac and Rebekah. He struggled with his twin brother Esau even in the womb and came out grasping his heel. Later he twice cheated him of his rights (see ESAU). He married Leah and Rachel, the daughters of **Laban**,* and by them and their maidservants he had the 12 sons from whom were descended the twelve tribes of **Israel**.* Genesis records two crucial episodes in his early life: (1) After stealing his father's blessing from Esau, he left home, stopping one night at a place where he dreamed of a ladder reaching to heaven on which angels were ascending and descending. Above it stood God, who promised that Jacob's descendants would be blessed and that the land on which he lay would be theirs (Genesis 28:10–22). (2) At a place he called

Peniel he wrestled all night with an unknown man, who touched the hollow of his thigh and put it out of joint, but Jacob refused to let go of him without a blessing. The man, whom he finally perceived to be God, renamed him **Israel** (Genesis 32:24–32). See LABAN.

JAEL Wife of Heber the Kenite. She offered refuge to the Canaanite general **Sisera**, who was fleeing from his defeat by the Israelites. Having invited him into her tent, she took one of the tent-pegs and hammered it through his temple while he slept. Her action is celebrated in the **Song of Deborah and Barak** (the Israelite commander).

The Song of Deborah and Barak (Judges 5:24–31)

24: Blessed above women shall Jael the wife of Heber the Kenite be, blessed shall she be above women in the tent.

25: He asked water, and she gave him milk; she brought forth butter in a lordly dish.

26: She put her hand to the nail, and her right hand to the workmen's hammer; and with the hammer she smote Sisera, she smote off his head, when she had pierced and stricken through his temples.

27: At her feet he bowed, he fell, he lay down: at her feet he bowed, he fell: where he bowed, there he fell down dead.

28: The mother of Sisera looked out at a window, and cried through the lattice, Why is his chariot so long in coming? why tarry the wheels of his chariots?

29: Her wise ladies answered her, yea, she returned answer to herself,

30: Have they not sped? have they not divided the prey; to every man a damsel or two; to Sisera a prey of divers colours, a prey of divers colours of needlework, of divers colours of needlework on both sides, meet for the necks of them that take the spoil?

31: So let all thine enemies perish, O LORD: but let them that love him be as the sun when he goeth forth in his might. And the land had rest forty years.

JAIRUS The ruler of a synagogue, whose 12-year-old daughter died while Jesus was on his way to heal her. On his arrival, Jesus said to the mourners, "*Why make ye this ado, and weep? the damsel is not dead, but sleepeth*" (Mark 5:39). He went in to her and with the words "*Talitha cumi*" brought her back from the dead.

JEHOSHAPHAT A king of Judah in the ninth century BC. His reign was godly, in spite of an ill-advised alliance with **Ahab**,* king of Israel, against Syria (1 Kings 22).

JEHOVAH see YAHWEH.

JEHU A king of Israel in the second half of the ninth century BC, anointed on **Elisha's*** instructions. He gained the throne by killing the reigning king of Israel, Ahab's son Joram. The watchman on the tower of Jezreel warned Joram of his approach with the words, "*and the driving is like the driving of Jehu the son of Nimshi; for he driveth furiously*" (2 Kings 9:20). Having dispatched Ahab's wife **Jezebel**,* his 70 sons, and all the worshippers of Baal, Jehu went on to found a new dynasty.

JEPHTHAH One of the judges who led Israel. He made a rash vow that if God gave him victory over the Ammonites he would sacrifice as a burnt offering whatever came out of his house to meet him on his return. It was his daughter, his only child, who came out to welcome him with timbrels and dances. Having made his vow, he was obliged to sacrifice her.

JEREMIAH A prophet in the late seventh and early sixth centuries BC who ended his life as an exile in Egypt. His reputation for gloom derives from his response in the Book of Jeremiah and in Lamentations (wrongly ascribed to him) to the woes that overtook both Israel and himself around the period of the fall of Jerusalem in 586 BC.

JERICHO A city just north of the Dead Sea that was destroyed by **Joshua*** soon after the Israelites crossed the Jordan into the Promised Land. On God's instructions, the Israelite army made a circuit of the city every day for six days, with seven priests carrying seven trumpets of rams' horns in front of the **ark of the covenant**.* The soldiers were not allowed to shout or speak. On the seventh day they made seven circuits, at the end of which the priests blew their trumpets, the people shouted, and the wall of Jericho fell down flat. In the course of the city's sack, **Achan**, one of the Israelites, stole some of the plunder reserved for God. He and his family were later stoned to death for the offense.

JEROBOAM The first king of Israel after the kingdom was divided following Solomon's death in ca. 922 BC. He led the ten tribes who broke away from the rule of Solomon's son **Rehoboam**.* Referred to in the Old Testament as "*Jeroboam the son of Nebat, who made Israel to sin*", he was regarded as a promoter of idolatry. The Israel that resulted from the partition survived for two turbulent centuries until overwhelmed by the Assyrians in 722 BC.

JERUSALEM A city in the north of Judah, close to the border with Israel. It was captured by King **David**,* who made it his capital. See BABYLON.

JESSE Father of David and an ancestor of Jesus.

JESUS Worshipped by Christians as the son of God, he was born ca. 4 BC in Bethlehem in the Roman province of Judaea. He grew up in Nazareth, where his mother's husband, Joseph, worked as a carpenter. At the age of 12, on a visit to Jerusalem, he went missing and was finally discovered by his parents in the Temple, conversing with the learned men. In answer to their reproaches, he spoke his first recorded words: "*How is it that ye sought me? wist ye not that I must be about my Father's business?*" (Luke 2:49). After his baptism by **John**,* he went into the wilderness where he was tempted by the Devil. He then began his ministry, calling his disciples, teaching, debating, performing miracles. In AD 29 or 30 he was arrested and executed by crucifixion. The gospels record that he rose from the dead two days after his crucifixion and ascended into heaven 40 days later. See especially ANNUNCIATION, CRUCIFIXION, NATIVITY, PASSION, TEMPTATIONS.

JEZEBEL Wife of King **Ahab*** of Israel. Her worship of Baal provoked the hostility of **Elijah*** and made her one of the most vilified figures in the Old Testament, whose name is still associated with vice. Her death at the hands of **Jehu*** after his murder of King Joram is recounted in the Book of Kings. When later Jehu sent men to bury her, there remained only the skull, the feet, and the palms of the hands. The rest had been eaten by dogs, according to the prophecy of Elijah.

Death of Jezebel (2 Kings 9:30–33)

30: And when Jehu was come to Jezreel, Jezebel heard of it; and she painted her face, and tired her head, and looked out at a window.
31: And as Jehu entered in at the gate, she said, Had Zimri peace, who slew his master?
32: And he lifted up his face to the window, and said, Who is on my side? who? And there looked out to him two or three eunuchs.
33: And he said, Throw her down. So they threw her down: and some of her blood was sprinkled on the wall, and on the horses: and he trode her under foot.

JOAB Commander of David's army, he was responsible for the killing of the king's son **Absalom**,* in spite of express orders against it. After David's death he backed Adonijah (another of David's sons) rather than Solomon for the succession, and was killed on Solomon's orders.

JOB The central figure of the Book of Job, he was an upright man from the land of Uz whose faith God tested by allowing Satan to inflict a series of unmerited sufferings on him. His torments were increased by the three friends – Job's comforters – who tried to persuade him that such suffering must be a retribution for sin. Guilty of nothing worse than pride in his own righteousness, Job was in the end restored to double his former prosperity.

Satan's Challenge (Job 1:6–12)

6: Now there was a day when the sons of God came to present themselves before the LORD, and Satan came also among them.

7: And the LORD said unto Satan, Whence comest thou? Then Satan answered the LORD, and said, From going to and fro in the earth, and from walking up and down in it.

8: And the LORD said unto Satan, Hast thou considered my servant Job, that there is none like him in the earth, a perfect and an upright man, one that feareth God, and escheweth evil?

9: Then Satan answered the LORD, and said, Doth Job fear God for nought?

10: Hast not thou made an hedge about him, and about his house, and about all that he hath on every side? thou hast blessed the work of his hands, and his substance is increased in the land.

11: But put forth thine hand now, and touch all that he hath, and he will curse thee to thy face.

12: And the LORD said unto Satan, Behold, all that he hath is in thy power; only upon himself put not forth thine hand. So Satan went forth from the presence of the LORD.

JOHN THE APOSTLE One of the sons of Zebedee, he and his brother James were given by Jesus the nickname **Boanerges**, sons of thunder. Identified as "the disciple whom Jesus loved," John alone among the apostles witnessed the crucifixion. The gospel that bears his name is distinct from the three synoptic gospels in various points of content and chronology as well as in its emphasis on the teachings of Jesus and their theological implications. Its opening words are well known:

1: In the beginning was the Word, and the Word was with God, and the Word was God.

2: The same was in the beginning with God.

3: All things were made by him; and without him was not any thing made that was made.

4: In him was life; and the life was the light of men.

5: And the light shineth in darkness; and the darkness comprehended it not.

John the Baptist (Matthew 3:3–4)

3: For this is he that was spoken of by the prophet Esaias, saying, The voice of one crying in the wilderness, Prepare ye the way of the Lord, make his paths straight.

4: And the same John had his raiment of camel's hair, and a leathern girdle about his loins; and his meat was locusts and wild honey.

JOHN THE BAPTIST So called from his practice of river baptism, John was a forerunner of Jesus, preaching a message of repentance. The representation of him in western art as a sort of wild man takes its cue from the biblical description (see panel). According to the gospels, his baptism of Jesus in the River Jordan was marked by the descent of the Holy Spirit in the likeness of a dove, and a voice from heaven, saying, in Matthew's version, *"This is my beloved Son, in whom I am well pleased."* John's criticism of Herod Antipas for marrying his sister-in-law Herodias led to his imprisonment and execution. See SALOME.

JONAH A minor prophet charged by God with reproving the inhabitants of the Assyrian capital Nineveh for their wickedness. Jonah tried to escape the task by taking ship from Joppa to Tarshish. When a storm arose, the sailors cast lots to find out who was responsible, and the lot fell upon Jonah. Thrown overboard, he was swallowed by a great fish and remained in its belly for three days and three nights until he prayed to God, whereupon the fish vomited him on to dry land. In the event, his mission to Nineveh was successful and the city repented, but Jonah himself was aggrieved that its inhabitants had escaped punishment. God's rebuke, with which the story ends, shows unaccustomed compassion: *"And should not I spare Nineveh, that great city, wherein are more than sixscore thousand persons that cannot discern between their right hand and their left hand; and also much cattle?"* (Jonah 4:11).

JONATHAN Son of King **Saul*** and devoted friend of **David**,* he died in the same battle against the Philistines as his father. His intense friendship with David is reflected in David's lament following his death.

David's lament for Saul and Jonathan (2 Samuel 1:19–27)

19: The beauty of Israel is slain upon thy high places: how are the mighty fallen!

20: Tell it not in Gath, publish it not in the streets of Askelon; lest the daughters of the Philistines rejoice, lest the daughters of the uncircumcised triumph.

21: Ye mountains of Gilboa, let there be no dew, neither let there be rain, upon you, nor fields of offerings: for there the shield of the mighty is vilely cast away, the shield of Saul, as though he had not been anointed with oil.

22: From the blood of the slain, from the fat of the mighty, the bow of Jonathan turned not back, and the sword of Saul returned not empty.

23: Saul and Jonathan were lovely and pleasant in their lives, and in their death they were not divided: they were swifter than eagles, they were stronger than lions.

24: Ye daughters of Israel, weep over Saul, who clothed you in scarlet, with other delights, who put on ornaments of gold upon your apparel.

25: How are the mighty fallen in the midst of the battle! O Jonathan, thou wast slain in thine high places.

26: I am distressed for thee, my brother Jonathan: very pleasant hast thou been unto me: thy love to me was wonderful, passing the love of women.

27: How are the mighty fallen, and the weapons of war perished!

JORDAN An important river in both the Old and New Testaments, the Jordan flows southwards from above the Sea of Galilee to the Dead Sea. When the Israelites entered the Promised Land, the flow of its waters was suspended so that they could cross on dry land.

JOSEPH The favorite son of Jacob, for whom he made a coat of many colors. The jealousy of his elder brothers was aggravated by Joseph's tactless relation of two dreams which suggested that he would reign over them as well as over his mother and father. When later he came to join them herding flocks, they conspired against him:

> And they said one to another, Behold, this dreamer cometh.
> Come now therefore, and let us slay him, and cast him into some pit, and we will say, Some evil beast hath devoured him: and we shall see what will become of his dreams. (Genesis 37:19–20)

Reuben,* the eldest brother, diverted them from killing him, but Joseph was stripped of his coat, cast into a pit, and then sold to some passing traders. He was taken by them to Egypt and there sold on into the household of **Potiphar**,* whose wife falsely accused him of trying to seduce her. He won his release from prison by interpreting two of Pharaoh's dreams (Genesis 41) as a warning that after seven years of plenty Egypt would suffer seven years of famine. Joseph himself was put in charge of food supplies – a position second in importance only to that of Pharaoh – and managed to preserve Egypt from disaster. Unaware of Joseph's eminence, his elder brothers traveled from famine-stricken Canaan to buy food in Egypt. After pretending to suspect them – "Ye are spies; to see the nakedness of the land ye are come" (Genesis 42:9) – Joseph finally revealed his identity and they were all reunited, including the youngest, Benjamin. The whole of Jacob's family then moved to Egypt, settling in the fertile area of Goshen.

JOSHUA The successor of Moses, he led the Israelites into the Promised Land and commanded them in the early wars of conquest. After taking the cities of **Jericho*** and Ai, he defeated an alliance of Amorites in decisive fashion by staying the course of the heavenly bodies in order to prolong the slaughter: "sun, stand thou still upon Gibeon; and thou, Moon, in the valley of Ajalon" (Joshua 10:12). Later he set up the six **cities of refuge** in which anyone who had killed unwittingly could be safe from blood vengeance. Along with **Caleb**,* Joshua was one of only two adults involved in the **Exodus*** who lived to enter the Promised Land.

JUDAH The territory to the west of the Dead Sea settled by the tribe of Judah. After the death of Solomon in ca. 922 BC his kingdom split into Israel and Judah (see REHOBOAM). Though Judah was much smaller, containing only the tribes of Judah and Benjamin, it outlasted Israel by almost a century and a half, surviving as an independent kingdom until Nebuchadnezzar's destruction of Jerusalem in 586 BC. Under Roman rule it became the province of Judaea.

JUDAS ISCARIOT The apostle who betrayed Jesus for 30 pieces of silver. In remorse he took the money back to the chief priests, saying: "I have sinned in that I have betrayed the innocent blood. And they said, What is that to us? see thou to that" (Matthew 27:4). Judas threw the pieces of silver down in the Temple, went out and hanged himself. The money was used to buy a field for the burial of strangers, which was afterwards called the field of blood (in Aramaic, Aceldama). A different version of Judas's end is given in Acts 1:18, where he is said to have purchased the field himself, "and falling headlong, he burst asunder in the midst, and all his bowels gushed out."

JUDGES The name given to the leaders of the Israelites in the period before the establishment of the monarchy. Among the most celebrated judges were **Deborah**,* **Gideon**,* and **Samson**.*

JUDITH A Jewish heroine whose story is told in the Book of Judith in the Apocrypha. Having won the confidence of the Assyrian general **Holofernes**, who was leading a campaign against the Israelites, she cut off his head while he was sleeping in his tent.

KORAH Leader of a rebellion against **Moses*** and **Aaron**.* His objections to the privileges of the priesthood were answered when the earth opened and swallowed him alive, along with his supporters.

LABAN Father of **Leah** and **Rachel**. He made **Jacob*** work seven years for the hand of Rachel but then deceived him into marrying Leah instead. Jacob had to work for another seven years in order finally to win Rachel. He stayed with Laban for a further six years before tricking him out of the best of his flocks and decamping with both daughters and Laban's household gods, which Rachel had stolen.

LAMB OF GOD The phrase is used by **John the Baptist*** when he sees Jesus coming to the Jordan for baptism: *"Behold the Lamb of God, which taketh away the sin of the world"* (John 1:29).

LAODICEA A city in what is now Turkey, criticized in Revelation for its lukewarm attitude to Christianity.

LAST JUDGMENT God's general judgment on humanity after the Resurrection of the Dead.

LAST SUPPER The last meal eaten by Jesus with his disciples in the Upper Room on the night of his arrest. It was at the Last Supper that he instituted the Eucharist.

LAZARUS (1) The brother of **Mary*** and **Martha**,* whom Jesus raised from the dead. Four days after Lazarus's death, Jesus went to the tomb, had the stone rolled away, and shouted to him to come forth: *"And he that was dead came forth, bound hand and foot with graveclothes: and his face was bound about with a napkin. Jesus saith unto them, Loose him, and let him go"* (John

11:44). (2) Lazarus was also the name given in one of Jesus's parables to the beggar who goes to heaven while the rich man at whose gate he sat goes to hell. See DIVES.

LEVIATHAN A sea-monster referred to most memorably in Job: "*Canst thou draw out leviathan with an hook? or his tongue with a cord which thou lettest down?*" (Job 41:1).

LEVITES Members of the tribe of Levi that provided the Israelite priesthood.

LEX TALIONIS The law of retaliation, summed up in Exodus 21:23–25:

> And if any mischief follow, then thou shalt give life for life,
> Eye for eye, tooth for tooth, hand for hand, foot for foot,
> Burning for burning, wound for wound, stripe for stripe.

LILITH A female demon, referred to in Isaiah as the screech-owl. One tradition affirms that she was Adam's first wife, before Eve. Unwilling to accept Adam's domination, she left Paradise.

Lord's Prayer, from the Book of Common Prayer (1662)

Our Father, which art in heaven, Hallowed be thy Name. Thy kingdom come. Thy will be done in earth, As it is in heaven. Give us this day our daily bread. And forgive us our trespasses, As we forgive them that trespass against us. And lead us not into temptation, But deliver us from evil. For thine is the kingdom, The power, and the glory, For ever and ever. Amen.

LION OF JUDAH A reference to Jesus in Revelation.

LORD'S PRAYER The prayer given as a model by Jesus to his disciples in the Sermon on the Mount. The familiar version from the Book of Common Prayer (see panel) differs slightly from the translation given in the King James Bible.

LOT Abraham's nephew. He and his wife and daughters were rescued from the fate of **Sodom*** after he had entertained and protected two angels who visited it before its destruction. As fire and brimstone rained down on the city, Lot's wife, contrary to God's command, looked back and was turned into a pillar of salt. Lot and his daughters escaped to a cave in the mountains, where, to preserve his family line, the daughters got him drunk and had sex with him. From their incest descended the Moabites and the Ammonites.

LUCIFER (Latin = *light-bearer*) Originally a reference to Venus, the morning star, it became one of the names for Satan.

LUKE A doctor and friend of **Paul**,* credited with writing the third gospel and Acts.

MACCABEES The Maccabee family led a revolt against Seleucid rule in Palestine (see p. 8), which was imposing an increasingly intrusive and sacrilegious Hellenism. In 164 BC **Judas Maccabeus** took Jerusalem and established it as the capital of an independent kingdom that was ruled by the Maccabee dynasty until **Pompey** (see p. 105) recaptured it for the Roman empire in 63 BC. See ALEXANDER.

MAGI The wise men in St. Matthew's gospel who came from the east, guided by a star, to worship the new-born Jesus. Later tradition fixed their number at three and turned them into kings, giving their names as Gaspar, Melchior, and Balthazar. They were represented as bringing gifts of gold, frankincense and myrrh, in allusion to Jesus's royalty, divinity, and future death. See INNOCENTS.

MAGNIFICAT (Latin = *magnifies*) The traditional name for Mary's hymn of praise when she visited her cousin Elizabeth after the **Annunciation**.* The familiar version from the Book of Common Prayer differs slightly from the translation given in the King James Bible (Luke 1:46–55).

MAMMON (Aramaic = *wealth, money*) The personification of mammon derives from the words of Jesus in the Sermon on the Mount: "*No man can serve two masters: for either he will hate the one, and love the other; or else he will hold to the one, and despise the other. Ye cannot serve God and mammon*" (Matthew 6:24). Medieval writers turned mammon into a Devil, and he appears as one of the fallen angels in Milton's *Paradise Lost*.

MANNA (Hebrew = *what is it?*) The food provided by God for the Israelites while they were in the wilderness. Like hoarfrost in appearance and sweet to the taste, it appeared every morning except the sabbath and was supplemented in the evening by quails. The gospel of St. John refers to it as "*bread from heaven*" (John 6:31).

MARTHA Sister of **Lazarus*** and of **Mary of Bethany**.* She is depicted as pre-occupied by household cares and resentful at being left to do the work while Mary talks with Jesus (Luke 10:38–42).

MARY The mother of Jesus, often called the Virgin Mary in reference to the belief that she conceived Jesus by the Holy Ghost while still a virgin. The dogma that she herself was conceived without Original Sin is referred to as the **Immaculate Conception**. See ANNUNCIATION, CRUCIFIXION, MAGNIFICAT, NATIVITY, VIRGIN BIRTH.

MARY OF BETHANY Sister of Lazarus and Martha, she is said by John to be the woman who anointed the feet of Jesus and wiped them with her hair. Another tradition has associated a slightly different version of this episode with **Mary Magdalene**.*

MARY MAGDALENE One of a group of women mentioned by Luke as accompanying Jesus and the apostles. Tradition has identified her with the unnamed woman in Matthew and Mark who pours a box of precious ointment over the head of Jesus, to the indignation of some of the disciples who say the money would have been better spent on the poor. Jesus defends her action: *"for ye have the poor always with you; but me ye have not always"* (Matthew 26:11). Mary was the first to see Jesus after the resurrection. Weeping beside the empty sepulcher, she was spoken to by someone she took for the gardener but who then revealed himself as Jesus. In a scene frequently depicted by western painters he warned her not to touch him — *Noli me tangere* in Latin — since he had not yet ascended into heaven. Mary's traditional characterization as a reformed prostitute is derived from the information in Mark and Luke that Jesus had delivered her from seven devils.

MASADA A fortress on the west bank of the Dead Sea where Jewish rebels mounted their last stand against the Romans. In AD 74 all but a handful of women and children committed suicide in the face of an overwhelming Roman attack.

MATTHEW A tax collector, he was one of the 12 apostles called by Jesus but is not thought to be the author of the gospel that bears his name.

MATTHIAS The disciple chosen to replace Judas as one of the Twelve.

MEPHIBOSHETH Son of **Jonathan**.* Lame in both feet, he was treated with great kindness by **David*** on account of his father. When told by David that he would be restored to all the lands of his grandfather Saul and would eat at the king's table, *"he bowed himself, and said, What is thy servant, that thou shouldest look upon such a dead dog as I am?"* (2 Samuel 9:8).

MERIBAH (Hebrew = *strife*) The name given to the place where the Israelites rose against **Moses*** and **Aaron**,* complaining of the lack of water in the desert. Moses gathered them together and with the words, "*Hear now, ye rebels; must we fetch you water out of this rock?*" (Numbers 20:10), struck the rock twice with his rod, producing an abundant stream of water. But God had told him merely to speak to the rock, and for this lapse of self-control he was denied entry into the Promised Land.

MESSIAH (Hebrew = *anointed one*) The term for the awaited savior who would deliver the Jewish people from their enemies. It is similar to the Greek word *christos*, Christ.

METHUSELAH Grandfather of **Noah**.* According to Genesis 5:27 he lived to the age of 969, the longest lifespan recorded in the Bible.

MIRIAM Sister of **Moses*** and **Aaron**,* she was a prophetess among the Israelites and led the celebrations for the crossing of the Red Sea. Later she was temporarily stricken with leprosy for criticizing the marriage of Moses to an Ethiopian woman.

MOAB The land of Moab was to the east of the Dead Sea, and there was frequent conflict between its people and the Israelites. The Moabites, of whom **Ruth*** was one, were supposedly descended from the incestuous union between **Lot*** and his elder daughter.

MOLOCH (or Molech) A middle-eastern god to whom children were sacrificed. Josiah, as king of Judah, tried with limited success to suppress his worship in the late seventh century BC. Moloch has since become a name for any devouring force to which precious goods or people must be sacrificed.

MORDECAI See ESTHER.

MOSES The leader of the Israelites who brought them out of slavery in Egypt. According to the story in Exodus, he barely escaped Pharaoh's edict that all male children born to the Israelites should be drowned in the Nile. His mother hid him in an ark of bulrushes at the edge of the river, where he was found by Pharaoh's daughter, who brought him up as her adopted son. After killing an Egyptian whom he saw ill-treating an Israelite, Moses fled to Midian, southeast of Palestine. There, "*a stranger in a strange land*" (Exodus 2:22), he married Zipporah, daughter of Jethro, a Midianite priest. Recalled by God at the age of 80 to deliver the Israelites from Egypt, he led them to freedom, dying just before they reached the Promised Land, which he himself was not allowed to enter (see MERIBAH). See also BURNING BUSH, EXODUS, PISGAH, PLAGUES, TEN COMMANDMENTS.

NAAMAN A Syrian general. He was cured of leprosy (probably a skin complaint rather than what we call leprosy today) by **Elisha**,* who sent him a message to bathe seven times in the River Jordan. Naaman was initially indignant – *"Are not Abana and Pharpar, rivers of Damascus, better than all the waters of Israel?"* (2 Kings 5:12) – but on the advice of his servants he carried out Elisha's instructions and was healed. See GEHAZI.

NABOTH Owner of a vineyard close to King **Ahab's*** palace. When Naboth refused to sell the vineyard to Ahab, **Jezebel*** arranged for him to be charged with blasphemy and stoned to death. Ahab went to take possession of the vineyard but was met by **Elijah**,* who prophesied the destruction of his house:

> Thus saith the Lord, In the place where dogs licked the blood of Naboth shall dogs lick thy blood, even thine.
> And Ahab said to Elijah, Hast thou found me, O mine enemy? (1 Kings 21:19–20)

NATHAN A prophet in the time of David. After David had engineered the killing of **Uriah**,* Nathan delivered God's sentence for his sin: internal strife in Israel and the death of his first child by Uriah's wife **Bathsheba**.*

NATIVITY The story of the birth of Jesus. Apart from the coming of the **Magi**,* most of the details – the Annunciation, the journey to Bethlehem, the manger, the shepherds – are found in St. Luke's gospel (see panel).

The Nativity (Luke 2:1–19)

1: And it came to pass in those days, that there went out a decree from Caesar Augustus, that all the world should be taxed.

2: (And this taxing was first made when Cyrenius was governor of Syria.)

3: And all went to be taxed, every one into his own city.

4: And Joseph also went up from Galilee, out of the city of Nazareth, into Judaea, unto the city of David, which is called Bethlehem; (because he was of the house and lineage of David:)

5: To be taxed with Mary his espoused wife, being great with child.

6: And so it was, that, while they were there, the days were accomplished that she should be delivered.

7: And she brought forth her firstborn son, and wrapped him in swaddling clothes, and laid him in a manger; because there was no room for them in the inn.

8: And there were in the same country shepherds abiding in the field, keeping watch over their flock by night.

9: And, lo, the angel of the Lord came upon them, and the glory of the Lord shone round about them: and they were sore afraid.

10: And the angel said unto them, Fear not: for, behold, I bring you good tidings of great joy, which shall be to all people.

11: For unto you is born this day in the city of David a Saviour, which is Christ the Lord.

12: And this shall be a sign unto you; Ye shall find the babe wrapped in swaddling clothes, lying in a manger.

13: And suddenly there was with the angel a multitude of the heavenly host praising God, and saying,

14: Glory to God in the highest, and on earth peace, good will toward men.

15: And it came to pass, as the angels were gone away from them into heaven, the shepherds said one to another, Let us now go even unto Bethlehem, and see this thing which is come to pass, which the Lord hath made known unto us.

16: And they came with haste, and found Mary, and Joseph, and the babe lying in a manger.

17: And when they had seen it, they made known abroad the saying which was told them concerning this child.

18: And all they that heard it wondered at those things which were told them by the shepherds.

19: But Mary kept all these things, and pondered them in her heart.

NAZARENE A person from Nazareth.

NAZIRITE Member of an ascetic group whose vows forbade them to take intoxicants, touch corpses, or cut their hair. **Samson*** was one of them, as was the prophet **Samuel**.*

NEBUCHADNEZZAR King of Babylon from 605 to 562 BC. He was responsible for the destruction of Jerusalem in 586 and the creation of the Hanging Gardens of Babylon. In the Book of Daniel he dreams of a huge image whose head is of gold, its breast and arms of silver, its belly and thighs of brass, its legs of iron, and its feet part iron and part clay. Daniel interprets this in terms of the future of the Babylonian kingdom through successive reigns (Daniel

2:31–45). In the dream the idol is broken in pieces because the admixture of clay in its feet makes it vulnerable – hence "feet of clay." A second dream that Daniel interpreted foretold Nebuchadnezzar's temporary expulsion from human society. Driven by what was presumably an attack of madness, he went out to live on grass like a beast in the field, his body wet with dew, his hair growing like eagles' feathers, and his nails like the claws of a bird. His reason returned when he recognized the authority of God.

NICODEMUS Mentioned in the gospel of St. John as a Pharisee who "*came to Jesus by night*" (John 3:2) to ask him questions. After the crucifixion he brought myrrh and aloes for Jesus's body and helped with the burial arrangements.

NIMROD Mentioned in Genesis 10:9 as "*a mighty hunter before the Lord.*" His name has become proverbial for skilled or enthusiastic hunters.

NINEVEH Capital city of the Assyrians, preached to by Jonah and inveighed against by the prophet Nahum: "*Woe to the bloody city! it is all full of lies and robbery*" (Nahum 3:1). See JONAH.

NOAH Genesis 6–9 tells how God, appalled by human wickedness, repented of his creation and decided to wipe it out with a great flood. Noah and his family alone were spared. On God's instructions they built an ark and took into it two of every living thing, which were thus preserved from destruction. The rain fell for 40 days and nights, covering the earth. As the waters began to recede, the ark came to rest in the seventh month on Mount Ararat. Noah knew that the flood was over when a dove that he had released from the ark returned in the evening with an olive leaf in her mouth, plucked from a tree. God promised that he would never again destroy the earth by flood and sealed the covenant by setting a rainbow in the sky. Having planted a vineyard, Noah got drunk on the wine and was seen naked in his tent by his son Ham. His two other sons, Shem and Japheth, managed to cover him with a garment, backing towards him to avoid seeing his nakedness. On waking, Noah cursed Ham's son for what his father had seen.

NOD The land "*on the east of Eden*" where **Cain*** goes to live after his murder of **Abel**.*

NUNC DIMITTIS See SIMEON.

OBADIAH A minor prophet, author of the shortest book in the Bible.

OG King of Bashan, defeated by the Israelites. He is reported in Deuteronomy 3:11 to have been a survivor of the race of giants, possessing an iron bedstead 9 cubits long by 4 cubits wide (i.e., about 13 feet by 6).

OLIVES, MOUNT OF A hill just to the east of Jerusalem, where the garden of **Gethsemane*** was situated.

ONAN A son of Judah. After his elder brother had been killed by God for wickedness, Onan was required by Judah to inseminate his sister-in-law Tamar on his brother's behalf: *"And Onan knew that the seed should not be his; and it came to pass, when he went in unto his brother's wife, that he spilled it on the ground, lest that he should give seed to his brother"* (Genesis 38:9). In spite of the current meaning of onanism, his sin, for which God duly killed him, was therefore *coitus interruptus* rather than masturbation.

ORIGEN (AD 185–254) Christian theologian from Alexandria who castrated himself in the service of God. His belief in universal salvation was condemned by many as heretical.

ORIGINAL SIN The doctrine, derived primarily from the writings of **St. Paul**,* that since the Fall human beings are born into a state of sin and can only be redeemed by divine grace.

PAPYRUS A kind of writing material used in ancient Egypt and made from the stem of the papyrus reed, which grew in the Nile delta.

PARADISE From the Persian word for a walled garden, it is used to refer both to the Garden of Eden and to the joys of heaven.

PASSION (Latin, *patior* = suffer) The word used for the suffering and death of Jesus. The main elements of the Passion are (1) the agony in the garden; (2) the arrest, during which one of the disciples drew a sword and cut off an ear of the high priest's servant, whom Jesus healed; (3) the trials before the Jewish **Sanhedrin*** and Pontius **Pilate**;* (4) the flogging by Roman soldiers; (5) the mockery of Jesus by dressing him in a purple robe and placing a crown of thorns on his head; (6) the journey to **Calvary*** (Via Dolorosa), on which Jesus (or, according to the synoptic gospels, **Simon of Cyrene**) was forced to carry the cross; (7) the crucifixion. See CRUCIFIXION, GETHSEMANE.

PASSOVER The Jewish festival that commemorates the Exodus from slavery in Egypt. The Israelites were instructed to kill a lamb – to be eaten roasted, with unleavened bread and bitter herbs – and daub its blood on the lintel and side-posts of their houses, which God would then pass over when he came through Egypt killing the firstborn children in the tenth and final plague: *"And thus shall ye eat it; with your loins girded, your shoes on your feet, and your staff in your hand; and ye shall eat it in haste: it is the Lord's passover"* (Exodus 12:11). See PLAGUES OF EGYPT.

PATRIARCH A term used for the immediate ancestors of the Israelites – **Abraham**,* **Isaac**,* and **Jacob**.*

PATRISTICS The study of the writings of the Fathers of the early Christian church.

PAUL Born in Tarsus in what is now Turkey, Paul (initially referred to in the Bible by his Jewish name, Saul) was also a Roman citizen. An orthodox Pharisee, who earned his living as a tent-maker, he became a persecutor of Christians until in ca. AD 34 he experienced a dramatic conversion on the road to Damascus. Blinded by a sudden light from heaven, he fell to earth and heard a voice saying,

> Saul, Saul, why persecutest thou me?
> And he said, Who art thou, Lord? And the Lord said, I am Jesus whom thou per-
> secutest: it is hard for thee to kick against the pricks. (Acts 9:4–5)

After three days of blindness in Damascus, he was visited by a disciple, **Ananias**, who put his hands over Saul's eyes and called on him to be filled with the Holy Ghost, *"And immediately there fell from his eyes as it had been scales: and he received sight forthwith, and arose, and was baptized"* (Acts 9:18). Qualified as an apostle by his personal experience of the risen Lord, Paul at once became an ardent champion of the new religion, to the point where the Jews of Damascus conspired to have him killed. He escaped by being let down the city wall in a basket. Thereafter he did much to shape Christian theology, preaching tirelessly, writing the epistles that form a substantial part of the New Testament, and undertaking three missionary journeys through Asia Minor and Greece. Arrested in Jerusalem, he exercised his right as a Roman citizen – *civis Romanus sum* – to appeal to Caesar (Acts 25:10–12) and was sent to Rome for judgment. There he continued to preach until he was beheaded in ca. 64 during Nero's persecutions.

The First Epistle of Paul the Apostle to the Corinthians

Chapter 13

1: Though I speak with the tongues of men and of angels, and have not charity, I am become as sounding brass, or a tinkling cymbal.

2: And though I have the gift of prophecy, and understand all mysteries, and all knowledge; and though I have all faith, so that I could remove mountains, and have not charity, I am nothing . . .

11: When I was a child, I spake as a child, I understood as a child, I thought as a child: but when I became a man, I put away childish things.

12: For now we see through a glass, darkly; but then face to face: now I know in part; but then shall I know even as also I am known.

13: And now abideth faith, hope, charity, these three; but the greatest of these is charity.

Chapter 15

54: So when this corruptible shall have put on incorruption, and this mortal shall have put on immortality, then shall be brought to pass the saying that is written, Death is swallowed up in victory.

55: O death, where is thy sting? O grave, where is thy victory?

PENTATEUCH The Greek name for the first five books of the Old Testament, known to Jews as the **Torah**, or Law. It was probably composed from a number of different sources between the tenth and sixth or fifth centuries BC.

PENTECOST A Jewish festival that acquired new significance when the apostles were filled with the Holy Ghost on that date and received the gift of tongues, enabling them to speak other languages. Today the feast is often called Whitsun.

PETER A Galilean fisherman whose real name was Simon. (The nickname Peter [= rock] was given later by Jesus.) He was one of the first disciples to be called by Jesus, who saw him and his brother Andrew casting nets into the Sea of Galilee: "*And he saith unto them, Follow me, and I will make you fishers of men*" (Matthew 4:19). He became one of the closest of the disciples and is represented, on the basis of Jesus's words in St.

Peter (Matthew 16:18–19)

18: And I say also unto thee, That thou art Peter, and upon this rock I will build my church; and the gates of hell shall not prevail against it.

19: And I will give unto thee the keys of the kingdom of heaven: and whatsoever thou shalt bind on earth shall be bound in heaven: and whatsoever thou shalt loose on earth shall be loosed in heaven.

Matthew, as holding the keys to the kingdom of heaven (see panel). Just before Jesus's arrest, he predicted that Peter would deny acquaintance with him three times in the course of the night. Immediately after the third denial, the cock crew: *"And Peter remembered the word of Jesus, which said unto him, Before the cock crow, thou shalt deny me thrice. And he went out, and wept bitterly"* (Matthew 26:75). His later apostleship was notable for the attempt to spread the word of God to Gentiles as well as Jews. Executed in ca. AD 65 in Nero's persecutions, he was said to have requested that he be crucified upside-down because he was unworthy to suffer the same death as Jesus.

PHARAOH Supreme ruler of ancient Egypt. The pharaoh who figures in the story of the Exodus was probably Ramses II (ca. 1279–1213 BC). His initial response to Moses's request that the Israelites be released was to set it down to idleness – *"Ye are idle, ye are idle: therefore ye say, Let us go and do sacrifice to the Lord"* (Exodus 5:17). Accordingly, he increased their workload, forcing them to make the same number of bricks each day but without any provision of straw – hence the phrase "make bricks without straw." Only after being visited with the ten plagues did he relent for long enough to let the Israelites go. See EXODUS, PLAGUES OF EGYPT.

PHARISEES A Jewish sect, formed in the second century BC, whose emphasis on strict observance of the **Torah** brought them into frequent conflict with Jesus.

PHILISTINES A sea-faring people who settled along the southern coast of ancient Palestine. They were often at war with the Israelites until **David*** finally defeated them. In spite of the meaning their name has acquired today, they seem to have had a relatively sophisticated culture.

PHYLACTERIES Small leather boxes containing texts from the **Pentateuch*** worn on the forehead and left arm by Jewish males when reciting prayers. Jesus accuses the scribes and Pharisees of making them unnecessarily broad in order to advertise their piety (Matthew 23:5).

PILATE, PONTIUS Governor of the Roman province of Judaea at the time of Jesus's arrest. He is represented in the gospels as willing to release Jesus but fearful of threats by the Jews to make trouble for him with the Emperor Tiberius: *"If thou let this man go, thou art not Caesar's friend: whosoever maketh himself a king speaketh against Caesar"* (John 19:12). Matthew 27:24–25 records the incident that has ever since been associated with his name:

When Pilate saw that he could prevail nothing, but that rather a tumult was made, he took water, and washed his hands before the multitude, saying, I am innocent of the blood of this just person: see ye to it.

Then answered all the people, and said, His blood be on us, and on our children.

See INRI.

PISGAH The mountain in Moab from which Moses was allowed to see the Promised Land before his death.

PLAGUES OF EGYPT The ten plagues visited on Egypt by God to persuade Pharaoh to release the Israelites (Exodus 7–12): (1) Aaron struck the waters of the Nile with his rod and they were turned to blood; (2) Aaron stretched his rod over the waters of Egypt and the land was covered by a plague of frogs; (3) Aaron struck the dust with his rod and produced a plague of lice; (4) a swarm of flies covered the land; (5) the cattle of Egypt were killed by an infectious disease (murrain); (6) the Egyptians were afflicted by boils; (7) then by destructive hail-storms; (8) then by a plague of locusts; (9) Egypt was stricken with darkness for three days; (10) finally, at midnight, God killed the firstborn child of every family in Egypt. See PASSOVER.

PLAIN, CITIES OF THE Five cities, of which **Sodom*** and **Gomorrah** were the most notorious, located on the plain southeast of the Dead Sea.

POTIPHAR One of Pharaoh's officers. He bought Joseph on his arrival in Egypt and promoted him within his household. **Potiphar's wife** later attempted to seduce Joseph, who fled, leaving his garment in her hand, whereupon she accused him of making advances to her (Genesis 39). Joseph was thrown into prison, from which he later secured his release by interpreting Pharaoh's dreams. See JOSEPH.

POTTER'S FIELD A cemetery near Jerusalem in which foreigners were buried. It was bought with the 30 pieces of silver earned by Judas for betraying Jesus. See JUDAS.

PRODIGAL SON The parable recorded in Luke of a younger son who squanders his inheritance on riotous living in a far country, then returns penitent to his father. To the dismay of the hard-working elder brother, their father kills the fatted calf and throws a party for the returned prodigal (see panel).

The Prodigal Son (Luke 15:11–32)

11: And he [Jesus] said, A certain man had two sons:

12: And the younger of them said to his father, Father, give me the portion of goods that falleth to me. And he divided unto them his living.

13: And not many days after the younger son gathered all together, and took his journey into a far country, and there wasted his substance with riotous living.

14: And when he had spent all, there arose a mighty famine in that land; and he began to be in want.

15: And he went and joined himself to a citizen of that country; and he sent him into his fields to feed swine.

16: And he would fain have filled his belly with the husks that the swine did eat: and no man gave unto him.

17: And when he came to himself, he said, How many hired servants of my father's have bread enough and to spare, and I perish with hunger!

18: I will arise and go to my father, and will say unto him, Father, I have sinned against heaven, and before thee,

19: And am no more worthy to be called thy son: make me as one of thy hired servants.

20: And he arose, and came to his father. But when he was yet a great way off, his father saw him, and had compassion, and ran, and fell on his neck, and kissed him.

21: And the son said unto him, Father, I have sinned against heaven, and in thy sight, and am no more worthy to be called thy son.

22: But the father said to his servants, Bring forth the best robe, and put it on him; and put a ring on his hand, and shoes on his feet:

23: And bring hither the fatted calf, and kill it; and let us eat, and be merry:

24: For this my son was dead, and is alive again; he was lost, and is found. And they began to be merry.

25: Now his elder son was in the field: and as he came and drew nigh to the house, he heard musick and dancing.

26: And he called one of the servants, and asked what these things meant.

27: And he said unto him, Thy brother is come; and thy father hath killed the fatted calf, because he hath received him safe and sound.

28: And he was angry, and would not go in: therefore came his father out, and intreated him.

29: And he answering said to his father, Lo, these many years do I serve thee, neither transgressed I at any time thy commandment: and yet thou never gavest me a kid, that I might make merry with my friends:

30: But as soon as this thy son was come, which hath devoured thy living with harlots, thou hast killed for him the fatted calf.

31: And he said unto him, Son, thou art ever with me, and all that I have is thine.

32: It was meet that we should make merry, and be glad: for this thy brother was dead, and is alive again; and was lost, and is found.

PROMISED LAND See CANAAN.

PROSELYTES Converts to Judaism.

From THE BOOK OF PROVERBS

Go to the ant, thou sluggard; consider her ways and be wise. (6:6)

Can a man take fire in his bosom and his clothes not be burned? Can one go upon hot coals, and his feet not be burned? (6:27–28)

Wisdom hath builded her house, she hath hewn out her seven pillars. (9:1)

Stolen waters are sweet, and bread eaten in secret is pleasant. (9:17)

He that spareth his rod hateth his son: but he that loveth him chasteneth him betimes. (13:24)

A soft answer turneth away wrath: but grievous words stir up anger. (15:1)

Better is a dinner of herbs where love is, than a stalled ox and hatred therewith. (15:17)

Pride goeth before destruction, and an haughty spirit before a fall. (16:18)

If thine enemy be hungry, give him bread to eat; and if he be thirsty, give him water to drink: For thou shalt heap coals of fire upon his head, and the Lord shall reward thee. (25:21–2)

Answer a fool according to his folly, lest he be wise in his own conceit. (26:5)

As a dog returneth to his vomit, so a fool returneth to his folly. (26:11)

Boast not thyself of to morrow; for thou knowest not what a day may bring forth. (27:1)

A fool uttereth all his mind: but a wise man keepeth it in till afterwards. (29:11)

Who can find a virtuous woman? for her price is far above rubies. (31:10)

RACHEL Jacob's second, and favorite, wife. She was the mother of Joseph and died giving birth to Benjamin. See LABAN.

RAHAB Referred to in the Book of Joshua as Rahab the harlot, she was a prostitute who helped the two Israelite spies sent by Joshua to Jericho. Having hidden them on the roof of her house, which was built into the city wall, she then let them down by a rope from the window. In exchange, the Israelites agreed that if she put a scarlet thread in the same window, she and her household would be spared when the city was sacked (Joshua 2).

RAPHAEL The archangel sent to help Tobit and his wife after Tobit had been stricken with blindness. He accompanied Tobit's son Tobias to recover a sum of money deposited in Media and on the way told him how to find a cure for his father's blindness by extracting the gall from a large fish that had attacked him. The story is told in the Book of Tobit in the Apocrypha.

REBEKAH Wife of Isaac and mother of **Esau*** and **Jacob**.* She helped Jacob, her favorite, to trick his father into giving him the blessing due to his elder brother. See ESAU.

RED SEA The Red Sea crossed by the Israelites in the Exodus is properly translated ''Sea of Reeds.'' Situated in the Suez canal area, it is different from the Red Sea that separates Africa and Arabia. See EXODUS.

REHOBOAM Solomon's son and successor as king of Israel. His refusal to compromise with Israelite demands for lighter taxation – *''My father made your yoke heavy, and I will add to your yoke: my father also chastised you with whips, but I will chastise you with scorpions''* (1 Kings 12:14) – was a cause of the break-up of Israel and Judah into a northern and a southern kingdom in 922 BC. Rehoboam was left ruling the tribes of Judah and Benjamin, while the other ten tribes broke away – *''to your tents, O Israel''* – to form the northern kingdom of Israel under Jeroboam.

REUBEN Jacob's firstborn son, by Leah. He lost preeminence after sleeping with his father's concubine. It was he who prevented the brothers from killing Joseph. See JOSEPH.

RUTH A young Moabite widow whose story is told in the Book of Ruth. After the death of her husband, Ruth, a foreigner, chose to stay with her widowed mother-in-law, Naomi:

> And Ruth said, Intreat me not to leave thee, or to return from following after thee: for whither thou goest, I will go; and where thou lodgest, I will lodge: thy people shall be my people, and thy God my God:
> Where thou diest, will I die, and there will I be buried: the LORD do so to me, and more also, if ought but death part thee and me. (Ruth 1:16–17)

Working at harvest-time in the fields of Naomi's rich kinsman Boaz, she was seen by him and later married him. Their son became the grandfather of David.

SABBATH (Hebrew = *rest*) The Jewish day of rest, taken on Saturday. (The word is sometimes incorrectly used of the Christian rest day on Sunday.)

SADDUCEES A conservative Jewish group, prominent at the time of Jesus. They emphasized observance of the written law laid down in the **Pentateuch**.*

SALOME Daughter of **Herodias*** by a son of Herod the Great, she is not actually named in the Bible. Her dancing at the birthday feast of her stepfather Herod Antipas so pleased him that he offered her anything she wished, up to half his kingdom. At the urging of her mother, whose marriage to Herod had been criticized by **John the Baptist**,* she asked for John's head in a charger (i.e., dish). Reluctantly, Herod ordered the execution (Matthew 14, Mark 6).

SAMARIA, WOMAN OF A woman to whom Jesus revealed himself as the messiah after he had asked her for a drink at Jacob's Well in Samaria.

SAMARITAN, GOOD The central figure in the parable by which Jesus answered the question, *"Who is my neighbour?"* The parable opens with the words, *"A certain man went down from Jerusalem to Jericho, and fell among thieves, which stripped him of his raiment, and wounded him, and departed, leaving him half dead"* (Luke 10:30). A priest and a Levite, Jews like the wounded man, came along the road but offered no help, passing by on the other side. Instead, it was one of the Samaritans, traditionally disliked by Jews, who proved himself the man's true neighbor by stopping to take care of him.

SAMSON One of the Judges of Israel, renowned for his strength and susceptibility to women. He was a **Nazirite*** and a formidable opponent of the Philistines, who at the time held the Israelites in subjection. On the way to see a Philistine woman he wanted to marry, he was attacked by a lion which he tore apart with his bare hands. As he returned, he saw that a swarm of bees had made honey in the carcase. At the marriage feast he posed the 30 Philistine guests a riddle – *"Out of the eater came forth meat, and out of the strong came forth sweetness"* (Judges 14:14) – and gave them seven days to answer it. If they succeeded, he would give them 30 sheets and 30 changes of clothing; if they failed, they would give the same to him. The Philistines pressured Samson's wife into getting the answer out of him – namely, that it referred to the lion he had killed. Samson paid them by going to Ashkelon, killing 30 other Philistines, despoiling them and taking their clothes. Meanwhile, his wife's father had given her away to someone else, in revenge for which Samson caught 300 foxes, tied their tails together, fixed firebrands in the knots and drove them into the Philistine cornfields to burn their crops. Thereupon the Philistines burnt to death his wife and her father. Samson retaliated by smiting them "*hip and thigh with a great slaughter*" (Judges 15:8). Fearful of Philistine retribution, the Israelites bound Samson and handed him over to them, but he broke free and killed a thousand more Philistines with the jawbone of an ass. While he was visiting a prostitute in Gaza, the Philistines tried to ambush him at the entrance to the city, but he simply picked up the city gate, posts and all, and walked away with it. After his betrayal by **Delilah**,* Samson, blinded and shorn, was set to work in Gaza grinding corn, until the occasion when he was brought to the house of an important Philistine to provide entertainment for a feast day. Grasping the pillars of the house, Samson pulled it down, killing himself and 3,000 Philistines in a final triumphant feat of strength.

SAMUEL A prophet and the last of Israel's Judges. Samuel led the fight-back against the Philistines and anointed Israel's first two kings, **Saul*** and **David**.*

SANHEDRIN The Jewish ruling council at the time of Jesus, who was brought before it for trial.

SATAN (Hebrew = *the enemy*) One of the names of the Devil.

SAUL The first king of Israel, anointed by Samuel. He lost God's favor by show-ing clemency to the defeated Amalekites, and thereafter his fortunes began to slide. The later years of his reign were marked by his uneasy relationship with David, whom he saw as an increasing threat. In his final battle, during which the victorious Philistines killed all three of his sons, Saul fell on his sword to avoid capture. David's lament following his death (see p. 35) pays him mov-ing tribute. See also AGAG, DAVID, ENDOR, JONATHAN.

SCAPEGOAT The modern meaning of the word derives from the practice described in Leviticus 16:20–22 of confessing Israel's sins over the head of a live goat and then sending it off into the wilderness to carry the people's sins away with it.

SCRIBES (Latin = *writers*) As referred to by Jesus in the gospels, they were the scholars responsible for interpreting and transmitting the Jewish Law. Along with the **Pharisees**,* they were targets of his anger: "*Woe unto you, scribes and Pharisees, hypocrites! for ye are like unto whited sepulchres, which indeed* *appear beautiful outward, but are within full of dead men's bones, and of all uncleanness"* (Matthew 23:27).

SECOND COMING The reappearance of Jesus that will mark the final establishment of God's kingdom on earth.

SENNACHERIB The king of Assyria who laid siege to Jerusalem in 701 BC. His attack on Judah melted away when, in answer to **Hezekiah's** prayer, God suddenly struck down a large part of his army (2 Kings 19:35) – presumably with pestilence. (The story is historically inaccurate.)

SERMON ON THE MOUNT A collection of Jesus's teachings which Matthew 5–7 presents as a sermon delivered by Jesus on a mountainside in Galilee, opening with the **Beatitudes**.* Since many phrases that are now part of our culture have their origin here, it is worth quoting extensively:

Chapter 5
13: Ye are the salt of the earth: but if the salt have lost his savour, wherewith shall it be salted? . . .
14: Ye are the light of the world. A city that is set on an hill cannot be hid.
15: Neither do men light a candle, and put it under a bushel, but on a candlestick; and it giveth light unto all that are in the house.

28: But I say unto you, That whosoever looketh on a woman to lust after her hath committed adultery with her already in his heart.
29: And if thy right eye offend thee, pluck it out, and cast it from thee: for it is profitable for thee that one of thy members should perish, and not that thy whole body should be cast into hell.

38: Ye have heard that it hath been said, An eye for an eye, and a tooth for a tooth:
39: But I say unto you, That ye resist not evil: but whosoever shall smite thee on thy right cheek, turn to him the other also.

45: . . . for he maketh his sun to rise on the evil and on the good, and sendeth rain on the just and on the unjust.

Chapter 6
3: But when thou doest alms, let not thy left hand know what thy right hand doeth:

19: Lay not up for yourselves treasures upon earth, where moth and rust doth corrupt, and where thieves break through and steal:

26: Behold the fowls of the air: for they sow not, neither do they reap, nor gather into barns; yet your heavenly Father feedeth them. Are ye not much better than they?

27: Which of you by taking thought can add one cubit unto his stature?

28: And why take ye thought for raiment? Consider the lilies of the field, how they grow; they toil not, neither do they spin:

29: And yet I say unto you, That even Solomon in all his glory was not arrayed like one of these.

34: Take therefore no thought for the morrow: for the morrow shall take thought for the things of itself. Sufficient unto the day is the evil thereof.

Chapter 7

1: Judge not, that ye be not judged.

2: For with what judgment ye judge, ye shall be judged: and with what measure ye mete, it shall be measured to you again.

5: Thou hypocrite, first cast out the beam out of thine own eye; and then shalt thou see clearly to cast out the mote out of thy brother's eye.

6: Give not that which is holy unto the dogs, neither cast ye your pearls before swine, lest they trample them under their feet, and turn again and rend you.

7: Ask, and it shall be given you; seek, and ye shall find; knock, and it shall be opened unto you:

8: For every one that asketh receiveth; and he that seeketh findeth; and to him that knocketh it shall be opened.

9: Or what man is there of you, whom if his son ask bread, will he give him a stone?

10: Or if he ask a fish, will he give him a serpent?

13: Enter ye in at the strait gate: for wide is the gate, and broad is the way, that leadeth to destruction, and many there be which go in thereat:

14: Because strait is the gate, and narrow is the way, which leadeth unto life, and few there be that find it.

15: Beware of false prophets, which come to you in sheep's clothing, but inwardly they are ravening wolves.

18: A good tree cannot bring forth evil fruit, neither can a corrupt tree bring forth good fruit.

19: Every tree that bringeth not forth good fruit is hewn down, and cast into the fire.

20: Wherefore by their fruits ye shall know them.

21: Not every one that saith unto me, Lord, Lord, shall enter into the kingdom of heaven; but he that doeth the will of my Father which is in heaven.

See also BEATITUDES, MAMMON.

SETH Third son of Adam and Eve, from whom Noah was descended.

SEVEN WORDS FROM THE CROSS See CRUCIFIXION.

SHADRACH, MESHACH, and ABEDNEGO The Babylonian names of Hananiah, Mishael, and Azariah, three Jews brought to Babylon after the fall of Jerusalem. When **Nebuchadnezzar*** set up a huge golden image, they refused to worship it and were bound and cast into a burning fiery furnace. The heat was so intense that it killed the men putting them in, but Shadrach, Meshach, and Abednego were completely unharmed. Nebuchadnezzar witnessed the miracle: *"lo, I see four men loose, walking in the midst of the fire, and they have no hurt; and the form of the fourth is like the Son of God"* (Daniel 3:25). Thereafter, he decreed that no one should speak against their God.

SHALMANESER The name of a number of Assyrian kings, particularly in the ninth and eighth centuries BC.

SHEBA, QUEEN OF She reigned over the Sabeans in southwest Arabia. Having come in impressive splendor to visit Solomon, she was herself impressed by what she found: *"and, behold, the half was not told me: thy wisdom and prosperity exceedeth the fame which I heard"* (1 Kings 10:7).

SHEKEL A unit of weight – 2/5 of an ounce (11.5 grams). Its use to measure silver and gold led to its adoption as a unit of currency.

SHIBBOLETH Its modern use to mean a password by which members of a group can identify one another (and hence an outmoded slogan or doctrine) comes from an episode in Judges 12:1–6. Having defeated the Ephraimites, the Gileadites under **Jephthah*** guarded the crossings of the Jordan to prevent the enemy from reaching safety. In order to identify fugitive Ephraimites trying to pass themselves off as Gileadites, those wanting to cross the river were required to say the word shibboleth (meaning *stream in flood*). The Ephraimites, who couldn't pronouce "sh," said "sibboleth" and were thus caught and killed.

SHIMEI A supporter of **Saul**,* who threw stones at **David*** and cursed him at the time of **Absalom's*** rebellion: *"Come out, come out, thou bloody man,* *and thou man of Belial . . ."* (2 Samuel 16:7). After his victory David was merciful but on his deathbed advised **Solomon*** to have Shimei killed.

SILAS A companion of **Paul*** on some of his missionary journeys. He also helped to write a number of Paul's epistles.

SILOAM A pool in Jerusalem. John records that Jesus healed a blind man by spitting on the ground, making clay of the spittle, then anointing the man's eyes and telling him to go and wash in the pool of Siloam. Jesus explained to his disciples that the man was not blind because of his sin or that of his parents but so that the works of God could be manifested in him: *"As long as I am in the world, I am the light of the world"* (John 9:5).

SIMEON (1) Jacob's second son, ancestor of the tribe of Simeon. (2) A devout old man to whom it had been revealed that he would not die until he had seen Jesus. He took the child in his arms in the Temple and spoke the song of praise known from the Latin version of its opening words as the Nunc Dimittis. At the same time Simeon predicted to Mary her own future suffering: *"Yea, a sword shall pierce through thy own soul also"* (Luke 2:35).

> **Nunc Dimittis (Luke 2:29–32)**
>
> *29:* Lord, now lettest thou thy servant depart in peace, according to thy word:
> *30:* For mine eyes have seen thy salvation,
> *31:* Which thou hast prepared before the face of all people;
> *32:* A light to lighten the Gentiles, and the glory of thy people Israel.

SIMON For Simon Peter, the apostle, see PETER.

SIMON MAGUS A sorcerer in Samaria who was converted by Philip. He was so struck by what the apostles could do that he offered money to receive similar powers from the Holy Ghost but was sternly rebuked by **Peter*** (Acts 8:9–24).

SINAI, MOUNT The mountain, also known as **Mount Horeb**, sacred to **Yahweh**.* It was here that **Moses*** saw the burning bush and later received the Ten Commandments.

SION (or Zion) A name for Jerusalem. It came to be used symbolically for the new Jerusalem, heaven itself.

SODOM AND GOMORRAH Two of the cities of the plain, near the Dead Sea. As punishment for their wickedness, they were destroyed by fire and brimstone from heaven. **Lot*** and his family were the only inhabitants allowed to escape. The connection between Sodom and sodomy is speculative, though the apparent intention of the townspeople to rape a couple of male guests (in fact, angels) staying with Lot suggests at the least a lack of discrimination.

SOLOMON (tenth century BC) **David's*** son by **Bathsheba*** and his successor as king of Israel. Asked by God in a dream what gift he would like, Solomon requested an understanding heart. He was rewarded with riches and long life as well. An early instance of his wisdom was given in the case of two prostitutes who appeared before him to dispute the ownership of a child. Both had given birth to a son, but the child of one had died in the night and she had exchanged it for the child of the other. To resolve the dispute Solomon proposed to cut the child in two and give half to each of the women. The true mother at once revealed herself by surrendering her claim in order to preserve the child's life. Solomon, who presided over a court of legendary splendor, was responsible for building the magnificent **Temple*** at Jerusalem. In later life his vast array of wives and concubines encouraged him in the worship of strange gods and cost him Jehovah's favor.

Song of Solomon, Chapter 4:1–7

1: Behold, thou art fair, my love; behold, thou art fair; thou hast doves' eyes within thy locks: thy hair is as a flock of goats, that appear from mount Gilead.
2: Thy teeth are like a flock of sheep that are even shorn, which came up from the washing; whereof every one bear twins, and none is barren among them.
3: Thy lips are like a thread of scarlet, and thy speech is comely: thy temples are like a piece of a pomegranate within thy locks.
4: Thy neck is like the tower of David builded for an armoury, whereon there hang a thousand bucklers, all shields of mighty men.
5: Thy two breasts are like two young roes that are twins, which feed among the lilies.
6: Until the day break, and the shadows flee away, I will get me to the mountain of myrrh, and to the hill of frankincense.
7: Thou art all fair, my love; there is no spot in thee.

STAR OF BETHLEHEM See MAGI.

STEPHEN The first Christian martyr. One of the seven men chosen to help the apostles in their ministry, he was stoned to death outside Jerusalem (Acts 6–7). His martyrdom was witnessed by Saul (**Paul***), one of the persecutors.

SUSANNA Her story is told in the Book of Susanna in the Apocrypha. A beautiful and virtuous woman, she excited the lust of two elders among the Jews. They spied on her in her garden and then threatened to testify that she'd been with a young man, not her husband, unless she agreed to have sex with them. She refused and was condemned to death on their evidence, but the young Daniel challenged the verdict and by questioning the elders separately exposed the falsehood of their testimony. Susanna was vindicated and the two elders executed.

Susanna (from The History of Susanna)

17: Then she said to her maids, Bring me oil and washing balls, and shut the garden doors, that I may wash me.
18: And they did as she bade them, and shut the garden doors, and went out themselves at privy doors to fetch the things that she had commanded them: but they saw not the elders, because they were hid.
19: Now when the maids were gone forth, the two elders rose up, and ran unto her, saying,
20: Behold, the garden doors are shut, that no man can see us, and we are in love with thee; therefore consent unto us, and lie with us.
21: If thou wilt not, we will bear witness against thee, that a young man was with thee: and therefore thou didst send away thy maids from thee.

TABERNACLE The sanctuary which the Israelites carried with them in the wilderness. It was divided in two: the main section, known as the Holy Place; and the inner sanctum, where the Ark of the Covenant was kept, known as the Holy of Holies. In Solomon's reign the tabernacle was replaced by the **Temple*** he constructed.

TABITHA (or **Dorcas** in the Greek form of the name) A disciple who was "*full of good works*" (Acts 9:36). When she died, the apostle **Peter*** came to Joppa and, with the words "*Tabitha, arise*" (Acts 9:40), brought her back to life.

TABOR, MOUNT A mountain to the west of the Sea of Galilee traditionally regarded as the site of Jesus's transfiguration.

TAMAR A daughter of **David**,* raped and abandoned by her half-brother Amnon, who had lured her to his bed by pretending to be ill and in need of her care. She was later avenged by her brother **Absalom**,* who had Amnon killed. For **Tamar** the wife of Judah, see ONAN.

TARSUS A town in Cilicia, the birthplace of **Paul*** the apostle. In Acts 21:39 he speaks of himself, with reference to Tarsus, as *"a citizen of no mean city."*

TEMPLE OF JERUSALEM The magnificent temple built by **Solomon*** and described in detail in 1 Kings 6–7. It was destroyed by the Babylonians in 586 BC and rebuilt on a smaller scale after the exile. A third temple, begun by Herod the Great in 19 BC, was destroyed by the Romans in AD 70 shortly after its completion.

TEMPTATIONS IN THE WILDERNESS The temptations of the Devil to which Jesus was subjected following his baptism by **John**:* (1) to turn stones into bread; (2) to throw himself from the Temple and thereby force God to preserve him from harm; (3) to worship the Devil in exchange for temporal power.

The Temptations in the Wilderness (Matthew 4:1–11)

1: Then was Jesus led up of the Spirit into the wilderness to be tempted of the Devil.

2: And when he had fasted forty days and forty nights, he was afterward an hungred.

3: And when the tempter came to him, he said, If thou be the Son of God, command that these stones be made bread.

4: But he answered and said, It is written, Man shall not live by bread alone, but by every word that proceedeth out of the mouth of God.

5: Then the Devil taketh him up into the holy city, and setteth him on a pinnacle of the temple,

6: And saith unto him, If thou be the Son of God, cast thyself down: for it is written, He shall give his angels charge concerning thee: and in their hands they shall bear thee up, lest at any time thou dash thy foot against a stone.

7: Jesus said unto him, It is written again, Thou shalt not tempt the Lord thy God.

8: Again, the Devil taketh him up into an exceeding high mountain, and sheweth him all the kingdoms of the world, and the glory of them;

9: And saith unto him, All these things will I give thee, if thou wilt fall down and worship me.

10: Then saith Jesus unto him, Get thee hence, Satan: for it is written, Thou shalt worship the Lord thy God, and him only shalt thou serve.

11: Then the Devil leaveth him, and, behold, angels came and ministered unto him.

TEN COMMANDMENTS The commandments given to **Moses*** on Mount Sinai (Exodus 20:1–17). They were inscribed on two tablets of stone by the finger of God. In his anger on seeing the **Golden Calf*** when he came down from the mountain, Moses flung them to the ground and broke them. Later, God wrote them out again and they were placed in the **Ark of the Covenant**.*

The Ten Commandments (from "A Catechism," Book of Common Prayer, 1662)

    I.   Thou shalt have none other gods but me.

    II.   Thou shalt not make to thyself any graven image, nor the likeness of any thing that is in heaven above, or in the earth beneath, or in the water under the earth. Thou shalt not bow down to them, nor worship them: for I the Lord thy God am a jealous God, and visit the sins of the fathers upon the children unto the third and fourth generation of them that hate me, and shew mercy unto thousands in them that love me, and keep my commandments.

    III.   Thou shalt not take the Name of the Lord thy God in vain: for the Lord will not hold him guiltless that taketh his Name in vain.

    IV.   Remember that thou keep holy the sabbath day. Six days shalt thou labour, and do all that thou hast to do; but the seventh day is the Sabbath of the Lord thy God. In it thou shalt do no manner of work, thou, and thy son, and thy daughter, thy man-servant, and thy maid-servant, thy cattle, and the stranger that is within thy gates. For in six days the Lord made heaven and earth, the sea, and all that in them is, and rested the seventh day: wherefore the Lord blessed the seventh day, and hallowed it.

    V.   Honour thy father and thy mother, that thy days may be long in the land which the Lord thy God giveth thee.

    VI.   Thou shalt do no murder.

    VII.   Thou shalt not commit adultery.

    VIII.   Thou shalt not steal.

    IX.   Thou shalt not bear false witness against thy neighbour.

    X.   Thou shalt not covet thy neighbour's house, thou shalt not covet thy neighbour's wife, nor his servant, nor his maid, nor his ox, nor his ass, nor any thing that is his.

TETRARCH (Greek = *ruler of a quarter*) The term was applied by the Romans to the rulers of certain petty states in the Middle East.

THEOPHILUS The person to whom St. Luke's gospel and Acts are addressed. The latter book opens with the words, "*The former treatise have I made, O Theophilus, of all that Jesus began both to do and teach.*"

THOMAS Named Didymus (= *twin*), he was one of the 12 apostles and is often referred to as Doubting Thomas because of his refusal to believe in the resurrection of Jesus when told of it by the other disciples: "*Except I shall see in his hands the print of the nails, and put my finger into the print of the nails, and thrust my hand into his side, I will not believe*" (John 20:25). Eight days later Jesus appeared to him and the other disciples in a room and Thomas at once acknowledged his divinity.

TOBIAS See RAPHAEL.

TONGUES, SPEAKING IN The ability to speak in foreign languages conferred on the apostles by the Holy Ghost at **Pentecost*** (Acts 2).

TORAH (Hebrew = *teaching*) See PENTATEUCH.

TRANSFIGURATION The episode when Jesus took Peter, James, and his brother John up a mountain and was revealed to them in the company of **Moses*** and **Elijah**,* his face shining like the sun and his clothing white as light.

TRINITY The doctrine of a three-personed God – Father, Son, and Holy Spirit – who nonetheless remains a unity.

TWELVE, THE A term used to refer to the 12 apostles chosen by Jesus. See APOSTLES.

UNLEAVENED BREAD Bread made without yeast. On the night of the **Passover*** God instructed the Israelites to eat unleavened bread (Exodus 12:8) and instituted the festival of unleavened bread in commemoration of it (Exodus 12:14–24).

URIAH THE HITTITE The husband of Bathsheba. **David*** seduced and impregnated his wife, then sent a letter to **Joab**,* the commander of his army, saying, "*Set ye Uriah in the forefront of the hottest battle, and retire ye from him, that he may be smitten and die*" (2 Samuel 11:15). Uriah was duly killed and David married Bathsheba. Nathan the prophet was sent by God to pass judgment on his actions. See BATHSHEBA, NATHAN.

VEIL OF THE TEMPLE The veil between the Holy of Holies and the Holy Place. See TABERNACLE.

VIA DOLOROSA The route, later followed by pilgrims, along which Jesus passed to his crucifixion on Calvary.

VIRGIN BIRTH The doctrine that Mary gave birth to Jesus without the normal prerequisite of sexual intercourse, having conceived him by the agency of the Holy Ghost.

VISITATION The visit that Mary paid, after the Annunciation, to her cousin Elizabeth, who was at the time pregnant with John the Baptist (Luke 1:39–56). See MAGNIFICAT.

XERXES Ruler of Persia from 486 to 465 BC. He was also known as Ahasuerus, under which name he appears in the Book of **Esther**.*

YAHWEH The Hebrew name for God, considered too sacred to pronounce. It was rendered YHWH and normally replaced by *Adonai*, meaning Lord. Jehovah, like Yahweh, is a version of YHWH made pronounceable by the insertion of vowels.

ZACCHAEUS A tax collector of Jericho who was too short to see Jesus, so climbed a sycamore tree to get a better view of him. Jesus went to stay at his house, in spite of murmuring among the crowd that he was thereby mixing with sinners.

ZADOK A priest who supported **David*** against **Absalom,*** and **Solomon*** against his elder brother **Adonijah**, for the throne of Israel. He was appointed chief priest, an office that remained in his family until the second century BC.

ZEALOTS Jewish opponents of Roman rule in the first century AD.

ZEBEDEE See APOSTLES.

ZEDEKIAH Last king of Judah, a puppet ruler installed by **Nebuchadnezzar**.* Contrary to **Jeremiah's*** advice, he rebelled against the Babylonians and was defeated. After being forced to witness the execution of his sons, he had his eyes put out and was taken in chains of brass to Babylon (2 Kings 25:1–7).

ZIGGURAT A temple built up in stages in the form of a stepped pyramid.

ZIPPORAH Wife of **Moses**.* When he returned to Egypt to lead the Israelites, she stayed in Midian, where her father was a priest.

Part 2

Surviving the Classics

The classical world can seem dauntingly remote, but it is at least relatively compact. Within a few hours you can find out enough to cope with most of the references you're likely to come across. In what follows I've tried to summarize the basic material so that this part can be either browsed through or used as a dictionary. The emphasis is on mythological rather than historical figures, because it is they who turn up most often as cultural points of reference.

In simplifying things, I have occasionally sacrificed precision. It's not always strictly accurate, for example, to identify the Greek gods and heroes with their Roman counterparts (whose names are given in brackets), but for the purposes of this book it seems a reasonable shorthand. Similarly, a large number of myths come in several versions. Rather than detailing the variant forms, I've usually opted for whichever has been most popular.

You'll find it easier to understand the context of these entries if you have some sense of the framework within which the classical myths developed. The prime movers in this patchwork of legend are the gods and goddesses living on Mount Olympus, who gained power by displacing the previous generation of gods, the **Titans**.* The loves, hates, and jealousies of the Olympians provide the motives for what goes on not just in their own sphere but also among the mortals in whose destinies they continually involve themselves. The ruler of Olympus is **Zeus** (Jupiter or Jove), whose jealous wife **Hera** (Juno) is the queen of heaven. **Poseidon** (Neptune) and **Hades** (Pluto or Dis) are the two brothers of Zeus, the former ruling the sea, the latter the Underworld. The twins **Apollo** and **Artemis** (Diana) are deities associated respectively with the sun and the moon.

Athene (Minerva), is the goddess of wisdom and war, **Hermes** (Mercury) the messenger of the gods, and **Ares** (Mars) the god of war. **Hephaestus** (Vulcan), who forges the armor of the gods in his smithy, is the god of fire, married to **Aphrodite** (Venus), goddess of beauty and love. These are the main figures in the classical pantheon.

The entries below give only a summary. To find out more, you should read Homer's *Iliad* and *Odyssey*, Virgil's *Aeneid*, and Ovid's *Metamorphoses*. There are other texts you could move on to, but these provide the best introduction to what lies behind the brief outlines given here. Modern translations are readily available (including reliable prose versions published by Penguin), but it can often be helpful to go back to the earlier ones that influenced contemporary writers. You may not want to read the whole of George Chapman's Homer (*Iliad*, 1611; *Odyssey*, 1614–15), Arthur Golding's *Metamorphoses* (1565–7) or Dryden's *Aeneid* (1697), but it's worth getting a flavor of them. For narrative accounts of classical mythology, Thomas Bulfinch's nineteenth-century compendium, *Bulfinch's Mythology* (Random House, 1998) and Robert Graves's *The Greek Myths* (Penguin, 1955) remain useful stand-bys. More recently, Richard Buxton's *Complete World of Greek Mythology* (Thames and Hudson, 2004) adds contextual detail to the familiar stories. Some literary explorations of myth are analyzed by Geoffrey Miles in his *Classical Mythology in English Literature: A Critical Anthology* (Routledge, 1999).

On p. 67 you'll find a map with most of the places mentioned in the following entries.

DICTIONARY

ACHATES The faithful friend of **Aeneas**.* The phrase *fidus Achates*, used by Virgil in the *Aeneid*, became a proverbial expression for a loyal and devoted companion.

ACHERON One of the rivers of the Underworld. Literally the *River of Sorrows*, it was later sometimes used as a synonym for the Underworld itself.

ACHILLES Son of Peleus and **Thetis**,* he was the greatest of the Greek heroes in the **Trojan War**.* Post-Homeric legend recounts how his mother dipped him as a child in the River **Styx**,* rendering his body invulnerable except for the heel by which she held him. It was by shooting him in this spot with an arrow that **Paris*** killed him – hence the phrase *Achilles' heel*. Educated by the centaur **Chiron**,* Achilles became king of the Myrmidons in Thessaly. It is said

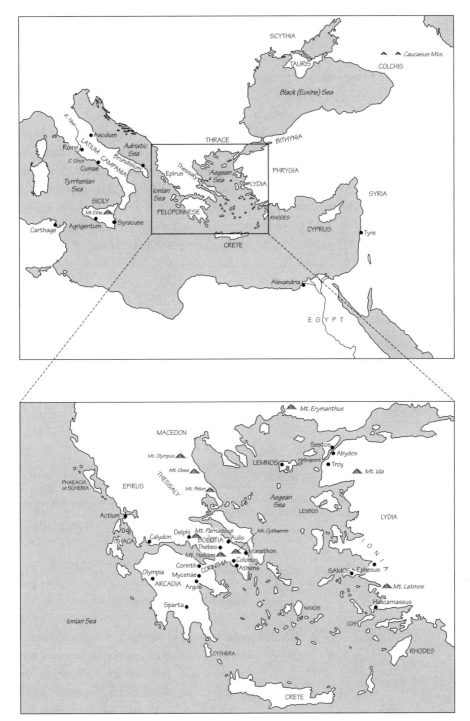

Map 2 The Classical World

that his mother offered him the choice between a long life lived in obscurity or a brief life of military glory. He chose the latter. In an effort to save him from the Trojan War, which she knew would be the scene of his death, Thetis sent him to the court of Lycomedes, where he was disguised as a woman. After **Odysseus*** had penetrated his disguise by tricking him into showing a preference for weapons over jewelry, Achilles agreed to join the war at the head of his Myrmidons. On their way to Troy, the Greeks were opposed by Telephus, a son-in-law of **Priam**,* who engaged them in battle and was wounded by Achilles. Informed by an oracle that the wound could only be cured by the one who had inflicted it, Telephus later sought out the Greeks at Troy and agreed to help them. In exchange, Achilles scraped some rust from his spear and applied it to the wound, thereby healing him. It is the anger of Achilles at a slight by **Agamemnon*** that provides the starting point of Homer's *Iliad*, and his slaying of Hector that marks its climax. See AGAMEMNON, HECTOR, HOMER, PATROCLUS.

ACIS See GALATEA.

ACTAEON A famous hunter who came upon Artemis and her attendants bathing. As punishment for this invasion of her privacy he was changed by the goddess into a stag and torn to pieces by his own hounds.

ADONIS A beautiful youth, loved by Aphrodite. He was killed by a wild boar while hunting. His role as a vegetation god is reflected in the legend that he was restored to life by **Persephone*** on condition that he spend six months of the year with her in the Underworld, the other six with Aphrodite.

AENEAS Trojan hero, son of Anchises and Aphrodite. At the fall of Troy Aeneas carried his elderly father through the flames of the city and set off on seven years of wanderings that led finally to Italy, where he became the ancestor of the Roman race. His story is told in the *Aeneid* of **Virgil**,* which includes (in Book 4) the account of his shipwreck near

---

From Percy Bysshe Shelley, "Adonais," Stanza 31 (The poet as Actaeon)

> . . . he, as I guess,
> Had gaz'd on Nature's naked loveliness,
> Actaeon-like, and now he fled astray
> With feeble steps o'er the world's wilderness,
> And his own thoughts, along that rugged way,
> Pursu'd, like raging hounds, their father and
>   their prey.

Virgil, *Aeneid*, Book 1, lines 1–6, trans. Dryden

> Arms, and the man I sing, who, forced by Fate,
> And haughty Juno's unrelenting hate,
> Expelled and exiled, left the Trojan shore.
> Long labours, both by sea and land, he bore,
> And in the doubtful war, before he won
> The Latian realm, and built the destined town . . .

Carthage and tragic love affair with its queen, **Dido**.* Other notable episodes in the legend of Aeneas (frequently referred to by Virgil as *pius Aeneas*) are the hero's descent into the Underworld (Book 6) to hear the future destiny of his line, and the culminating battle with **Turnus**, a local king, for the hand of **Lavinia**.*

AEOLUS God of the winds – hence the name of the Aeolian harp. In the *Odyssey* Aeolus gave **Odysseus*** all the winds unfavorable to his voyage tied securely in a bag. Within sight of home, the inquisitive crew let them out and Odysseus's ships were driven back to Aeolia.

AESCHYLUS (525–456 BC) The first of the great Athenian writers of tragedy. Of some eighty plays by him only seven survive: the *Persians*, the *Seven Against Thebes*, *Prometheus Bound*, the *Suppliants*, and, most famously, the *Oresteia*, a trilogy of plays about **Orestes*** made up of the *Agamemnon*, the *Choephori*, and the *Eumenides*. An unfounded legend has it that Aeschylus died when an eagle dropped a tortoise on his bald head, mistaking it for a convenient rock.

AESOP Credited with inventing the literary form of the fable, he is said to have been a Phrygian slave living in the sixth century BC.

AGAMEMNON King of Mycenae and commander of the Greek forces in the **Trojan War**.* His insistence on taking possession of **Briseis**, a female captive allotted to **Achilles**,* sparked the quarrel that opens the *Iliad*. On his return from Troy, Agamemnon was murdered by his wife **Clytemnestra** and her lover Aegisthus. See IPHIGENIA.

AGES OF MAN The poet **Hesiod*** distinguishes five ages through which the human race has passed: the Golden under Cronos, the Silver under Zeus, the Bronze under Poseidon, the Heroic under Ares, and the Iron, which is our present age, under Hades. In the way of these things, each age is held to represent a decline from the one before, the first and best being the Golden Age in which humankind lived in harmony and prosperity.

AIAS (Ajax) Better known by his Roman name of **Ajax**, he was the greatest of the Greek warriors, with the exception of Achilles. Son of Telamon, he is designated Telamonian Aias by Homer to distinguish him from another Aias, who also took part in the Trojan War. Though an impressive fighter, Ajax left behind a reputation, exploited by Shakespeare in *Troilus and Cressida*, for being slightly dense. When the armor of the slain Achilles was awarded to Odysseus, he went mad and killed himself.

ALCESTIS The wife of Admetus, king of Pherae in Thessaly. In return for kindness shown to Apollo, Admetus was granted redemption from death if he could find someone to take his place. Alcestis loyally sacrificed herself for her husband but was rescued from the Underworld by **Heracles**.*

ALCIBIADES (ca. 450–404 BC) A disciple of **Socrates**,* he became a famous Athenian general, who twice changed sides in the **Peloponnesian War*** between Athens and Sparta.

ALCMENE (or **Alcmena**). Daughter of the king of Argos, she was promised in marriage to Amphitryon. Captivated by her beauty, Zeus took the form of Amphitryon to deceive her, delaying the sunrise so that he could spend three nights with her in the space of one. **Heracles*** was born of their union.

ALCYONE (or **Halcyone**) When her husband **Ceyx** died in a shipwreck, she threw herself into the sea. The two of them were changed into birds which are said to keep the sea calm while they are nesting – hence the term *halcyon days*.

ALEXANDER (III) THE GREAT (356–323 BC) Son of Philip II of Macedon, he became king on his father's death in 336 and was proclaimed divine five years later by the oracle at **Siwa** in Egypt. During his reign he conquered most of the ancient world, leading his armies through Asia as far as India. In spite of a tyrant's whims – the drunken murder of a friend (Clitus) who failed to rate his achievements highly enough, the torture and execution of a tutor (Callisthenes) who declined to worship him as a god, the burning of Persepolis at the urging of his courtesan **Thais** – he was generally enlightened in his treatment of those he conquered. He died of fever at Babylon when only 32. His horse **Bucephalus**, which none but he could ride, has acquired its own place in legend. See DIOGENES, GORDIAN KNOT.

AMAZONS A mythical race of female warriors, located by **Herodotus*** in Scythia. Their name (Greek = *without breast*) was supposed to derive from the practice of cutting off their right breast to make it easier to use a bow.

AMBROSIA The food of the gods. Their drink is **nectar**.

ANACREON A Greek lyric poet of the sixth century BC who famously celebrated love and wine.

ANDROCLES A runaway slave who removed a thorn from the paw of a lion. Captured and sentenced to death in the Roman arena, Androcles was confronted by the same lion. Instead of tearing him apart, it repaid his earlier kindness with a display of grateful affection.

ANDROMACHE Wife of **Hector*** and mother of **Astyanax**. She presents a tragic figure in the *Iliad*, both in her parting from Hector and in her mourning for his death. After the fall of Troy, she was among the spoils of battle awarded to **Neoptolemus**,* who had killed her son.

ANDROMEDA Daughter of the king of Ethiopia. When her mother Cassiope boasted that Andromeda was more beautiful than the **Nereids**,* the infuriated Poseidon sent a sea-monster to lay waste the land. Andromeda was chained to a rock as a sacrifice to the monster, but **Perseus**,* fresh from his defeat of **Medusa**,* rescued her by showing the Gorgon's head to the monster and thereby turning it to stone.

ANTAEUS A giant, son of Poseidon and **Ge*** (the Earth). He was a mighty wrestler, drawing new strength from his mother every time his body touched the ground. **Heracles*** defeated him by holding him in the air and squeezing him to death.

ANTIGONE Daughter of **Oedipus*** and **Jocasta**, sister of **Polynices** and **Eteocles**.* In defiance of the orders of her uncle **Creon**, she buried the body of Polynices, who had perished in an attempt to retake Thebes from their brother Eteocles. She was sentenced to be buried alive but forestalled the punishment by taking her own life. Creon's son **Haemon**, who was in love with her, killed himself on her grave. See ETEOCLES.

ANTINOUS A youth of outstanding beauty, loved by the Emperor **Hadrian**.* He drowned in the Nile in AD 130.

ANTONY, MARK (ca. 83–30 BC). The anglicized name of Marcus Antonius, Roman general and supporter of **Julius Caesar**.* Along with **Octavian*** and **Marcus**

Lepidus, he became one of the triumvirate that took power after Caesar's assassination. Having defeated **Marcus Brutus** and **Cassius Longinus** (leaders of the conspiracy against Caesar) at the **battle of Philippi** (42 BC), the triumvirs divided the Roman world between them. It was as ruler of the eastern provinces that Antony came under the spell of **Cleopatra**.* In spite of his subsequent marriage to Octavian's half-sister, tensions between the two men led finally to civil war and Antony's inglorious defeat at the naval **battle of Actium** (31 BC). A year later, as Octavian closed in on Alexandria, he committed suicide. See CLEOPATRA.

APHRODITE (Venus) Goddess of love and beauty, she emerged from the foam of the sea (Greek *aphros* = foam) off the island of Cythera. Married to **Hephaestus**,* she was the lover of **Ares**,* by whom she became the mother of **Eros**.*

APOLLO God of light, music, and poetry, he is also associated with archery and medicine. The son of Zeus and **Leto** (Latona), and twin brother of Artemis, he was portrayed as the image of manly beauty and often referred to as **Phoebus** (= *radiant*) Apollo. His oracle at Delphi was the most famous in the ancient world. See PYTHON.

ARACHNE According to Ovid, she challenged the goddess Athene to a tapestry-weaving contest. When the jealous goddess destroyed her work – a flawless depiction of the loves of the Olympians – Arachne tried to kill herself but was pitied by Athene and turned into a spider.

ARCADIA A mountainous region of the Peloponnese, where **Pan*** was supposed to live. It became identified with a pastoral idyll in which nymphs and shepherds lived a life of rustic simplicity and contentment. The phrase *Et in Arcadia ego* (Even in Arcadia I am present), referring to Death, has its origin in a seventeenth-century painting by Guercino, in which shepherds contemplate a skull.

ARCHIMEDES (ca. 287–212 BC) Greek scientist and mathematician from Syracuse in Sicily. He invented the Archimedes screw for raising water and also recognized the principle of the lever, reportedly saying, *"Give me a place to stand, and I will move the earth."* Most famously, he discovered the principle of specific gravity when he noticed the way his body displaced water in the bath, at which point he is said to have run into the street shouting *"Eureka!"* ("I have found it").

72

ARES (Mars) God of war and lover of Aphrodite.

ARGONAUTS The Greek heroes who sailed with **Jason*** aboard the *Argo* to recover the **Golden Fleece*** from Colchis, on the Black Sea. Their story is recounted in the *Argonautica* of the Alexandrian poet **Apollonius Rhodius** (third century BC). Among their exploits was a stay on Lemnos to repopulate the island, which at the time was inhabited entirely by women who had murdered their husbands. At a later stop in Bithynia, where the king liked to challenge visitors to a fatal boxing match, **Pollux** took up the challenge and killed him. Further on, the Argonauts delivered a local king from the persecution of the **harpies**.* After avoiding destruction by the clashing rocks known as the **Symplegades**, they finally reached Colchis. For the recovery of the Golden Fleece, see JASON.

ARGUS (1) A monstrous figure with a hundred eyes. Jealous of **Io**, a nymph whom Zeus had raped and then turned into a heifer by way of camouflage, Hera set Argus to keep watch on her; but Hermes lulled the monster to sleep with his lyre and killed him. Hera set his hundred eyes in the peacock's tail. (2) Odysseus's faithful dog. Homer tells us that after 20 years he recognized the hero on his return to Ithaca, wagged his tail in greeting, and died.

ARIADNE Daughter of King **Minos*** of Crete and **Pasiphae**. She fell in love with **Theseus*** and supplied him with a thread that enabled him to escape from the **Minotaur's*** labyrinth. After killing the Minotaur, Theseus took Ariadne away with him but abandoned her on the island of Naxos, where she hanged herself in despair. Another legend has it that she became the wife of **Dionysus**.*

ARISTOPHANES (ca. 450–ca. 380 BC) The greatest of the Greek comic dramatists. Of some fifty works eleven survive, including the *Clouds*, the *Birds*, the *Wasps*, the *Frogs*, and *Lysistrata*. (The term *cloud cuckoo land* is taken from the imaginary city built by the birds in his play of that name.)

ARISTOTLE (384–322 BC) Greek philosopher. After studying under **Plato*** in Athens, he was later appointed by Philip of Macedon to be tutor to his son **Alexander (the Great)**.* His school of philosophy is known as the Peripatetic after the cloister (*peripatos*) of the Lyceum, where he taught. His most celebrated works are the three treatises: *Ethics*, *Poetics*, and *Politics*. See also p. 254.

ARTEMIS (Diana) Twin sister of Apollo, the goddess was a virgin and huntress associated with the moon. Her temple at Ephesus was one of the Seven Wonders of the World. In a bid to make his name immortal, **Herostratus** burnt it to the ground in 356 BC on the night that Alexander the Great was born.

ASCLEPIUS (Aesculapius) God of healing. A son of Apollo, he was taught medicine by the centaur **Chiron**.* When his miraculous ability to restore people to life led to complaints from Hades, ruler of the Underworld, Zeus struck him dead with a thunderbolt. The snake was sacred to Asclepius, and a cock was traditionally offered to him as a sacrifice for a cure.

ASPASIA The beautiful and highly educated mistress of **Pericles**.*

ATALANTA A heroine of Greek legend, famous as an athlete. It was Atalanta who drew first blood in the hunting of the **Calydonian Boar** (see MELEAGER). Vowed to chastity, she forced her many suitors to run against her in a race: if they won, she would be theirs; if not, she would kill them. She invariably won, until Hippomenes (or, in another version, Milanion) distracted her during the race by throwing down in turn three golden apples from the Garden of the **Hesperides**,* given to him for the purpose by Aphrodite.

ATHENE, or **Athena (Minerva)** Goddess of war, wisdom, and crafts, she sprang fully armed from the head of Zeus, who had swallowed her mother Metis in fear that their offspring would be more powerful than himself. When Athene and Poseidon quarreled over the sovereignty of Attica, it was decided that supremacy should go to whichever of them provided the most useful gift. Poseidon's was the horse (or a spring), Athene's the olive. She was judged the victor and gave her name to Athens, the capital city. Often called Pallas Athene, she is usually represented with helmet, spear, and shield. In the Trojan War she was a powerful ally of the Greeks, and of Odysseus in particular.

ATHENS The main city of Attica, it was originally called Cecropia after its legendary founder Cecrops. Athens began its rise to prominence in the seventh century BC under a system of government by annually elected magistrates, known as **Archons**. Its defeat of the invading Persians at the battles of **Marathon** (490) and **Salamis** (480) took it to the height of its power as a city state (*polis*). In the mid-fifth century BC, under the rule of **Pericles**,* Athenian culture enjoyed a Golden Age that produced the architecture of the **Acropolis**, the sculpture of **Phidias**, and the plays of **Aeschylus**,* **Sophocles**,* and **Euripides**.* The **Peloponnesian War*** in the last decades of the century broke Athens's military and political power, but figures such as **Plato**,* **Aristotle**,* and **Aristophanes*** ensured that it maintained its cultural preeminence.

ATLANTIS A fabled island, mentioned by Plato and later located in the Atlantic, which was supposed to have been lost beneath the sea.

ATLAS One of the **Titans**.* For his part in their war against Zeus he was condemned to uphold the heavens on his shoulders. On one occasion **Heracles*** gave him a brief respite by taking over from him. According to another legend, he was a king in northwest Africa who failed to show **Perseus*** due hospitality. By way of retribution, Perseus turned **Medusa's*** head on him, transforming him into a huge mountain.

ATREUS King of Argos and father of **Agamemnon*** and **Menelaus**.* To revenge himself on his brother Thyestes for seducing his wife, Atreus invited him to a banquet at which he served the flesh of Thyestes' own children, fathered on Atreus's wife. Thyestes fled in horror, calling down a curse on the House of Atreus.

AUGUSTUS, Gaius Julius Caesar Octavianus (63 BC–AD 14) Adoptive son of **Julius Caesar**.* After defeating **Mark Antony*** at the **battle of Actium** (31 BC), Octavian was left undisputed ruler of Rome. In 27 BC he became the first Roman emperor, though with an eye for public relations he claimed to be no more than "first among equals" in the Senate, preferring to call himself princeps (= first citizen). His title of Augustus was taken by all subsequent Roman emperors.

AURORA Roman goddess of the dawn. She is commonly represented driving a rose-colored chariot across the sky.

AUTOLYCUS Son of Hermes and grandfather of Odysseus, he was a noted thief and trickster.

AVERNUS A lake in Campania, thought by the ancients to be an entrance to the Underworld.

BASILISK Also known as a **cockatrice**, it was a fabulous reptile supposed to have been hatched from a cock's egg by a serpent. Its look had the power to kill.

BAUCIS Wife of **Philemon**. The old couple offered hospitality to Zeus and Hermes when the gods were traveling in Phrygia. Zeus transformed their house into a temple, making them its priest and priestess. They died at the same moment, as they had requested, and were turned into two trees growing side by side.

BELISARIUS (sixth century) The greatest of **Justinian's** generals, he was later accused of conspiring against the emperor. A fanciful tradition has him dying blinded and in beggary.

BELLEROPHON Hero who slew the **Chimaera**, a fire-breathing monster with the head of a lion, the body of a goat, and the tail of a serpent. He was helped in the task by the winged horse **Pegasus**,* on which, according to another legend, he later attempted to fly to heaven. Zeus sent a gadfly to make the horse rear and throw Bellerophon off.

BOETHIUS, Annius Manlius Severinus (d. 524) Roman philosopher who served the emperor Theodoric until he was imprisoned for treason and subsequently executed. While in prison he wrote the highly influential *De Consolatione Philosophiae* (*The Consolation of Philosophy*), which was translated by Alfred the Great, Chaucer, and Queen Elizabeth I.

BOREAS The North wind, worshipped as a deity by the ancient Greeks.

CADMUS The brother of **Europa**,* father of **Semele**,* and legendary founder of the city of **Thebes**. Directed by the Delphic oracle to follow a cow and build a city at the place where it lay down, he was led to a spring in Boeotia. Having killed the spring's guardian dragon, he sowed its teeth, from which sprang a crop of armed men. At the prompting of Athene, he threw a stone into their midst, triggering a fight between them which left only five survivors. These five helped him found the city of Thebes. Later, Cadmus and his wife were unlucky enough to be persecuted by Hera. As a release from their sufferings, Zeus turned them into serpents. The legend that Cadmus introduced the alphabet into

Greece is alluded to by Byron in *Don Juan*: "*You have the letters Cadmus gave – /Think ye he meant them for a slave?*"

CAESAR, Gaius Julius (d. 44 BC) Roman general who conquered Gaul, invaded Britain, and went on to become supreme ruler in Rome. His invasion of Italy provoked a civil war in which he was opposed by **Pompey,*** whom he defeated at the **battle of Pharsalus** in 48 BC. Among his many mistresses was **Cleopatra.*** Resentment at his dismantling of the Republic led to his assassination on the Ides (15th) of March 44 BC by a group of conspirators that included his friend **Brutus**.

CALIGULA (Latin = *little boot*) Nickname of the Roman Emperor Gaius, who ruled for just under four years, until he was murdered in AD 41. He is remembered chiefly for his cruelty and debauchery. Among his more benign extravagances, he appointed his favorite horse, Incitatus, to the offices of high priest and consul.

CALLISTO A nymph seduced by Zeus. Jealous Hera turned her into a bear, but at the moment when her own son was about to kill her in the chase, Zeus raised them to the sky as the constellation of the bear. One of several alternative versions suggests that Callisto was killed by Artemis, who had mistaken her for a real bear.

CALYPSO A nymph, daughter of Atlas, whose home was the island of Ogygia. **Odysseus*** spent seven years there as her lover but refused her offer of immortality and continued his wanderings.

CAMILLA Queen of the Volsci in Latium. A formidable warrior and athlete, she was so swift that she could run over a field of corn without bending it, or over the sea without wetting her feet. She was killed in battle while helping Turnus against **Aeneas.***

CARYATIDS Draped female statues used to support entablatures. Legend has it that when the Greeks enslaved the women of Caryae for siding with the Persians, they marked the episode by using statues of them in place of columns.

Alexander Pope, *An Essay on Criticism*, lines 370–3

When Ajax strives, some rock's vast weight to throw,
The line too labours, and the words move slow:
Not so, when swift Camilla scours the plain,
Flies o'er th'unbending corn, and skims along the main.

CASSANDRA A daughter of **Priam*** and **Hecuba**.* Smitten by her beauty, Apollo gave her the gift of prophecy, but when she failed to respond he ordained that no one would believe what she prophesied. At the fall of Troy she was assigned to **Agamemnon*** and later murdered by his wife **Clytemnestra**.

CASTOR AND POLLUX Twin sons of Zeus and **Leda**,* known as the **Dioscuri**. They joined the expedition of the **Argonauts*** and were ultimately granted immortality as the constellation of Gemini. Their twin sister was **Helen*** of Troy.

CATO THE CENSOR (234–149 BC) Roman senator noted for his uncompromising austerity at a time of increasing license. He recognized the danger to Rome posed by Carthage, repeatedly calling for the city's destruction: *Delenda est Carthago*. His great-grandson was another Cato, famous for his dedication to the Republican ideals that **Julius Caesar*** was eroding. This second Cato killed himself in 46 BC when it became clear that opposition to Caesar had failed.

CENTAURS Fabulous creatures, half man and half horse, said to have lived in Thessaly. At the wedding of **Pirithous**, king of the Lapiths, the centaurs got drunk and began assaulting the female guests, which led to the celebrated battle between the centaurs and the Lapiths. It was the centaur **Nessus** who attempted to rape Heracles's wife **Deianira*** and who was ultimately responsible for the death of **Heracles*** himself. See CHIRON, DEIANIRA, IXION.

CERBERUS The dog with three heads (fifty, according to **Hesiod***) that guarded the entrance to the Underworld. **Heracles*** had to bring him up to earth as one of his labors; **Orpheus*** had to lull him to sleep with his lyre when he went for Eurydice; and **Aeneas*** could only pass into the Underworld when Cerberus had been put out of action with a drugged cake.

CHARON The ferryman who conducted the souls of the dead across the River **Styx**.* The toll was an *obol* (a small coin), which had to be placed under the tongue of the dead person as part of the funeral rites. The living could only be ferried on presentation of a golden bough, given to them by the **Sibyl**.* Charon was once imprisoned for having allowed **Heracles*** to cross without it.

CHIMAERA See BELLEROPHON.

CHIRON The most famous of the **centaurs**.* His skill in medicine, music, and archery made him a valued teacher to the heroes of the age, including

Achilles* and **Jason**.* After receiving a mortal wound, accidentally inflicted by **Heracles**,* he was raised by Zeus to become the constellation of Sagittarius.

CICERO, Marcus Tullius (106–43 BC) Roman statesman and writer. A staunch Republican, he was one of those proscribed and killed when **Octavian**,* **Mark Antony**,* and **Lepidus** formed their ruling triumvirate. His writings have made him revered since the early Middle Ages as both a political thinker and a prose stylist.

CINCINNATUS, Lucius Quinctius (fifth century BC) A historical figure who came to typify an ideal of Roman virtue. Called from his plow in 458 BC to rescue Rome from the threat of the neighboring Aequi, he reluctantly assumed the dictatorship, defeated the Aequi, and then returned to his farm, declining further honors – all within the space of 16 days.

CIRCE A sorceress who lived on the island of Aeaea, visited by **Odysseus*** as he returned from the **Trojan War**.* She turned his men into pigs, but Odysseus secured their release, having himself escaped enchantment by virtue of a herb called Moly, given to him by Hermes.

CLEOPATRA (ca. 70–30 BC) Queen of Egypt. She was established on the throne by **Julius Caesar**,* whose son she bore. Later she became the lover of **Mark Antony**,* with whom she fought and lost the **battle of Actium** (31 BC) against **Octavian**.* After Antony's suicide the following year, she killed herself by the bite of an asp.

COCLES, Publius Horatius See HORATIUS.

COLOSSUS OF RHODES A vast bronze statue of Apollo that stood at the entrance to the harbor. One of the Seven Wonders of the World, it was cast in the first half of the third century BC and destroyed by an earthquake in 224 BC.

CORNUCOPIA The horn of plenty, frequently depicted in western art as a horn overflowing with fruit, flowers, and corn. According to legend, it belonged to the goat that suckled Zeus.

CROESUS (sixth century BC) The last king of Lydia, proverbial for his wealth. He boasted to the philosopher **Solon*** that he was the happiest of men, but

Solon replied, "*Call no man happy until he is dead.*" Later, when his kingdom had been conquered by the Persian king **Cyrus**, Croesus was ordered to be burnt alive. On the point of death he called out Solon's name three times. When told the reason for this, Cyrus spared his life and became his friend.

CRONOS (or **Kronos**) One of the Titans, identified by the Romans with **Saturn**.* He castrated his father **Uranus*** and became ruler of the gods, marrying his sister **Rhea**. For greater security, he devoured his children as they were born, but Rhea concealed the birth of Zeus, Poseidon, and Hades, giving Cronos stones to swallow instead. Zeus later dethroned him and inaugurated the rule of the Olympians.

CYBELE The mother-goddess whose cult, celebrated with orgiastic rites, passed from Phrygia to Greece and thence to Rome. She is identified with **Rhea**, the wife of Cronos and mother of Zeus, Poseidon, Hades, and Hera. Central to the cult of Cybele was the figure of her shepherd lover **Attis**, who castrated himself after breaking a vow of celibacy taken when he became guardian of her temple.

CYCLOPS A race of giants with one eye in the middle of their foreheads. Supposed to live in Sicily, they were credited with great skill as builders, and supplied the workers for **Hephaestus**.* See POLYPHEMUS.

DAEDALUS Legendary Athenian craftsman and engineer who built the labyrinth for King **Minos*** of Crete. Having lost the king's favor, he was imprisoned on the island but constructed wings for himself and his son **Icarus*** so that they could escape by flight. See MINOTAUR.

DAMOCLES A courtier of Dionysius the Elder, ruler of Syracuse in the fourth century BC. In an attempt to flatter the tryant, Damocles pronounced him the happiest of men. To demonstrate the reality of his situation, Dionysius responded by seating Damocles at a sumptuous banquet with a sword suspended above his head by a single hair – hence the phrase *sword of Damocles*.

DAMON AND PYTHIAS (or **Phintias**) Legendary friends. When Pythias was sentenced to death by Dionysius of Syracuse, Damon agreed to stand bail for him while he returned home to set his affairs in order. Just in time to save his friend, Pythias came back to face execution, but Dionysius was so impressed by the fidelity of the pair that he pardoned him.

DANAE Daughter of Acrisius, king of Argos. Warned by an oracle that he would be killed by his daughter's son, the king imprisoned her in a bronze tower, but Zeus gained access to her in the form of a shower of gold. Their son was **Perseus**,* who later fulfilled the oracle by accidentally killing his grandfather with a quoit.

DANAIDS The 50 daughters of Danaus, king of Argos. They married the 50 sons of Danaus's brother Aegyptus, but Danaus, fearful of his future sons-in-law, made his daughters promise to kill their husbands on their wedding night. All but one carried out their promise and, according to later legend, were punished in Hades by the endless task of collecting water in vessels full of holes.

DAPHNE A nymph pursued by Apollo. As she fled from him, she begged the gods for help and was turned into a laurel tree.

DARIUS THE GREAT King of Persia and father of **Xerxes**,* he reigned from 521–486 BC. His invasion of Greece ended in failure when the Persian army was defeated by the Athenians at the battle of **Marathon** in 490 BC.

DEIANIRA Wife of **Heracles**.* On one occasion she was carried across a swollen stream by the centaur Nessus, who then tried to rape her. Seeing this from the other bank, Heracles shot Nessus with a poisoned arrow. The dying centaur gave his blood-stained tunic to Deianira, telling her that it would act as a love-charm on an unfaithful husband. When Heracles later fell in love with Iole, Deianira sent him the garment. As soon as he put it on, the tunic began to torture his flesh. To escape the pain, Heracles flung himself on a burning pyre, or, according to another version, succumbed to the poison and was placed on a pyre. In despair, Deianira killed herself.

DEMETER (Ceres) A Greek corn goddess, she was the mother of **Persephone**.*

DEMOSTHENES (ca. 384–322 BC) Celebrated Athenian orator who made his name in a series of speeches warning the Greeks of the threat posed by Philip of Macedon – hence the term *philippic*. According to legend, he overcame a stammer by rehearsing speeches with pebbles in his mouth.

DEUCALION A Greek version of Noah. The son of **Prometheus**,* he was told by his father to build a ship to escape the flood with which Zeus was about to overwhelm the earth. Afterwards, he and his wife Pyrrha repopulated the world by throwing stones behind them; those thrown by Deucalion turned into men and those by Pyrrha into women. Deucalion was the father of **Hellen**, legendary ancestor of the Greek race – hence Hellenes, Hellas, hellenic, etc.

DIANA See ARTEMIS.

DIDO Daughter of a king of Tyre, she sailed to the coast of North Africa after the murder of her husband and was there granted as much land as could be covered by the hide of a bull. By cutting the bull's hide into thin strips she enclosed the parcel of land that became Carthage, of which she was queen. Later she fell in love with Aeneas, who had been shipwrecked there after the fall of Troy. When he was ordered away by the gods, she killed herself.

DIOGENES (d. ca. 324 BC) Greek philosopher whose followers were called Cynics. He lived in Athens with ostentatious frugality, preaching simplicity of lifestyle, indifference to riches, and disregard for convention. He is supposed to have carried around a barrel or earthenware jar that served him for accommodation. One time he took a lantern through the streets in broad daylight, claiming to look for an honest man. When **Alexander the Great*** asked what he could do for him, Diogenes replied, "*Get out of the light.*" A graceful loser on this occasion, Alexander remarked that if he were not Alexander, he would wish to be Diogenes.

John Milton, *Comus*, lines 46–53

Bacchus, that first from out the purple grape
Crushed the sweet poison of misusèd wine,
After the Tuscan mariners transformed,
Coasting the Tyrrhene shore, as the winds listed,
On Circe's island fell. (Who knows not Circe,
The daughter of the Sun? whose charmèd cup
Whoever tasted, lost his upright shape,
And downward fell into a groveling swine.)

DIONYSUS (Bacchus) God of wine. He was associated with music, poetry, the shedding of inhibitions, and the celebration of ecstatic fertility cults. See ARIADNE, SEMELE.

DIS See HADES.

DRACO Athenian lawgiver of the seventh century BC. His enthusiasm for the death penalty resulted in a penal code of extreme severity – hence *draconian*.

DRYADS and **HAMADRYADS** Tree-nymphs. Hamadryads were thought to die at the same time as the trees that had been their home.

ECHO A nymph deprived of independent speech by Hera. When Zeus was making love to other nymphs on the mountainside, she distracted Hera by her chatter, allowing the nymphs to escape. It was for this that Hera punished her. Echo fell in unrequited love with **Narcissus*** and pined away until nothing remained but her voice.

ELECTRA Daughter of **Agamemnon*** and **Clytemnestra**, she encouraged her brother **Orestes*** to murder their mother in revenge for the killing of Agamemnon. Her devotion to her father and hatred of her mother prompted Freud to give her name to the Electra complex, counterpart of the Oedipus complex.

ELYSIUM (or **Elysian Fields**) The paradise where immortal heroes dwelt after their life on earth.

EMPEDOCLES (fifth century BC) A poet and philosopher from Agrigentum in Sicily, he embraced the Pythagorean belief in the transmigration of souls. Convinced that he was a god, or perhaps just resolved to die, he is said to have thrown himself into the crater of Mount Etna.

ENDYMION A beautiful young shepherd whom the moon saw sleeping on Mount Latmos. She fell in love with him and made him sleep forever so that she could continue to look on his beauty.

EPICURUS (341–270 BC) Greek philosopher who founded the Epicurean school. Popularly interpreted as a hedonistic philosophy, epicureanism was in fact more concerned with the pursuit of happiness through a tranquil detachment from worldly ambitions.

EROS (Cupid) Son of Aphrodite. He is the god of love, usually represented as a winged child with bow and arrows. See PSYCHE.

ETEOCLES Son of **Oedipus*** and **Jocasta**. After the death of Oedipus it was agreed that he and his brother **Polynices** should reign over Thebes in alternate years, but when Eteocles's term expired, he refused to surrender the kingship. Polynices collected an

Geoffrey Chaucer, General Prologue to *The Canterbury Tales*, lines 331–8

A Frankeleyn was in his compaignye.
Whit was his berd as is the dayesye;
Of his complexioun he was sangwyn.
Wel loved he by the morw a sop in wyn;
To lyven in delit was evere his wone,
For he was Epicurus owene sone,
That heeld opinioun that pleyn delit
Was verray felicitee parfit.

army headed by seven champions – the **Seven against Thebes** – and attacked the city at each of its seven gates. He and Polynices killed each other, leaving the city to be ruled by their uncle **Creon**. The story of the Seven against Thebes is the subject of the *Thebaid*, an epic by the Roman poet **Statius** (ca. AD 45–96) which enjoyed great popularity in the Middle Ages. See ANTIGONE.

EURIPIDES (ca. 480–406 BC) Younger than **Aeschylus*** or **Sophocles**,* he was the most skeptical and innovative of the three great classical tragedians. For this reason, perhaps, he won relatively few prizes at Athens's dramatic festivals and became a target for the satire of **Aristophanes**.* Of over ninety plays by him, eighteen survive, including *Alcestis, Medea, Electra,* and the *Bacchae.*

EUROPA Sister of **Cadmus**,* she was seduced by Zeus in the form of a bull. While she played by the seashore, he induced her to climb on his back and then carried her away to Crete, where she bore him three sons: **Minos**,* **Rhadamanthus**,* and **Sarpedon**.

FASCES (Latin *fascis* = bundle) The sheaf of elm or birch rods, bound with a red band and carried by the Roman lictors as an emblem of authority. (Outside Rome the sheaf was surmounted by an axe-head to indicate the power of execution.) It was from this symbol that the Italian fascist party took its name.

FATES The three sister goddesses (known to the Greeks as the *Moirae* and to the Romans as the *Parcae*) who preside over human destiny: Clotho, Lachesis, and Atropos. **Clotho** presides over the moment of birth; **Lachesis** spins the thread of the individual's life; **Atropos**, with her shears, cuts it at the moment of death. Even the gods cannot alter their decrees.

FLORA The Roman goddess of flowers and spring.

FURIES Allecto, Megaera, and Tisiphone. They were the ministers of vengeance of the gods, visiting war and pestilence on the earth, and punishing the sins of individuals with pangs of remorse. They were known to the Greeks as the *Erinyes*, or, in euphemistic propitiation, the *Eumenides* ("Kindly Ones").

GALATEA (1) The name given to the figure sculpted by **Pygmalion**.* (2) A sea-nymph pursued by the Cyclops **Polyphemus**.* Her love for the young shepherd **Acis** excited the jealousy of Polyphemus, who crushed his rival with a huge rock. Acis was then transformed into a river at the foot of Mount Etna.

GANYMEDE A Trojan youth of such beauty that Zeus had him carried away on an eagle to become his cup-bearer. Later he became identified as a type of the homosexual's minion, and the word *catamite* was derived from the Latin form of his name.

GE, or **Gaea (Terra,** or **Thea)** A personification of the Earth, mother of the **Titans*** and also of the **Giants.***

GIANTS (Gigantes) Sons of Ge and Uranus (Earth and Heaven) who rebelled against the Olympians and tried to scale the heavens by piling **Mount Pelion** on **Mount Ossa** – hence the phrase *to heap Pelion on Ossa*, meaning to add difficulty to difficulty, trouble to trouble, etc. With the help of **Heracles**,* the Giants were defeated but not before most of the Olympians had fled to Egypt in terror. (The Giants are sometimes confused with the Titans, but the two groups are distinct.)

GOLDEN FLEECE The object of **Jason's*** expedition with the **Argonauts.*** Its history goes back to the previous generation. Phrixus was the son of the king of Thebes, hated by his stepmother. Warned of her machinations against his life, he escaped with his sister Helle on the back of a winged ram whose fleece was of gold. On the way, his sister fell off and drowned in what thereafter became known as the Hellespont. Phrixus himself reached Colchis on the Black Sea, sacrificed the ram to Zeus (or, in another version, Ares), and dedicated the Golden Fleece to him in a sacred grove.

GORDIAN KNOT Gordius was a peasant who became king of Phrygia and dedicated his wagon to Zeus. Its yoke was attached to the pole with a knot so ingenious that a legend arose that whoever could untie it would rule the empire of Asia. **Alexander the Great*** took advantage of the legend by simply cutting through it with his sword – hence the phrase *to cut the Gordian knot*, used of a single decisive solution to any awkward problem.

GORGONS Three monstrous sisters with snakes for hair, teeth like the tusks of a wild boar, hands of brass, and bodies covered with impenetrable scales. They turned to stone all who looked on them. The most famous of the three was **Medusa.***

GRACES Three daughters of Zeus who personified grace and beauty. They dispensed kindness and were often represented as attendants of Aphrodite.

GYGES A Lydian shepherd to whom King **Candaules** showed his wife naked. In revenge, the queen prompted Gyges to murder Candaules and seize his throne.

Intertwined with this myth is the story told by Plato that Gyges acquired a ring conferring invisibility. By means of it he gained access to the queen, then killed her husband, married her, and took the throne.

HADES (Pluto) Also known as **Dis**, he was the God of the Underworld, whose name later came to be used of the Underworld itself. In this sunless region the ghosts of the dead, Homer tells us, flitted to and fro like bats. Its deepest pit was **Tartarus** – a place of punishment for those guilty of the most serious crimes, where Zeus imprisoned the **Titans**.*

HADRIAN Roman emperor (r. AD 117–38) responsible for the building of "Hadrian's Wall" in Britain as a defense against incursions from the north by the Picts and Scots. See ANTINOUS.

HANNIBAL (247–ca. 183 BC) Carthaginian general who became one of Rome's most formidable opponents. The first **Punic War** (Latin *Punicus* = Carthaginian), from 264 to 241 BC, had driven Carthage out of Sicily; the second was provoked by Hannibal in 218 BC. With extraordinary boldness he led the Carthaginian army, including its fearsome elephants, out of Spain and across the Alps to invade Italy. After inflicting crushing defeats on the Roman army at the battles of **Trasimene** (217 BC) and **Cannae** (216 BC), he missed the opportunity to march on Rome. Over the next 14 years his army was held at bay by the guerilla tactics of **Fabius Maximus** (nicknamed *Cunctator* = Delayer). When the Roman general **Scipio*** took the fight to Africa and threatened Carthage, Hannibal was forced to return. He was defeated by Scipio at the battle of **Zama** (202 BC). Suspected by the Romans some years later of plotting further rebellion, Hannibal committed suicide to avoid capture. Carthage itself was destroyed at the end of the third Punic War (149–146 BC), which had been brought on by Rome's fears that the city might again pose a threat.

HARPIES Loathsome winged monsters with the head and breasts of a woman.

HEBE Goddess of youth. She was the daughter of Zeus and Hera, and cup-bearer to the gods.

HECATE An ancient goddess associated with death and the Underworld. She has a special care for witches and sorcerers.

HECTOR Son of Priam and Hecuba, he was the greatest of the Trojan heroes in Homer's *Iliad*. In revenge for the death of **Patroclus**,* he was killed by **Achilles**,* who dragged his body round the walls of Troy at the rear of his chariot.

He stretched his arms towards his child, but the boy cried and nestled in his nurse's bosom, scared at the sight of his father's armour, and at the horse-hair plume that nodded fiercely from his helmet. His father and mother laughed to see him, but Hector took the helmet from his head and laid it all gleaming upon the ground. Then he took his darling child, kissed him, and dandled him in his arms, praying over him the while to Jove and to all the gods. "Jove," he cried, "grant that this my child may be even as myself, chief among the Trojans; let him be not less excellent in strength, and let him rule Ilius with his might. Then may one say of him as he comes from battle, 'The son is far better than the father.' May he bring back the blood-stained spoils of him whom he has laid low, and let his mother's heart be glad."

HECUBA Wife of **Priam*** and mother of **Hector**.* Her sufferings during and after the Trojan War drove her mad with grief. One legend has her transformed into a dog.

HELEN Daughter of Zeus and **Leda**.* Her legendary beauty was the cause of the ten-year Trojan War. Married to **Menelaus**,* she was seduced by **Paris**,* who took her back to Troy. Menelaus then gathered an army to recover her. After the fall of Troy she was reconciled with her husband and returned to Greece with him.

HELIOS The Greek sun-god, later identified with Hyperion and Apollo.

HEPHAESTUS (Vulcan, or Mulciber) God of fire. The son of Zeus and Hera, he was thrown from heaven by his father for attempting to intervene on Hera's behalf in a marital dispute. His fall to earth on the island of Lemnos nine days later left him permanently lame. He was, however, an ingenious smithy, and set up a forge on Mount Etna. Homer tells in the *Odyssey* how he caught his wife Aphrodite in the embraces of Ares (Mars) by means of a cunningly made net of metal concealed above the bed.

From Christopher Marlowe, *Doctor Faustus*, Act 5, Scene 1, lines 96–102

Was this the face that launched a thousand ships,
And burnt the topless towers of Ilium?
Sweet Helen, make me immortal with a kiss
Her lips suck forth my soul, see where it flies!
Come, Helen, come, give me my soul again.
Here will I dwell, for heaven is in thy lips,
And all is dross that is not Helena.

John Milton, *Paradise Lost*, Book 1, lines 738–46

Nor was his name unheard or unadored
In ancient Greece, and in Ausonian land
Men called him Mulciber; and how he fell
From heav'n, they fabled, thrown by angry Jove
Sheer o'er the crystal battlements: from morn
To noon he fell, from noon to dewy eve,
A summer's day; and with the setting sun
Dropped from the zenith like a falling star,
On Lemnos th'Aégean isle . . .

Though he lived on Olympus after reconciliation with his father, he seems to have been paid scant respect by the other Olympians.

HERA (Juno) Sister and wife of Zeus, she was worshipped as queen of the Olympians and the goddess of marriage. Incorrigibly jealous, she pursued her husband's many lovers with inventive malice. The peacock was considered sacred to her.

HERACLES (Hercules) Son of Zeus and Alcmene, he was renowned for his superhuman strength and courage. Heracles (sometimes called **Alcides**) is often represented with a bow or club and wearing a lion skin. While still in the cradle, he strangled a couple of snakes sent to kill him by the slighted Hera. Thereafter he earned fame by completing **twelve labors** set for him by Eurystheus, king of Argos, whom Heracles had been obliged to serve in expiation for killing his own children in a fit of madness sent by Hera. The labors were as follows:

1   Kill the **Nemean lion**. (Heracles strangled it and afterwards wore its skin.)
2   Kill the **Hydra*** of Lerna.
3   Capture a stag with golden horns and brazen feet, sacred to Artemis.
4   Capture a huge wild boar that had been ravaging the area round Mount Erymanthus.
5   Cleanse the **stables of Augeas**, where 3,000 oxen had been kept for years. (Heracles diverted the course of two rivers so that they ran through the stables.)
6   Kill the **Stymphalian birds** – carnivorous monsters that lived around Lake Stymphalus.
7   Capture a wild bull that had been terrorizing Crete.
8   Capture the **mares of Diomedes**, king of Thrace, who had been accustomed to give them human flesh to eat. (Heracles fed him to his own horses.)
9   Obtain the **girdle of Hippolyta**, queen of the Amazons.
10   Steal the cattle of the three-bodied giant **Geryon**.
11   Take the golden apples from the garden of the **Hesperides**.*
12   Bring back from the Underworld the triple-headed dog **Cerberus*** that guarded its entrance.

In the course of his final labor, Heracles took the opportunity to rescue **Theseus*** and **Pirithous**, who had been confined in Hades for their attempt to carry off **Persephone**.* See ALCESTIS, ANTAEUS, ATLAS, CHARON, CHIRON, DEIANIRA, GIANTS, PHILOCTETES, PROMETHEUS.

HERACLITUS (ca. 500 BC) Greek philosopher from Ephesus who emphasized the transitory nature of existence, teaching that everything is in a state of flux ("*You cannot step into the same river twice . . .*"). He should not be confused with the Heraclitus referred to in W. J. Cory's poem ("*They told me, Heraclitus, they told me you were dead . . .*"), who was a poet from Halicarnassus, living in the third century BC.

HERMAPHRODITUS According to Ovid, he was the son of Hermes and Aphrodite, with whom the nymph Salmacis fell in love. When he rejected her, she embraced him, calling on the gods to unite the two of them in a single body.

HERMES (Mercury) Messenger of the gods, identified by his winged hat and sandals and the herald's staff he carried. He was the patron of travelers and thieves.

HERO A priestess of Aphrodite at Sestos. She was loved by **Leander**, a native of Abydos, who used to swim across the **Hellespont** by night to visit her, guided by the burning torch she held as a beacon for him. One night a storm put out the torch, and Leander drowned. In despair, Hero threw herself into the sea.

HERODOTUS (ca. 484–425 BC) Greek historian, celebrated for his account of the wars between Greece and Persia. His concern for ordering his material and testing its accuracy has led him to be called the father of history.

HESIOD (ca. 700 BC) One of the earliest Greek poets. He is the author of the *Works and Days*, a description of farming life in his native Boeotia, and of the *Theogony*, a genealogy of the gods that is the source of many later myths.

HESPERIDES Three nymphs, daughters of Hesperus (the evening star), who guarded a tree of golden apples that grew in a garden beyond the sea, protected by a fierce dragon. For his eleventh labor **Heracles*** was required to steal the apples. According to one tradition, he killed the dragon and brought them back himself; another version has it that **Atlas*** procured them while Heracles temporarily upheld the heavens for him. See ATALANTA.

HESTIA Greek counterpart of the Roman hearth goddess. See VESTA.

HIPPOCRATES (born ca. 460 BC) Celebrated Greek physician who established his school of medicine at Cos. He is remembered now for the Hippocratic Oath, which sets out the ethical obligations of the medical profession.

HIPPOMENES See ATALANTA.

HOMER (? eighth century BC) The great epic poet credited with authorship of the *Iliad* and the *Odyssey*. The *Iliad*, which tells of the **Trojan War**,* begins with the fateful quarrel between **Achilles*** and **Agamemnon*** that sends Achilles off to sulk in his tent while the war rages on, until the death of **Patroclus*** spurs him to take up arms again and kill **Hector**.* The *Odyssey* recounts the adventures of **Odysseus*** during his return from the Trojan War. Nothing is known of Homer's life, though seven Greek cities dispute the claim to be his birthplace. He is traditionally represented as blind.

HORACE (Quintus Horatius Flaccus, 65–8 BC) Roman poet of humble origins whose works include the *Satires*, *Epodes*, *Epistles*, *Ars Poetica* (*Art of Poetry*), and, most famously, the *Odes*. Witty, tolerant, epicurean, he enjoyed the friendship of **Gaius Maecenas**, one of the great patrons of the age and a personal friend of the Emperor Augustus. Horace's advice in *Ars Poetica* to mingle profit with pleasure and instruct the reader while giving delight has often been taken as a text by later writers and critics.

HORATII The three Roman brothers, triplets, who, according to the legend recounted by Livy, decided the war between Rome and Alba by meeting the three Curatii in single combat. Two of the Horatii and all three of the Curatii were killed. When the survivor returned, his sister was unwise enough to display grief for one of the Curatii, to whom she'd been betrothed. Incensed by what he took to be lack of patriotism and family solidarity, he stabbed her to death. The unbending singleness of purpose shown by the three brothers became a symbol of austere Roman virtue.

HORATIUS (Publius Horatius Cocles) Roman hero who held a bridge over the Tiber against the whole of **Lars Porsenna's*** Etruscan army, while his companions destroyed the bridge behind him. When Porsenna's line of advance was cut, the wounded Horatius jumped into the Tiber and swam to the shore without abandoning his arms. His feat is the subject of the best known of Macaulay's *Lays of Ancient Rome*.

HYACINTHUS A beautiful Spartan youth, loved by both Apollo and **Zephyrus**. His preference for Apollo led the jealous Zephyrus (a personification of the West Wind) to blow off course a discus thrown by the god, so that it struck and killed Hyacinthus. From his blood sprang the flower that took his name.

HYDRA A many-headed monster killed by Heracles. As soon as one of the heads was cut off, two more grew in its place. The problem was overcome through the help of Heracles's companion, who cauterized each of the severed necks with a burning brand. By dipping his arrows in the Hydra's blood, Heracles ensured that any wound they inflicted would be mortal.

HYMEN The god of marriage, traditionally represented as a youth wearing a wreath of flowers and carrying a torch and a veil.

HYPERBOREANS A legendary race that worshipped Apollo and lived in perpetual sunshine beyond the North Wind (*Boreas*). The association with sunshine has now been lost, and the term *hyperborean* is used to refer to the cold regions of the north.

HYPERION One of the Titans. Hyperion was a sun-god, sometimes identified by poets with the sun itself.

ICARUS Son of **Daedalus**,* he escaped from Crete with his father by means of the wings Daedalus had made for them. Intoxicated by the sensation of flight, Icarus ignored his father's warnings and flew too close to the sun. The wax that held his wings together melted, and he plunged to his death in the Aegean Sea.

IDOMENEUS A king of Crete, who sailed with the Greeks to the Trojan War. Caught in a tempest on the way home, he made a rash vow to Poseidon that if he escaped the storm he would sacrifice to the god the first living creature he saw on reaching Crete. It was his son. Idomeneus fulfilled his vow and was banished by the Cretans in retribution.

IPHIGENIA Daughter of **Agamemnon*** and **Clytemnestra**. When the Greek fleet was at **Aulis**, prevented by contrary winds from sailing to Troy, it was decided that for the good of the expedition Iphigenia must be offered as a sacrifice to Artemis, whom Agamemnon had offended. At the last moment the goddess, moved by her innocent distress, rescued her from the altar, carrying her off to become a priestess at her shrine in **Tauris**. There Iphigenia supervised the sacrifice of all strangers who landed on the peninsula, until her brother **Orestes*** was about to become one of the victims. Together they escaped, taking with them the statue of the goddess.

IRIS A messenger of the gods, who used the rainbow to travel between earth and sky.

ISIS Egyptian deity, wife and sister of Osiris, mother of Horus. Her cult spread widely around the Mediterranean.

IXION A king of the Lapiths who murdered his father-in-law, and then, after being purified by Zeus, attempted to seduce Hera. Zeus deceived him by creating a cloud in Hera's likeness, on whom Ixion engendered the Centaurs. His punishment in the afterlife was to be bound on an endlessly revolving wheel.

JANUS Roman god of the doorway (Latin, *ianua*), represented as having two faces looking in opposite directions. The doors of his temple were left open when Rome was at war and closed in times of peace.

JASON Son of the king of Iolchos in Thessaly. The throne which should have been Jason's was usurped by his uncle Pelias, and Jason himself was driven away, to be brought up by the centaur **Chiron**.* When he later returned to claim his inheritance, Pelias agreed to hand over the crown provided that he would first fetch the **Golden Fleece*** from Colchis. To this end Jason organized the expedition of the **Argonauts**.* Once in Colchis, he was able to secure the fleece through the help of the king's daughter **Medea**,* a sorceress who fell in love with him and advised him how to accomplish the tasks imposed by her father as a condition of surrendering the fleece. These were actually designed to kill Jason, who was ordered, among other things, to yoke a pair of fire-breathing bulls. Another task was to sow dragon's teeth that produced a crop of armed adversaries. Jason turned them against one another by throwing a stone into their midst. Finally, with Medea's herbs, he drugged the guardian dragon and made off with the fleece. After marrying and abandoning Medea, he did little of note, dying unheroically when a beam from his ship the *Argo* fell and crushed him.

JOCASTA See OEDIPUS.

JUNO See HERA.

JUPITER See ZEUS.

LAESTRYGONES Cannibal giants encountered by **Odysseus**.* They sank 11 of his 12 ships.

LAIS Famous Greek courtesan of the fourth century BC whose favors were enjoyed by, among many others, **Alcibiades*** and **Diogenes*** the Cynic. The orator **Demosthenes*** journeyed to Corinth for her sake but thought better of it when told how much she charged, remarking that he would not buy repentance at so high a price. After leaving Corinth, Lais was murdered by the jealous women of Thessaly.

LAOCOÖN A priest of the Trojans who tried to dissuade them from bringing the wooden horse into the city. In retribution for this attempt to thwart the will of the gods, he and his two sons were crushed to death by a pair of huge serpents that emerged from the sea while he was sacrificing to Poseidon.

LAPITHS See CENTAURS.

LARES Roman gods of the home, similar to *penates*. The phrase "*lares* and *penates*" came to refer to those household effects that embody the spirit of an individual's home.

LARS PORSENNA According to Livy, an Etruscan chieftain who besieged Rome to put the exiled King Tarquinius Superbus back on the throne. See HORATIUS, SCAEVOLA.

LAVINIA Daughter of the king of Latium. In spite of her betrothal to Turnus, king of the Rutuli, she was offered by her father to **Aeneas**.* His defeat of Turnus in single combat, described by Virgil, made Aeneas the heir to Latium and thereby ancestor of the Roman race.

LEANDER See HERO.

LEDA Wife of Tyndareus, king of Sparta. Raped by Zeus in the form of a swan, she gave birth to two eggs, from one of which came **Castor*** and **Clytemnestra**; from the other, **Pollux** and **Helen**.* Other versions of the legend make Tyndareus the father of Castor and Clytemnestra.

LIVY (Titus Livius, 59 BC–AD 17) Roman historian who wrote a history of Rome in 142 books (of which 35 survive) from the foundation of the city in 753 BC to his own times.

LONGINUS (1) The philosopher traditionally credited with authorship of an influential treatise *On the Sublime*, probably written in the first century AD (see p. 255). (2) The name legend gives to the Roman soldier who pierced Christ's side with a spear. See CRUCIFIXION (p. 17).

LOTUS-EATERS A people encountered by **Odysseus**.* They fed on a fruit so entrancing that it deprived the eater of all desire to return to his native land.

LUCAN (Marcus Annnaeus Lucanus, AD 39–65) Roman poet who was author of the *Pharsalia*, a ten-book epic poem on the civil war between **Caesar*** and **Pompey**.* After joining a conspiracy against the Emperor **Nero**,* he was forced to commit suicide.

LUCIAN (second century AD) A Greek writer whose satirical works, including *Dialogues of the Dead* and *Dialogues of the Gods*, have influenced many western writers, from Erasmus to Thomas Love Peacock.

LUCRETIA The virtuous Roman wife of Tarquinius Collatinus. Raped by Sextus, the son of **Tarquinius Superbus**, she told her husband and father what had happened, and then stabbed herself. This outrage led to the expulsion of the Tarquins from Rome and the inauguration of the Republic.

LUCULLUS (ca. 115–ca. 50 BC) Roman noble who, after a distinguished military career, devoted himself to a life of luxury. His wealth supported a magnificent lifestyle that included banquets which made his name a byword for extravagant feasting.

LYCAON A king of Arcadia who tried to trick Zeus into eating a dish of human flesh, for which the god turned him into a wolf (Greek *lucos* = wolf).

LYCURGUS Legendary lawmaker who was supposed to have given **Sparta*** its constitution and the austere military regime that went with it.

MANES The spirits of the dead, which for the Romans had the status of a divinity to be propitiated with appropriate ceremonies.

MARS See ARES.

MARSYAS A Phrygian flute player who challenged Apollo to a contest of musical skill. The victorious god tied Marsyas to a tree and flayed him alive.

MEDEA Daughter of the king of Colchis. She fell in love with **Jason*** and by her power as a sorceress helped him to secure the **Golden Fleece*** before sailing back with him in the *Argo*. To delay the inevitable pursuit, she tore her brother apart and scattered the pieces for their father to pick up. After marrying Jason, she magically restored his aged father Aeson to the vigor of youth. When the daughters of Jason's usurping uncle **Pelias** wanted to try the same feat, she misled them into chopping him up and boiling him. After a period of harmony, Jason abandoned her. Medea responded by murdering in his presence two of their children and then escaping in a chariot drawn by winged dragons. Later, she is said to have married Theseus's father Aegeus. According to one tradition, she ended up after death as the consort of **Achilles*** in the Elysian Fields.

MEDUSA The only one of the three **Gorgons*** who was mortal. She was killed by **Perseus*** with the help of the gods. Unable to look at her without being turned to stone, he used his shield as a mirror and struck off her head. From her blood sprang the winged horse **Pegasus**.*

MELEAGER One of the Argonauts, famous for killing the **Calydonian boar**, a monstrous creature sent by Artemis to lay waste the countryside around Calydon, whose king, Meleager's father, had slighted her. When the hero was born, the Fates decreed that he would live only as long as a brand that was on the fire at the time remained unconsumed. His mother snatched it up and preserved it until Meleager killed her brothers in a quarrel after the boar-hunt. On hearing of this she threw the brand into the fire, thereby ending her son's life.

MEMNON A handsome son of **Tithonus*** and **Eos**, said to have been killed by **Achilles*** in the Trojan War. He owes his fame to a colossal statue near present-day Luxor, actually of an Egyptian pharaoh but for long thought to represent Memnon. Damaged by an earthquake, the statue gives off a curious musical note at sunrise.

MENANDER (ca. 342–292 BC) Athenian dramatist. As the foremost author of New Comedy (more realistic and contemporary than its predecessors), he had an important influence on **Plautus*** and **Terence**,* and through them on European comic drama.

MENELAUS King of Sparta, brother of **Agamemnon*** and husband of **Helen**.* It was her desertion of him that led to the Trojan War.

MENIPPUS A cynic philosopher of the third century BC who gave his name to the literary genre known as Menippean satire, a mixture of prose and verse.

MESSALINA Wife of the Roman Emperor **Claudius** and a byword for depravity. She was executed by her husband in 48 AD for allegedly plotting against him.

MIDAS A king of Phrygia. In recompense for entertaining the satyr **Silenus**,* he was granted his wish that everything he touched should turn to gold. When he discovered that this applied even to his food, he begged for the favor to be withdrawn and was ordered to bathe in the River Pactolus, whose sands were thereafter tinged with gold. Another legend tells how he judged Pan a superior flute player to Apollo and was given a pair of ass's ears by the angry god. They could not be concealed from his barber, who whispered the secret into the ground, but reeds grew up and repeated it to the world.

MINERVA See ATHENE.

MINOS King of Crete. He was the husband of **Pasiphae** and had the labyrinth constructed to house the **Minotaur**,* her monstrous offspring. After his death he became one of the three judges of the Underworld, along with Aeacus and

Rhadamanthus.* He gives his name to the Minoan Period, referring to bronze age civilization in Crete.

MINOTAUR Angered by Minos, Poseidon made his wife **Pasiphae** fall in love with a bull. By constructing a hollow cow for her to get inside, **Daedalus*** enabled her to mate with the bull. Their offspring, half-human and half-bull, was the Minotaur. It was confined in the labyrinth, where it received an annual tribute of seven youths and seven maidens from Athens. With **Ariadne's*** help, **Theseus*** succeeded in killing it.

MITHRAS A Persian sun-god whose cult became popular among the Roman army during the period of the Empire.

MITHRIDATES VII, THE GREAT (d. 63 BC) A king of Pontus, and one of Rome's most persistent and successful enemies. Facing defeat by **Pompey**,* he was unable to poison himself, having secured immunity by taking repeated small doses of various poisons. He was dispatched by a sword at his own request.

MORPHEUS The son of Sleep and bringer of dreams — hence the name given to morphine.

MUSES The nine daughters of Zeus and **Mnemosyne** (Memory) that preside over the arts and sciences. The most celebrated are **Calliope** (epic poetry), **Clio** (history), **Melpomene** (tragedy), and **Terpsichore** (lyric poetry and dance). Among places sacred to the Muses were Mounts **Helicon**, **Pierus**, and **Parnassus**,* and the two fountains, **Castalia** and **Hippocrene**.

MYRMIDONS Thessalian followers of Achilles at the siege of Troy, known for their brutality.

NAIADS Nymphs of lakes, fountains, and rivers.

NARCISSUS A beautiful youth who fell in love with his own reflection in the waters of a spring. He pined away for love of it (or, according to another version, killed himself in despair) and was turned into a flower. See ECHO.

NAUSICAA In Homer's *Odyssey*, the daughter of Alcinous, king of the Phaeacians. Playing by the seashore with her maids, she found **Odysseus**,* shipwrecked and naked. After bringing him food and clothes, she took him to be entertained by her father. Her sadness at his departure breathes a sense of unrealized possibilities.

NEMESIS In Greek mythology the personification of divine retribution.

NEOPTOLEMUS (or **Pyrrhus**) Son of Achilles, he played a courageous but cruel part in the final stage of the Trojan War. Having entered the city in the wooden horse, he went on to kill Hector's son Astyanax and carried off the child's mother **Andromache*** among the spoils of war. But he had angered the gods by killing **Priam*** at the altar of Zeus and was himself later murdered in the temple of Delphi.

NEREIDS Sea nymphs, the daughters of the sea-god Nereus.

NERO Roman emperor from AD 54 to 68 who became notorious for his cruelty. He was thought by many to have been responsible for the fire in AD 64 that partially destroyed Rome, during which he was said to have played his lyre and sung of the fate of Troy. His artistic pretensions stayed with him to the last. Faced with an unstoppable rebellion, he committed suicide, exclaiming *Qualis artifex pereo* ("What an artist dies with me").

NESTOR King of Pylos. He appears in Homer as an old man, respected among the Greek chiefs for his wisdom.

NIKE (**Victoria**) The winged goddess of Victory.

NIOBE Daughter of **Tantalus**.* She had seven sons and seven daughters (estimates of the number vary), but made the mistake of boasting herself superior on this account to the Titan **Leto**, who only had two children, Apollo and Artemis. Leto avenged the insult by sending the pair to kill all but one of Niobe's children with their arrows. Niobe in her grief was turned to stone, the tears still trickling down her petrified form.

NISUS A Trojan who followed **Aeneas*** to Italy and whose friendship with **Euryalus** became proverbial. After the two had made a successful raid on the Latin camp, Euryalus fell into the hands of the enemy. Nisus went to his rescue and the two died together.

OCTAVIAN See AUGUSTUS.

ODYSSEUS (Ulysses) King of Ithaca, husband of **Penelope**,* father of **Telemachus**.* He figures in Homer's *Iliad* as a bold and resourceful leader among the Greeks and in later legend is awarded the arms of **Achilles*** after the hero's death. The *Odyssey* relates the wanderings that finally take him back to Ithaca after an absence of 20 years. On his return he kills the suitors who have been laying siege to his wife Penelope. Non-Homeric legend gives us an Odysseus whose hallmark is unscrupulous cunning. In more modern times he figures as the archetypal wanderer. The main adventures described in the *Odyssey* are his encounters with the following: the **Lotus-Eaters**,* the **Cyclops**,* **Aeolus**,* the **Laestrygones**,* **Circe**,* **Tiresias*** and the **souls of the dead**, the **Sirens**,* **Scylla*** and **Charybdis**, **Calypso**,* **Nausicaa**.*

Alfred Tennyson, "Ulysses," lines 1–17

It little profits that an idle king,
By this still hearth, among these barren crags,
Matched with an agèd wife, I mete and dole
Unequal laws unto a savage race,
That hoard, and sleep, and feed, and know not me.
I cannot rest from travel: I will drink
Life to the lees: all times I have enjoyed
Greatly, have suffered greatly, both with those
That loved me, and alone; on shore, and when
Through scudding drifts the rainy Hyades
Vexed the dim sea: I am become a name;
For always roaming with a hungry heart
Much have I seen and known; cities of men
And manners, climates, councils, governments,
Myself not least, but honoured of them all;
And drunk delight of battle with my peers;
Far on the ringing plains of windy Troy . . .

OEDIPUS The son of **Laius**, king of Thebes, and **Jocasta**. Warned by an oracle that he would die at the hands of his son, Laius ordered him to be killed. Oedipus was exposed on Mount Cithaeron, suspended from a tree by a twig passed through a hole bored in his foot (Greek, *Oedipus* = swollen foot). Rescued by a shepherd, he grew up unaware of his parentage and later killed Laius in a quarrel over precedence at a cross-roads. He went on to Thebes, killed the **Sphinx*** that was terrorizing the region and in reward was given the throne of Thebes and its widowed queen, Jocasta. From their unwitting incest were born two sons, **Polynices** and **Eteocles**,* and two daughters, **Ismene** and **Antigone**.* It was only much later, when he was seeking the cause of a plague afflicting Thebes, that he discovered the truth, whereupon he blinded himself and left the city. Led by his daughter Antigone, he came finally to a grove near Colonus, the appointed place of his death.

OENONE A nymph of Mount Ida who fell in love with **Paris**,* the son of Priam, while he was still living as a shepherd. Their marriage was happy until he cruelly abandoned her to pursue **Helen**.* Wounded at Troy by an arrow from **Philoctetes**,* Paris turned to Oenone for help, but she refused to save him. On hearing of his death, she killed herself in remorse.

ORESTES Son of **Agamemnon*** and **Clytemnestra**. In revenge for the murder of his father, he killed Clytemnestra and her lover Aegisthus. **Aeschylus*** shows him finally purified of this act by the intervention of Athene, who calms the Furies that pursue him. In **Euripides*** his purification can only be obtained by bringing the statue of Artemis from the land of the Tauri to Greece, which he does with the help of his sister **Iphigenia*** and his loyal friend **Pylades**.

ORION A giant and hunter who was placed among the stars after his death.

ORPHEUS A poet whose skill on the lyre was such that he could charm the wild beasts with his music and stir even the rocks and trees. When his wife **Eurydice** died, he went down into the Underworld to win her back, his music earning from Dis the promise of her release as long as he did not turn to look at her until they reached the upper earth. At the last moment he looked back, and Eurydice vanished. He wandered through Thrace, singing of his grief, until Thracian women, enraged by jealousy, tore him to pieces in a Dionysian frenzy. The Muses gathered up and buried the fragments of his body, except for the head which, still singing, floated on the waves to **Lesbos**.

Alexander Pope, "Ode for Musick, on St. Cecilia's Day," lines 113–17

Yet ev'n in Death *Eurydice* he sung,
Eurydice still trembled on his Tongue,
Eurydice the Woods,
Eurydice the Floods,
Eurydice the Rocks, and hollow Mountains rung.

OVID (Publius Ovidius Naso, 43 BC–AD 18) Roman poet whose works include the *Amores*, the *Fasti*, and, most famously, the *Metamorphoses*, from which western literature has taken many of its versions of Greek mythology. In 8 AD Ovid was banished to **Tomis** (present-day Costanza) on the Black Sea, having earlier offended the puritanical Emperor Augustus by his *Ars Amatoria* (Art of Love). He died in exile.

PALINURUS The helmsman of **Aeneas,*** who nodded off to sleep and fell into the sea between Africa and Italy. He reached the shore but was murdered by the local inhabitants.

PALLADIUM A statue of Pallas Athene, supposed to have fallen from heaven during the building of Troy. It protected the city until carried off by **Diomedes** and **Odysseus**.* Another version has it that **Aeneas*** rescued the statue at the fall of Troy and carried it with him to Italy, where it was venerated in Rome.

PAN A fertility god with a special care for shepherds. Half-human and half-goat, he invented the flute with seven reeds, was noted for his lechery, and could inspire sudden fits of alarm (*panic*).

PANDARUS An ally of the Trojans who figures in the *Iliad* as a courageous archer. His role as go-between (hence the term *pander*) in the love affair of **Troilus** and **Cressida** is a medieval addition.

PANDORA A woman created from clay by Hephaestus at the command of Zeus, who wished to exact revenge for **Prometheus's*** impious championship of man. From the gods she received every gift of nature, but along with them Zeus presented her with a box that she was to give to the man she married. Though Prometheus himself was too suspicious of divine favors to accept her, his brother Epimetheus was less cautious. He married Pandora and opened the box. Out of it flew all the evils and diseases that have afflicted humankind ever since. Hope alone remained at the bottom of the box to make life tolerable.

PARIS Son of **Priam*** and **Hecuba**,* who were warned in a dream that he was destined to bring destruction on Troy. Exposed on **Mount Ida**, he was found and brought up by shepherds. For a time he lived happily as the husband of **Oenone**,* but the gods intervened by appointing him to settle a dispute between Aphrodite, Hera, and Athene that had arisen at the wedding of Peleus and Thetis, the parents of Achilles. **Eris** (Strife) had appeared uninvited at the celebration and thrown down an apple marked "for the fairest," a title at once claimed by each of the three goddesses. The **Judgment of Paris** went in favor of Aphrodite, who had promised him in return the most beautiful woman in the world. Unfortunately, this turned out to be **Helen**,* already married to **Menelaus**.* Her subsequent flight with Paris to Troy was the cause of the Trojan War, during which Paris himself was fatally wounded by an arrow from the archer **Philoctetes**.*

PARNASSUS A mountain in Greece near Delphi. One of its peaks was sacred to Apollo and the Muses, the other to Dionysus. Its association with the arts is reflected in the term *Parnassian* for the nineteenth-century art for art's sake movement.

PARTHIANS A people who lived south of the Caspian Sea and proved a troublesome presence on the fringe of the Roman empire. They were famous for their cavalry tactic of turning to shoot back at an enemy from whom they were retreating – hence *Parthian shot*. It was while attempting to invade Parthia in 53 BC that **Marcus Crassus** led seven legions to one of the most terrible defeats in Roman history at the **battle of Carrhae**.

PASIPHAE See MINOTAUR.

PATROCLUS The dear friend of **Achilles**,* killed by **Hector**.* In Homer's *Iliad* his death spurs Achilles to take up arms again.

PEGASUS A winged horse, born from the blood of **Medusa*** when **Perseus*** cut off her head. He carried Perseus to the rescue of **Andromeda**,* and **Bellerophon*** to the conquest of the **Chimaera**. By stamping his hoof on **Mount Helicon**, Pegasus created the spring known as **Hippocrene**, sacred to the Muses.

PELOPONNESIAN WAR (431–404 BC) A war in two main stages between Athens and Sparta, supported by their respective allies. Its primary cause, according to **Thucydides**,* was Sparta's fear of its neighbor's growing imperial power. After ten years of inconclusive conflict, a peace was agreed in 421, but it broke down six years later when Athens launched an ill-judged invasion of Sicily that resulted in the virtual destruction of the Athenian fleet. In 404, with its military and political power broken, Athens finally surrendered.

PENELOPE Wife of **Odysseus**.* In an attempt to hold off the suitors who beset her during her husband's absence at the siege of Troy, she declared that she would make choice of them only when she had finished weaving a shroud for her father-in-law. Until the ruse was discovered, she unpicked each night the threads she had woven by day, thus turning it into a never-ending task. In post-Homeric legend she figures as a model of fidelity and domestic virtue.

PENTHESILEA Queen of the Amazons. She came to fight for the Trojans after the death of **Hector*** and was killed by **Achilles**,* who, when he stripped her of her arms, was touched by her beauty and mourned her death. See THERSITES.

PERICLES The general and statesman who controlled Athens at the peak of its military and artistic power. He directed the affairs of the city from 460 BC until his death in 429 BC.

PERSEPHONE (Proserpina) Daughter of Demeter and Zeus. Her story reflects the annual cycle of death and rebirth in nature. While gathering flowers, she was carried off by Dis to be queen of the Underworld. Beseeched by her distraught mother, Zeus granted that she should be returned to the upper air, provided that she had eaten nothing in the Underworld. But Persephone had tasted some pomegranate seeds. Finally, it was decided that she should spend six months of each year in the Underworld and six months among the living.

> **John Milton, *Paradise Lost*, Bk. 4, lines 268–75**
>
> Not that fair field
> of Enna, where Prosérpine gathering flow'rs,
> Herself a fairer flow'r, by gloomy Dis
> Was gathered, which cost Ceres all that pain
> To seek her through the world; nor that sweet grove
> Of Daphne by Orontes, and th'inspired
> Castalian spring, might with this Paradise
> Of Eden strive . . .

PERSEUS Son of Zeus and **Danae**.* His most famous exploits were the killing of **Medusa*** and the rescue of **Andromeda**.* For the former task the gods equipped him with a helmet that made him invisible, a shield that shone like a mirror (so that he could avoid direct contact with the gorgon's petrifying gaze), and a pair of wings for his feet.

PHAEDRA The daughter of **Minos*** and Pasiphae, she married **Theseus*** but fell in love with her stepson **Hippolytus**, who was Theseus's son by the amazon **Hippolyta**. Rejected by the virtuous Hippolytus, she accused him of making advances to her. Theseus banished his son and begged Poseidon to exact retribution. The sea-monster sent in answer to this plea panicked Hippolytus's horses, who trampled him to death. In despair, Phaedra hanged herself.

PHAETON A son of Phoebus Apollo who persuaded his father to allow him to drive the chariot of the sun. Unable to control the horses, he would have burnt up the earth if Zeus had not struck him with a thunderbolt and hurled him into the River Po. His grieving sisters were turned into trees, and their tears became amber that dropped from the branches into the river.

PHALARIS A tyrant of Agrigentum, noted for roasting his victims inside the hollow belly of a brazen bull.

PHILEMON See BAUCIS.

PHILOCTETES A Greek hero, renowned for his archery, who inherited the arrows of **Heracles**,* dipped in the blood of the **Hydra*** and fatal to any whom they struck. At the start of the expedition to Troy he was left behind on the island of Lemnos because of a foul-smelling wound in his foot. Ten years later, it was revealed by an oracle that Troy could only be taken with his help, so **Odysseus*** and **Neoptolemus*** (or in some versions **Diomedes**) were sent to fetch him. Among the many Trojans he killed with the arrows of Heracles was **Paris**.*

PHILOMELA A daughter of Pandion, king of Athens. Her sister **Procne** married King **Tereus** of Thrace and obtained permission for Philomela to join her. Tereus went to fetch Philomela from Athens but on the way back raped her and cut out her tongue to prevent her telling what had happened. Having confined Philomela in a castle, Tereus returned to Thrace where he told Procne that her sister had died on the journey. But Philomela managed to reveal her story by weaving it into a tapestry which was conveyed to Procne, who then took revenge by murdering her six-year-old son Itys and serving him up for Tereus to eat. Just as Tereus drew his sword to strike her down, the three were changed into birds: Tereus into a hoopoe, Philomela into a nightingale, Procne into a swallow.

T. S. Eliot, *The Waste Land*, Part 2: "A Game of Chess," lines 97–103

Above the antique mantel was displayed
As though a window gave upon the sylvan scene
The change of Philomel, by the barbarous king
So rudely forced; yet there the nightingale
Filled all the desert with inviolable voice
And still she cried, and still the world pursues,
"Jug Jug" to dirty ears.

PHLEGETHON One of the rivers of the Underworld.

PHOENIX A fabulous bird from Egypt or Arabia reputed to build itself a funeral pyre every 500 years and disappear in flames. From its ashes the phoenix rises again, reborn.

PINDAR (ca. 518–ca. 438 BC) Greek lyric poet. Four books of his Odes, written in praise of victors at the Olympic Games, have survived and been widely imitated by western writers.

PLATO (ca. 428–ca. 347 BC) Greek philosopher. A pupil of **Socrates*** and teacher of **Aristotle**,* he taught in the olive grove of Academus outside Athens, which gave its name to his Academy. Among his most famous works, almost all of which survive, are the Dialogues known as the *Republic*, the *Symposium*, the *Laws*, the *Timaeus*, the *Phaedo*, and the *Apology*. See also p. 254.

PLAUTUS, Titus Maccius (ca. 254–184 BC) Roman comic dramatist whose plays have had a continuing influence on European theater. The stock figure of the boastful soldier, the *miles gloriosus*, had its origin in his work.

PLEIADES The seven daughters of **Atlas**,* who were raised to the heavens to form a constellation after their death.

PLUTARCH (ca. AD 45–ca. 125) Greek biographer best known for his *Parallel Lives* of celebrated Greeks and Romans, arranged in 23 pairs. The Elizabethan translation of this work by Sir Thomas North was used by Shakespeare as a source for a number of his plays.

POLYPHEMUS A son of Poseidon, and the most famous of the **Cyclops**.* He captured **Odysseus*** along with 12 of his followers and shut them in his cave, eating two of them each day. Odysseus escaped by getting him drunk and driving a burning stake through his one eye. He and his surviving companions then concealed themselves under the bellies of Polyphemus's rams as they went out to pasture. See GALATEA.

POMPEY THE GREAT (Gnaeus Pompeius) (106–48 BC) Outstandingly successful Roman general who cleared the western Mediterranean of pirates and ruled Rome as part of the First Triumvirate with **Julius Caesar*** (his father-in-law) and **Marcus Crassus**. Conflict with Caesar led to civil war, which ended with Pompey's defeat at the **battle of Pharsalus** (48 BC). He escaped to Egypt but was murdered as he went ashore.

POSEIDON (Neptune) Brother of Zeus and ruler of the seas, he was also the god of horses and earthquakes.

PRAXITELES Celebrated Athenian sculptor of the fourth century BC. His work is known from a statue of Hermes carrying the infant Dionysus and from Roman copies of his "Aphrodite of Cnidos."

PRIAM The last king of Troy, killed by Achilles's son **Neoptolemus*** at the fall of the city.

PRIAPUS A fertility god said to be the offspring of Aphrodite and Dionysus, usually represented with a prominent phallus.

PROCNE See PHILOMELA.

PROCRIS Wife of Cephalus. Inspired with jealousy by her rival **Eos** (the Dawn), she spied on him while he was out hunting. He mistook her for prey and killed her with his spear, which never missed its mark.

PROCRUSTES A robber of Attica, killed by **Theseus**.* He had a bed to which he tied his victims. To make them fit exactly, he either stretched their limbs or lopped them off – hence the term *Procrustean bed* for a crude attempt to impose uniformity.

PROMETHEUS A Titan who was supposed to have created man out of clay and then stolen for him the gift of fire. In revenge, Zeus sent **Pandora**.* Prometheus was punished by being chained to a rock on Mount Caucusus where an eagle (according to some, a vulture) preyed endlessly on his liver. After 30 years **Heracles*** released him by killing the bird.

PROTEUS Shepherd of Poseidon's flocks, he was granted the gift of prophecy but could only be questioned with difficulty since he continually changed shape until firmly held – hence *protean*.

PSYCHE A beautiful girl loved by **Eros*** (Cupid), who visited her by night, leaving at sunrise. In spite of the god's warnings, she could not resist the temptation to look at him. Woken by a drop of hot oil from her lamp, Eros fled, abandoning her to despair. Later, Zeus took pity on her and the two were reunited. Her story has been taken as an allegory of the relationship between the soul and love.

PTOLEMY (second century AD) Egyptian mathematician and astronomer who devised a model of the heavenly bodies, with the earth at the center of the universe. The Ptolemaic system was accepted for many centuries and only displaced by the Copernican (see p. 166) after fierce resistance from the church.

PYGMALION A king of Cyprus who sculpted the figure of a woman so beautiful that he fell in love with the statue. In answer to his prayers, Aphrodite brought it to life. He named the woman, who later bore him a son, **Galatea**.

PYRAMUS A Babylonian youth, in love with **Thisbe**. The two agreed to meet under a white mulberry tree at the tomb of Ninus. Thisbe arrived first but was scared by a lion and fled, dropping her veil, which the lion tore with its blood-stained jaws. Pyramus then came up, saw the veil and, assuming the worst, killed himself. When Thisbe returned to find Pyramus dying, she stabbed herself with the same sword. Stained with their blood, the roots of the tree produced fruit of a deep red color which the mulberry has ever since retained.

PYRRHUS (1) See NEOPTOLEMUS. (2) A king of Epirus who won a costly victory over the Romans at Asculum in AD 279, leaving his own army badly depleted – hence the term *pyrrhic* for a victory whose cost outweighs its benefits.

PYTHAGORAS (sixth century BC) Greek philosopher and mathematician, credited with discovering the geometrical theorem that bears his name. He believed in the transmigration of souls and taught that the heavenly bodies move according to the laws of musical harmony – hence the music of the spheres. Among the more outlandish legends that grew up about him was the claim that one of his thighs was made of gold.

PYTHON A monstrous serpent that arose from the mud after **Deucalion's*** flood. It was killed by Apollo, who instituted the Pythian Games to mark his victory. The priestess of Apollo at Delphi, who delivered the oracle, took her name, Pythia, from this event.

RHADAMANTHUS Son of Zeus and **Europa**,* he became one of the judges of the dead in the Underworld. The adjective *rhadamanthine* reflects his reputation for stern and uncompromising justice.

RHEA See CYBELE.

ROME According to tradition, the city was founded by **Romulus*** in 753 BC. Its period of greatness began with the establishment of a Republic after the expulsion of **Tarquin*** the Proud (Tarquinius Superbus), Rome's last monarch, at the end of the sixth century BC. Under a system of government by two annually elected **consuls** and a number of subordinate magistrates, Rome managed over the next two and a half centuries to dominate the rest of Italy. It was the start of an empire that by the end of the first century AD encircled the Mediterranean and reached up into Britain and northern Europe. As the Roman army gained in strength and importance, the Republic had become increasingly vulnerable to the power of ambitious military commanders. The struggle for control of Rome in the early second century BC between the two generals **Marius** (157–86 BC) and **Sulla** (138–78 BC) foreshadowed the later civil wars between **Pompey*** and **Julius Caesar**,* and **Octavian** and **Mark Antony**.* It was the second of these wars that finally brought the Republic to an end. In 27 BC Octavian became the first Roman emperor, adopting the title of **Augustus**.* The empire survived for five centuries, reaching its zenith in the age of the Antonines (**Nerva, Trajan, Hadrian,*** **Antoninus Pius, Marcus Aurelius**), who ruled from AD 96 to 180. The breach that emerged between an eastern and a western empire was briefly healed by **Constantine the Great** (d. AD 337), Rome's first Christian emperor, but the pressures of disunity and economic decline left the empire fatally exposed to barbarian invasion. The sack of Rome, first by Visigoths in 410 and then by Vandals in 455, was followed in 476 by the deposition of the last Roman emperor of the West.

ROMULUS Twin brother of **Remus**, and legendary founder of Rome. The twins, fathered by Mars, were born to the daughter of the king of Alba. Her uncle, who had usurped the throne of Alba, had them thrown into the Tiber, but they survived and were suckled by a she-wolf. Later, when they came to found the city of Rome, Romulus killed Remus in a quarrel over precedence.

ROSCIUS Celebrated Roman actor of the first century BC. His name has since been used to refer to any actor of outstanding talent.

RUBICON The river that separated Italy from Gaul. By crossing it at the head of an army in 49 BC, **Julius Caesar*** effectively committed himself to civil war – hence the phrase *to cross the Rubicon*, used of an irrevocable step that commits one to a course of action with important consequences.

SABINE WOMEN, RAPE OF THE Livy tells the legend of how **Romulus**,* needing women for his newly founded city, invited the neighboring Sabines to a celebration during which the youth of Rome carried off the Sabine women. The Sabines in consequence became the first people to take up arms against the Romans.

SAPPHO (ca. seventh century BC) Greek poet from **Lesbos**, supposed to have leapt to her death in the sea out of unrequited love for **Phaon**, a handsome youth. Her association with lesbianism was based on the passionate sentiments expressed in her poetry for some of the women in her circle.

SATURN A Roman god of agriculture identified with **Cronos**.* His festival was the Saturnalia, a period of license subsequently incorporated in New Year's festivities. Later writers associated the reign of Saturn with the Golden Age.

SATYR A woodland spirit, represented in Roman art with budding horns and the legs, ears, and tail of a goat. The lustful disposition of satyrs is reflected in the modern term *satyriasis*.

SCAEVOLA, G. Mucius A Roman of legendary fortitude. He entered the Etruscan camp in disguise, determined to assassinate **Lars Porsenna**,* who was at the time besieging Rome. Captured and brought before the Etruscan chief, he calmly placed his hand on an altar of burning coals and held it there without flinching to demonstrate what Porsenna was up against. Duly impressed, Porsenna abandoned his siege.

SCIPIO AFRICANUS MAJOR, Publius Cornelius (236–ca. 183 BC) The Roman general who defeated **Hannibal*** and the Carthaginian army at the battle of **Zama** (202 BC), bringing to an end the **Second Punic War**. It was as the conqueror of **Carthage** that he was accorded the name "Africanus." Livy records that on one occasion he refused to exercise his rights over a beautiful captured princess and sent her back to her family with gifts for her intended husband. Scipio's Dream (the *Somnium Scipionis*) refers to an episode in Cicero's *Republic*, when Scipio the Younger dreams that his ancestor appears to him.

SCYLLA A six-headed monster who, along with the whirlpool **Charybdis**, guarded the passage through the straits of Messina. Later accounts say she was originally a beautiful nymph, changed into this hideous form by the jealousy of **Circe**.*

SEMELE A daughter of **Cadmus**,* loved by Zeus. Jealous Hera prompted her to beg the god to appear to her in all his divine splendor, armed with his thunderbolts. The sight destroyed her, but their unborn child **Dionysus*** was rescued by Zeus.

SENECA, Lucius Annaeus (d. AD 65) Stoic philosopher and writer of tragedies. He acted as tutor to the Emperor **Nero*** but was later accused of complicity in **Piso's conspiracy** against the emperor. Nero ordered him to commit suicide, which he did with exemplary firmness by opening his veins.

SEVEN AGAINST THEBES See ETEOCLES.

SEVEN SLEEPERS OF EPHESUS Seven Christian youths, fleeing the persecution of the emperor Decius in the mid-third century, who took refuge in a cave where they were walled up by order of the emperor. They escaped death, however, by falling into a miraculous sleep that lasted for almost two hundred years.

SIBYL OF CUMAE The most famous of the divinely inspired prophetesses of classical legend. Apollo loved her when she was young and offered her a wish. She asked for as many years of life as she held grains of sand in her hand but forgot to ask for continuing health and youth. She is glimpsed in Petronius's *Satyricon*, wishing only to die. It was she who instructed Aeneas, in Virgil's epic, to pick the golden bough required for access to the Underworld, and predicted that the Tiber would foam with blood in the wars that awaited him in Italy. She is often identified with the sibyl who, according to the story in Livy, offered nine books of prophecies to King Tarquin II at a seemingly exorbitant price. When he rejected them, she went off and burned three of them, returning with the other six, which she offered at the same price. Again they were rejected, and she burned another three. Returning with the last three, she once more demanded the same price. At this point Tarquin agreed and bought the three remaining Sibylline Books for the price of the original nine. Thereafter they were preserved with great reverence and consulted by the Senate in times of crisis. It was the sibyl's custom to write her prophecies on leaves and place them at the entrance to her cave, where they risked being scattered by the wind before they could be read.

SILENUS A **satyr*** who acted as tutor to the young **Dionysus**.* He is usually represented as fat and drunk, often riding on an ass and garlanded with flowers. See MIDAS.

> **Sir Thomas Browne, *Urn Burial*, chapter 5**
>
> What song the Syrens sang, or what name Achilles assumed when he hid himself among women, though puzzling questions, are not beyond all conjecture . . .

SIMEON STYLITES A fifth-century Syrian ascetic, who was reputed to have spent some thirty or forty years living on top of a pillar near Antioch. A number of other Stylites practiced the same form of asceticism but without gaining his renown.

SIRENS Sea-nymphs who lured sailors to destruction by the beauty of their singing. **Odysseus*** ordered his crew to plug their ears with wax, while he himself was lashed to the mast so that he could hear their song. The sirens are sometimes represented as having a woman's body above the waist and a bird's below.

SISYPHUS A king of Corinth condemned in the Underworld to roll a huge stone up a hill. Just as he reached the top, the stone would roll down, forcing him to begin the task again.

Albert Camus, last paragraph of _The Myth of Sisyphus_ (1942)

I leave Sisyphus at the bottom of the mountain! One always finds one's burden again. But Sisyphus teaches the higher fidelity that says No to gods and lifts up boulders. He too judges that all is well. This universe, henceforth without master, seems to him neither sterile nor pointless. Each particle of this stone, each flash of mineral in this night-filled mountain constitutes its own world. The struggle towards the summits is itself enough to fill a man's heart. We must think of Sisyphus as happy.

SOCRATES (ca. 469–399 BC) Athenian philosopher. He wrote nothing himself but his characteristic method of acting as midwife to the truth by interrogating the opinions and assumptions of his interlocutors is recorded in Plato's Dialogues. His unflinching integrity put him at odds with the authorities, and he was condemned to death as a corrupter of youth. His final scene, in which he drank hemlock, is described in Plato's _Phaedo_. Among the personal details recorded of him, apart from his ugliness, is his marriage to **Xanthippe**, whose reputation for shrewishness has lived on through the centuries.

SOLON (ca. 638–ca. 560 BC) Celebrated Athenian statesman and lawgiver, famed for his wisdom. He moderated the harshness of **Draco's*** code. See CROESUS.

SOPHOCLES (496–406 BC) Along with Aeschylus and Euripides, one of the three great Athenian tragic dramatists. Of his many plays only seven survive, among them _Oedipus Tyrannus_ (_Oedipus the King_), _Oedipus at Colonus_, and _Antigone_.

SPARTA Also known as **Lacedaemon**, it became the dominant city-state in the southern Peloponnese from the seventh century BC until its decline in the fourth century BC. Spartan society was based on a rigorous military regime supposed to have been instituted by the legendary lawgiver **Lycurgus**. Its narrow dedication to the art of war depended on the existence of a slave class of **helots**, who had been the original inhabitants of the region. Babies considered sickly or imperfect were exposed to die. The military focus of this culture inevitably brought it into conflict with its neighbor Athens, and the resulting Peloponnesian War, though Sparta emerged victorious in 404 BC, left it drained and vulnerable. Within thirty years its star had begun to wane. Among many stories told of the fortitude inculcated by Sparta's harsh discipline is that of the boy who rather than reveal the stolen fox-cub he had hidden under his tunic accepted a painful death by allowing it to gnaw away at his vitals. See PELOPONNESIAN WAR, THERMOPYLAE.

SPARTACUS A Thracian gladiator who led a rebellion against Rome from 73 to 71 BC. He was eventually defeated by the legions of **Marcus Crassus**. Spartacus himself died in the final battle, and thousands of his followers were crucified along the Appian Way between Rome and Capua.

SPHINX A monster of Greek legend, usually represented with a human head and the body of a lion. In the **Oedipus*** story it terrorized the region around Thebes, killing all who failed to answer its riddle: what animal walks on four legs in the morning, two at midday, and three in the evening? When Oedipus answered correctly that it was Man (who moves on all fours at the start of life, then walks upright, and finally uses a stick), the Sphinx hurled itself from its rock and was killed.

STENTOR A Greek warrior mentioned in the *Iliad* as having a voice as loud as the voices of 50 other men – hence the word *stentorian*.

STOICS A school of Greek philosophers founded by **Zeno** of Citium (in Cyprus) towards the end of the fourth century BC. Their commitment to reason and self-control, and their indifference to good or ill fortune, provided an ideal of virtue that recommended itself to many Romans. **Seneca**,* the philosopher **Epictetus**, and the emperor **Marcus Aurelius** were among followers of the Stoic school.

STYX The gloomy river of the Underworld across which the dead were ferried by **Charon*** – hence the adjective *Stygian*.

SYBARIS A Greek colony in southern Italy notorious in the seventh and sixth centuries BC for the luxurious and self-indulgent lifestyle of its inhabitants – hence the word *sybarite*. (Seneca tells of a native of Sybaris who complained of being unable to sleep one night because of a rose-leaf doubled under him.)

SYCOPHANTS Much-despised figures in ancient Athens who acted as informers, frequently blackmailing their victims with the threat of slanderous accusations. The modern word *sycophant*, a servile flatterer, has shifted the meaning slightly.

SYMPOSIUM Literally a drinking party, and hence the discussion arising from it. Both **Plato*** and **Xenophon*** gave the title to one of their Dialogues.

SYRINX An Arcadian nymph. Pursued by Pan, she begged the gods for help and was changed into a reed.

TACITUS, Gaius Cornelius (ca. AD 55–ca. 120) Roman historian who recorded in sharp, epigrammatic prose the early history of the Roman empire from **Augustus*** to the death of the emperor Domitian. Of his surviving works the best known are the *Agricola*, the *Germania*, the *Histories*, and the *Annals*.

TANTALUS A son of Zeus who was variously supposed to have stolen **ambrosia*** for mortal consumption and to have served the flesh of his son Pelops in a banquet for the gods. He was punished in Hades by being set in a pool of water up to his chin, with a bough of fruit above his head. Each time he bent to drink or reached up to eat, the water or food receded, leaving him tormented by perpetual thirst and hunger – hence the word *tantalize*.

TARPEIAN ROCK The rock on the Capitoline Hill from which criminals were thrown to their death in ancient Rome. According to the legend recorded by Livy, its name was derived from Tarpeia, daughter of the citadel's governor, who agreed to let the Sabines into the city if they would give her their bracelets. Instead, they crushed her to death with their shields.

TARQUIN The family of the early kings of Rome. The last was Tarquinius Superbus (late sixth century BC), whose son committed the rape on **Lucretia*** that led to the family's expulsion from Rome and the founding of the Republic.

TELEMACHUS Son of **Odysseus*** and **Penelope**.* When his father failed to return from the Trojan War, Telemachus set out to look for him. Later, he helped Odysseus to kill Penelope's suitors.

TERENCE (Publius Terentius Afer) (ca. 190–ca. 159 BC) Roman comic dramatist, who initially came to Rome from North Africa as a slave. His six comedies, which draw heavily on the Greek dramatist **Menander**,* enjoyed great popularity among his contemporaries and were an important influence on later European theater. Among other figures, he created the soldier **Thraso**, whose boastfulness became proverbial.

THEMISTOCLES (ca. 525–460 BC) Athenian general who defeated the Persians in the great naval battle of **Salamis** (480 BC). Later, he was accused of treachery and banished from Athens. He threw himself on the mercy of the Persian king, was honorably treated, and died in Magnesia.

THEOCRITUS (third century BC) Greek pastoral poet best known now for his *Idylls*.

THERMOPYLAE A narrow pass leading from Thessaly into southern Greece. In 480 BC it was the scene of a heroic defense by a small force of Greeks who held it for three days against the overwhelming might of Xerxes's Persian army. In the end, after the Greek position had been betrayed, a band of 300 Spartans under **Leonidas** made the last stand and died to a man. The epitaph for them written by the Greek poet Simonides has been rendered in a well-known translation: "*Go tell the Spartans, stranger passing by, / That here, obedient to their laws, we lie.*"

> **Lord Byron, *Don Juan*, canto 3**
>
> Must we but weep o'er days more blest?
> Must we but blush? – Our fathers bled.
> Earth! Render back from out thy breast
> A remnant of our Spartan dead!
> Of the three hundred grant but three,
> To make a new Thermopylae!

THERSITES A scurrilous and cynical member of the Greek host, who cuts a uniquely anti-heroic figure in Homer's *Iliad*. According to post-Homeric legend, he was killed by **Achilles*** for mocking the latter's grief over the death of **Penthesilea**.*

THESEUS A son of Poseidon or, according to other legends, of Aegeus, he performed many heroic feats and became king of Athens. Among his exploits was the killing of the **Minotaur**,* in which he was helped by **Ariadne**.* On his return to Athens, he forgot to change the black sail on his boat. This had been the agreed signal of failure, and Aegeus, assuming his son to be dead, threw himself into the sea. As king of Athens in succession to him, Theseus defeated the Amazons and fathered **Hippolytus** by their queen, Hippolyta. He also took part in the battle of the **Lapiths** and **Centaurs*** at the wedding of his friend **Pirithous**, with whom he later went

down to the Underworld in an unsuccessful attempt to carry off **Persephone**.*
Imprisoned there, the two of them were later rescued by **Heracles**.*

THESPIS Greek poet of the sixth century BC who is said to have invented tragedy by introducing an actor with a role separate from the Chorus – hence the word *thespian*.

THETIS One of the **Nereids**,* she became mother of **Achilles**.*

THISBE See PYRAMUS.

THUCYDIDES (ca. 460–ca. 400 BC) Athenian historian, who spent much of his later life in exile after leading an unsuccessful expedition to prevent the Spartans capturing a town on the Thracian coast. His *History of the Peloponnesian War*, which covers the progress of the struggle between Athens and Sparta up to 411 BC, is marked by an innovative concern with factual accuracy and with the political causes and consequences of the events described.

THULE An island thought by the ancients to be at the extremity of the north sea, and so referred to as *ultima Thule* (farthest Thule). It came to represent the end of the world, or, figuratively, the limit of what can be reached.

TIMON A citizen of fifth-century Athens whose legendary misanthropy is recorded by **Plutarch**.*

TIRESIAS A Theban seer who, according to one myth, was blinded by Athene when he came upon her bathing. Later she gave him the gift of prophecy by way of compensation. Ovid favors a more colorful story. Tiresias, he tells us, once saw two snakes mating, struck them with his staff, and was turned into a woman. Seven years later he saw the same pair, struck them again, and was this time turned back into a man. When Zeus and Hera were disputing whether men or women get more pleasure from sex, they appealed to Tiresias as someone who had the requisite experience. His answer – that women get ten times the pleasure of men – offended Hera, who struck him blind. Zeus, in compensation, gave him the gift of prophecy and extended his life to seven times that of ordinary mortals.

TITANS The generation of gods, children of **Ge*** and **Uranus**,* who preceded the Olympians and were displaced by them. See CRONOS, URANUS.

TITHONUS A beautiful youth, son of the king of Troy, who was loved by **Eos**, the Dawn. She granted him eternal life, but he forgot to ask for eternal youth so was condemned to live on with all the vile infirmities of age. Finally, out of compassion or disgust, Eos turned him into a grasshopper.

TITYUS One of the **Giants**,* so huge his body covered nine acres of land. He attempted to rape **Leto**, mother of Apollo and Artemis, and was punished in Tartarus by a vulture that endlessly devoured his liver.

TRITON A powerful sea-god – half-man, half-dolphin – who was the son of Poseidon and Amphitrite. He is usually represented blowing a conch-shell.

TROILUS A son of Priam, killed by Achilles. The story of his love for **Cressida** and her betrayal of him with **Diomedes** is a product of the Middle Ages.

Shakespeare, *The Merchant of Venice*, V, i, 3–13

Lorenzo   . . . in such a night
Troilus, methinks, mounted the Trojan walls,
And sighed his soul towards the Grecian tents
Where Cressid lay that night.

Jessica   In such a night
Did Thisbe fearfully o'ertrip the dew
And saw the lion's shadow ere himself,
And ran dismayed away.

Lorenzo   In such a night
Stood Dido with a willow in her hand
Upon the wild sea banks, and waft her love
To come again to Carthage.

Jessica   In such a night
Medea gatherèd the enchanted herbs
That did renew old Aeson.

TROJAN HORSE The stratagem by which the Greeks finally took Troy. A huge wooden horse was constructed, and then the Greeks set sail, having put about the rumor that the horse was an offering to the gods for their safe return home. The Trojans dragged it into the city, unaware that its hollow interior was filled with Greeks. At night the hidden soldiers let themselves out, killed the guards, and opened the gates of the city to the Greek armies.

TROJAN WAR The abduction of **Helen**,* the wife of **Menelaus**, by the Trojan prince **Paris*** was the legendary cause of the war. A coalition of Greek states mounted an expedition to recover her, led by Menelaus's brother **Agamemnon**.* Among the principal Greek chieftains were **Achilles**,* **Ajax**,* **Odysseus**,* and **Diomedes**; on the side of the Trojans, the preeminent figure was **Hector**,* brother of **Paris*** and son of King Priam. For ten years the Greeks besieged Troy, heroes battling against heroes, until the **Trojan Horse*** finally allowed them to break in and sack the city. The subject of Homer's *Iliad* and the source of numerous other legends, the Trojan War is central to our understanding of the heroic ideals of the early classical age.

***From* W. H. Auden, Introduction to *The Portable Greek Reader* (1948)**

The Homeric hero has the military virtues of courage, resourcefulness, magnanimity in victory, and dignity in defeat to an exceptional degree. His heroism is manifested in exceptional deeds which can be judged by others who are forced to admit "He achieved what we could not have achieved." His motive is to win admiration and glory from his equals whether they are on his side or the enemy's. The code by which he lives is a code of honor which is not a universal requirement like law but an individual one, that which I require of myself and that which in view of my achievements I have a right to demand of others.

TROY (or **Ilium**) A city near the Hellespont which stood on the site of present-day Hissarlik. Its ruins were discovered by **Heinrich Schliemann** in 1873. Archeological evidence suggests that the war which resulted in Troy's destruction was probably in the twelfth or thirteenth century BC.

TURNUS See AENEAS.

URANUS The oldest of the gods, a personification of the sky. He married Ge, the Earth, and by her became father of the **Titans**, whom he kept in cruel confinement. Cronos, however, escaped. With a scythe supplied by his mother, he castrated Uranus and replaced him on the throne.

VENUS See APHRODITE.

VESTA The goddess of the hearth, worshipped in Roman households. She had a temple in the forum, where the sacred fire – supposedly brought from Troy

– was tended by six vestal virgins. These had to serve for 30 years, during which they were highly honored but risked burial alive if they lost their virginity.

VIRGIL (Publius Vergilius Maro) (70–19 BC) Roman poet born near Mantua, and hence sometimes referred to as the "swan of Mantua." He was the author of a group of pastoral poems (the *Eclogues*) and a didactic poem about agriculture (the *Georgics*), but his crowning achievement was the *Aeneid*, an epic poem in 12 books recounting the story of **Aeneas**.* His status in the Middle Ages was so high (partly because be was believed to have foretold the birth of Christ in his fourth, or Messianic, Eclogue) that people used his works as a means of fortune-telling, opening one of them at random to see what it said – the so-called *Sortes Virgilianae*.

VULCAN See HEPHAESTUS.

WOODEN HORSE OF TROY See TROJAN HORSE.

XENOPHON (ca. 430–ca. 355 BC) Greek historian who joined the force raised by **Cyrus the Younger** to march against his brother, the Persian King Artaxerxes. After the defeat and death of Cyrus at the battle of **Cunaxa** (401 BC), Xenophon was elected one of the generals who had to manage the perilous retreat of the Greek army, which he achieved successfully. This became the subject of his most famous work, the *Anabasis*.

XERXES I King of Persia from 486 to 465 BC. Determined to avenge the defeat of his father, **Darius the Great**,* at **Marathon** (490 BC), he built a bridge of boats across the Hellespont and invaded Greece. His setback at **Thermopylae*** was only the prelude to a crushing defeat at **Salamis** (480 BC) which destroyed his fleet and put an end to the invasion. Among the more eccentric details recorded by **Herodotus*** is his order that the sea be whipped in retribution for a storm that had destroyed his bridge across the Hellespont.

ZENOBIA Queen of Palmyra in Syria during the second half of the third century AD. A woman of courage and ambition, she invaded Asia Minor and Egypt in defiance of Rome but was finally defeated and captured in 272 by the armies of the Emperor Aurelian. After appearing in his triumph, she was allowed to live in considerable luxury near Tibur (present-day Tivoli).

ZEUS (Jupiter, Jove) The supreme god of the Olympians, wielder of the thunderbolt. Only the Fates were outside the power of his decrees.

ZEUXIS (late fifth century BC) Celebrated Greek painter whose representations of reality were so lifelike that birds were said to have pecked at a bunch of grapes he painted. He was bested, however, in a competition with **Parrhasius**, who painted a curtain with such skill that Zeuxis tried to draw it back, imagining it to be a real veil behind which the painting was concealed.

Part 3

Surviving History

There are three elements to this part of the book: (1) a series of timelines; (2) a dictionary of background information; (3) a short list of dates. The emphasis throughout is on English (as opposed to British or American) history, and in particular on those aspects of it that became part of the nation's mythology.

For a clearer sense of how the historical context helped to shape the literature of the time, it's worth looking at one or two brief histories of English literature. Among those available at the moment are Michael Alexander's *History of English Literature* (Palgrave Macmillan, 2000), *The Routledge History of Literature in English* (Routledge, 2001) by Ronald Carter and John McRae, and the new edition of Andrew Sanders's *Short Oxford History of English Literature* (Oxford University Press, 2004). In each case there are differences of method and perspective, but all of them reinforce the value of approaching literature with some grasp of its historical background.

TIMELINES

The point of this section is to make it easier to see historical links between the literature of a given period and what was going on in other spheres. Too much detail can make it difficult to keep track of these broad correlations, so I've tried to keep the timelines simple. They are not intended to provide a history of English literature, political changes, scientific discoveries, or anything else. I've simply picked out a few titles and a few events in order to highlight the main lines of development.

There is no single way to make use of timelines. The fact that Chaucer's *Troilus and Criseyde* was written at about the time of the Peasants' Revolt may be no more than an interesting sidelight, but the same information about *Piers Plowman* could change one's reading of the poem. How important were the unsolved Ripper murders to the success of Sherlock Holmes a year or two later? Is it worth knowing that Linnaeus was naming plants at the same time as Johnson was defining words, or that Maxim was inventing his machine gun while Rider Haggard was writing *King Solomon's Mines*? Like the publication of Blake's *Songs of Innocence* in the same year as the mutiny on the *Bounty* and the outbreak of the French Revolution, such coincidences are suggestive enough to prompt lines of thought; and this is probably as much as one can hope for. Often, the links will be far more tenuous. To know that mail coaches, plate glass, and metal water closets were all coming on the scene in the late eighteenth century is unlikely to transform our view of Sheridan's plays or Crabbe's poetry, but such knowledge is not therefore worthless. If it colors our understanding of the writer's world, it will have served its purpose.

LITERATURE	DATE	POLITICAL HISTORY
	First century BC	Roman invasions (55 and 54 BC)
	First century AD	Roman colonization from AD 43
	Fifth century	Roman legions leave Britain (410) Invasions of Jutes, Angles, and Saxons (ca. 450)
Old English Literature (seventh–tenth centuries)	**Seventh–ninth centuries**	Conversion of England to **Christianity** (seventh century)
Caedmon (seventh century)		
Bede, *Historia Ecclesiastica Gentis Anglorum* (731) **Dream of the Rood** (? eighth century)		**Offa** is king of Mercia (757–96) **Lindisfarne** sacked by Viking raiders (793)
Beowulf (? eighth century)		**Alfred the Great** is king of Wessex (871–99)
Cynewulf (late eighth/early ninth century)		**Danelaw** established following Alfred's victory over the Danish invaders at the battle of Edington (878)

LITERATURE	DATE	POLITICAL HISTORY
Anglo-Saxon Chronicle (from late ninth century)	**Tenth century**	
Battle of Brunanburh (tenth century)		**Athelstan**, king of the English, defeats an invading force of Scots at **Brunanburh** (937)
"**The Wanderer**" and "**The Seafarer**" (? tenth century) *Battle of Maldon* (? end of tenth century) **Aelfric**, *Lives of the Saints* (end of tenth century)		**Battle of Maldon**: Viking invaders defeat a force of local Essex men (991)
Wulfstan, *Sermo lupi ad anglos* (? 1014)	**Eleventh century**	**Norman Conquest** (1066)
Geoffrey of Monmouth, *Historia Regum Britanniae* (ca. 1130s) **Marie de France**, *Lais* (late twelfth century)	**Twelfth century**	The future Henry II's marriage to **Eleanor of Aquitaine** (1152) brings a vast area of France to the English crown
Layamon, *Brut* (late twelfth or early thirteenth century) *The Owl and the Nightingale* **Romances** (e.g., *King Horn, Floris and Blauncheflour, Sir Orfeo*)	**Thirteenth century**	**King John loses Normandy** to the French (1204–5) **Magna Carta** (1215) **Simon de Montfort** leads a revolt of the Barons against Henry III (1264)
Mystery Plays *The Travels of Sir John Mandeville* (mid-fourteenth century) *Sir Gawain and the Green Knight* (late fourteenth century) **William Langland**, *Piers Plowman* (late fourteenth century) **Julian of Norwich**, *Revelations of Divine Love* (? late fourteenth century) **John Gower**, *Confessio Amantis* (ca. 1390) **Geoffrey Chaucer**, *The Canterbury Tales* (1390s)	**Fourteenth century**	**Hundred Years War** (1337–1453) **Black Death** (1348) **Peasants' Revolt** (1381)

LITERATURE	DATE	POLITICAL HISTORY
Thomas Hoccleve (ca. 1369–1426) **John Lydgate** (ca. 1370–1449) *The Kingis Quair* (ca. 1424) **Thomas Malory**, *Le Morte Darthur* (completed ca. 1470)	**Fifteenth century**	Battle of **Agincourt** (1415) French victory at the **battle of Castillon** (1453) marks the end of the Hundred Years War **Wars of the Roses** (1455–85)
Robert Henryson (d. ca. 1505), *The Testament of Cresseid* ***Everyman*** (Morality play, ca. 1495) **William Dunbar**, "Lament for the Makars" (ca. 1506) **Thomas More**, *Utopia* (1516) **John Skelton**, "Speke Parrot" (written 1521) **Sir Thomas Elyot**, *The Boke Named the Governour* (1531) **Thomas Wyatt** (ca. 1503–42) and **Henry Howard, earl of Surrey** (ca. 1517–47). Poems by them included in *Tottel's Miscellany* (1557)	**1485–1558** **Henry VII** (1485–1509) **Henry VIII** (1509–47) **Edward VI** (1547–53) **Mary** (1553–8)	**Battle of Bosworth** (1485) brings the Wars of the Roses to an end. Henry Tudor comes to the throne as Henry VII, the **first Tudor monarch** **Early voyages of exploration** **Battle of Flodden**: invading Scots routed by the English under the earl of Surrey (1513) Start of the **Reformation** in Europe (1517) **Henry VIII breaks with Rome** (1530s) **Persecution of Protestants** under Mary (1550s)
Thomas Norton and **Thomas Sackville**, *Gorboduc* (blank-verse drama) (1561–2) **Philip Sidney**, *Arcadia* (written 1580) **Christopher Marlowe**, *Tamburlaine* (ca. 1587) **Richard Hakluyt**, *Voyages and Discoveries* (1589)	**1558–1603** **Elizabeth I** (1558–1603)	**Roman Catholic plots** and uprisings against Queen Elizabeth Beginnings of the English **slave trade** (1560s) Execution of **Mary, Queen of Scots** (1587) **Spanish Armada** (1588)

LITERATURE	DATE	POLITICAL HISTORY
Edmund Spenser, *The Faerie Queene* (Bks I–III, 1590) **William Shakespeare**, *A Midsummer Night's Dream* (ca. 1595) **John Donne**, *Songs and Sonets* (written 1590s and 1600s)	**1558–1603**	**Earl of Essex leads an abortive rebellion** against the Queen (1601)
William Shakespeare, *Othello* (ca. 1603) **John Marston**, *The Malcontent* (1603–4) **Francis Bacon**, *The Advancement of Learning* (1605) **Ben Jonson**, *The Alchemist* (1610) **John Webster**, *The Duchess of Malfi* (ca. 1614) **Robert Burton**, *The Anatomy of Melancholy* (1621) **John Ford**, *'Tis Pity She's a Whore* (1632–3) **John Milton**, *Lycidas* (1637) **Robert Herrick**, *Hesperides* (1648) **Richard Lovelace**, *Lucasta* (1649) **Andrew Marvell**, "Upon Appleton House" (written ca. 1652)	**1603–60** **James I** (1603–25) **Charles I** (1625–49) **Commonwealth & Protectorate** (1649–60)	James VI of Scotland comes to the throne as James I, the **first Stuart monarch** **Gunpowder Plot** (1605) **Authorised Version** of the Bible is published (1611) **Pilgrim Fathers** sail for America aboard the *Mayflower* (1620) **Charles I dismisses Parliament** and rules without it (1629–40), supported by **Strafford** and **Laud** **English Civil War** (1642–9) **Commonwealth** is established (1649)
Samuel Pepys, *Diary* (written 1660–9) **George Etherege**, *The Comical Revenge, or Love in a Tub* (1664) **John Milton**, *Paradise Lost* (1667) **William Wycherley**, *The Country Wife* (1675) **John Bunyan**, *The Pilgrim's Progress* (1678)	**1660–99** **Charles II** (1660–85) **James II** (1685–9) **William III and Mary** (1689–1702)	**Restoration** of the monarchy (1660) **Recurrent trade wars** with the Dutch **Great Plague of London** (1665) **Great Fire of London** (1666) **Religious tensions** between Roman Catholics, Protestants, and Dissenters

LITERATURE	DATE	POLITICAL HISTORY
John Dryden, *Absalom and Achitophel* (1681) **Aphra Behn**, *Oroonoko* (1688) **William Congreve**, *Love for Love* (1695) **John Vanbrugh**, *The Relapse* (1696)	**1660–99**	Influx of French **Huguenots** following the revocation of the Edict of Nantes (1685) **Glorious Revolution** brings the staunchly Protestant William of Orange and Mary to the throne (1688) **Bank of England** founded (1694) to manage the national debt
George Farquhar, *The Beaux' Stratagem* (1707) **Joseph Addison** and **Richard Steele** publish *The Spectator* (1711) **Alexander Pope**, *The Rape of the Lock* (1712, 1714) **Daniel Defoe**, *Robinson Crusoe* (1719) **Jonathan Swift**, *Gulliver's Travels* (1726) **John Gay**, *The Beggar's Opera* (1728) **Samuel Richardson**, *Pamela: or, Virtue Rewarded* (1740) **Henry Fielding**, *Tom Jones* (1749)	**1700–49** **Anne** **(1702–14)** **George I** **(1714–27)** **George II** **(1727–60)**	**Act of Union** with Scotland (1707) creates Great Britain **War of the Spanish Succession** (1702–14): military victories of Marlborough **Last trial for witchcraft** in England (1712) **South Sea Bubble** bursts (1720), causing numerous bankruptcies **Walpole** is prime minister (1722–42) **War of Jenkins's Ear** (1739) **Jacobite rebellion** of 1745 is crushed at the **battle of Culloden** (1746)
Tobias Smollett, *The Adventures of Peregrine Pickle* (1751) **Samuel Johnson**, *A Dictionary of the English Language* (1755) **Laurence Sterne**, *Tristram Shandy* (1759–67) **Oliver Goldsmith**, *She Stoops to Conquer* (1773)	**1750–99** **George III** **(1760–1820)**	**Lisbon earthquake** causes massive loss of life (1755) **Seven Years War** (1756–63) extends Britain's colonial power, notably in India and North America

LITERATURE	DATE	POLITICAL HISTORY
R. B. Sheridan, *The Rivals* (1775)	**1750–99**	**American Revolution** (1775–83)
William Blake, *Songs of Innocence* (1789)		**French Revolution** (1789–99)
William Wordsworth and **Samuel Taylor Coleridge**, *Lyrical Ballads* (1798)		**Wars with France** (from 1792)
William Wordsworth, *The Prelude* (early version completed 1805)	**1800–49** **Regency (1811–20)** **George IV (1820–30)** **William IV (1830–7)**	**Act of Union** (1800) creates the United Kingdom of Great Britain and Ireland
Lord Byron, *Childe Harold's Pilgrimage* (first two cantos, 1812) **Jane Austen**, *Mansfield Park* (1814)		**Napoleonic Wars**, marked by decisive victories against the French at Trafalgar (1805) and Waterloo (1815)
John Keats, "Ode to a Nightingale" (1819) **Walter Scott**, *Woodstock* (1826)	**Victoria (1837–1901)**	"Peterloo Massacre" (1819)
Thomas Love Peacock, *Crotchet Castle* (1831) **Charles Dickens**, *Nicholas Nickleby* (1838–9) **Robert Browning**, *Sordello* (1840) **Edward Lear**, *A Book of Nonsense* (1846) **Charlotte Brontë**, *Jane Eyre* (1847) **W. M. Thackeray**, *Vanity Fair* (1847–8)		**Chartism** is launched (1838) **Repeal of the Corn Laws** (1846) **Irish Famine** (1845–9) **European revolutions** (1848)
Alfred Tennyson, *In Memoriam* (1850)	**1850–99** **Victoria (1837–1901)**	**Population of London** trebles during the reign of Victoria
Elizabeth Gaskell, *Cranford* (1851–3) **Elizabeth Barrett Browning**, *Aurora Leigh* (1856) **Thomas Hughes**, *Tom Brown's Schooldays* (1857) **Anthony Trollope**, *Barchester Towers* (1857) **Christina Rossetti**, *Goblin Market and Other Poems* (1862)		**The Great Exhibition** (1851) **Crimean War** (1854–6) **Indian Mutiny** (1857–8) **American Civil War** (1861–5)

LITERATURE	DATE	POLITICAL HISTORY
Charles Dickens, *Our Mutual Friend* (1864–5) **Matthew Arnold**, "Culture and Anarchy" (1869) **George Eliot**, *Middlemarch* (1871–2) **Thomas Hardy**, *The Return of the Native* (1878) **Rudyard Kipling**, *Plain Tales from the Hills* (1888) **A. Conan Doyle**, *The Sign of Four* (Sherlock Holmes) (1890) **Oscar Wilde**, *The Importance of Being Earnest* (1895) **H. G. Wells**, *The Island of Doctor Moreau* (1896)	**1850–99**	Opening of the **Suez Canal** (1869) facilitates trade with the east **Social legislation**: abolition of imprisonment for debt (1869); Education Act (1870); introduction of bank holidays (1871) **Expansion of British empire**, especially in Africa "**Jack the Ripper**" murders (1888) **Second Boer War** (1899–1902)
Joseph Conrad, *Nostromo* (1904) **George Bernard Shaw**, *Major Barbara* (1905) **John Galsworthy**, *The Man of Property* (1906) **Arnold Bennett**, *Clayhanger* (1910) **Edward Marsh** (ed.), *Georgian Poetry I* (1912) **W. B. Yeats**, *Responsibilities* (1914) **D. H. Lawrence**, *The Rainbow* (1915) **James Joyce**, *A Portrait of the Artist as a Young Man* (1916) **Siegfried Sassoon**, *Counter-Attack* (1918) **T. S. Eliot**, *The Waste Land* (1922) **Agatha Christie**, *The Murder of Roger Ackroyd* (1926) **Virginia Woolf**, *To the Lighthouse* (1927) **Aldous Huxley**, *Brave New World* (1932)	**1900–49** **Edward VII** **(1901–10)** **George V** **(1910–36)** **Edward VIII** **(1936)** **George VI** **(1936–52)**	**Suffragettes** campaign for votes for women. **Industrial unrest**, particulary among miners, dockers, and rail workers **World War I** (1914–18) **Easter Rising** in Ireland (1916) **Russian Revolution** (1917) **Mussolini** and **Stalin** come to power in Italy and Russia, respectively (1922) **General Strike** (1926) Women in the UK achieve **voting equality** with men (1928) **Hitler** comes to power in Germany (1933)

LITERATURE	DATE	POLITICAL HISTORY
W. H. Auden and **Christopher Isherwood**, *The Ascent of F6* (1936)	**1900–49**	**Abdication** of Edward VIII (1936)
		Spanish Civil War (1936–9)
George Orwell, *The Road to Wigan Pier* (1937)		
Graham Greene, *Brighton Rock* (1938)		**Munich Agreement** (1938)
Louis MacNeice, *Autumn Journal* (1939)		**World War II** (1939–45)
W. H. Auden, *New Year Letter* (1941)		
Henry Green, *Loving* (1945)		Atomic bombs dropped on **Hiroshima** and **Nagasaki** (1945)
J. B. Priestley, *An Inspector Calls* (1945)		Details of the **Holocaust** begin to emerge (1945)
Evelyn Waugh, *Brideshead Revisited* (1945)		**National Health Service** is introduced following the victory of the Labour Party in the 1945 British general election; several industries and public services are nationalized
		The **United Nations** is founded (1945) in place of the League of Nations
Dylan Thomas, *Deaths and Entrances* (1946)		
George Orwell, *Nineteen Eighty-Four* (1949)		
E. M. Forster, *Two Cheers for Democracy* (1951)	**1950–2005**	**Korean War** (1950–3)
Samuel Beckett, *Waiting for Godot* (in French, 1953)	**Elizabeth II** (1952–)	America explodes the **first hydrogen bomb (1952)**
John Osborne, *Look Back in Anger* (1956)		**Suez crisis** (1956)
Sam Selvon, *The Lonely Londoners* (1956)		

LITERATURE	DATE	POLITICAL HISTORY
John Le Carré, *The Spy Who Came in from the Cold* (1963)	1950–2005	Assassination of John F. Kennedy, American president (1963)
Harold Pinter, *The Basement* (1967)		Six Day War (1967): Israel defeats a coalition of Arab states, making territorial gains that will be a source of continuing conflict
Alan Bennett, *Forty Years On* (1968)		Vietnam War sparks widespread protests against American actions
Ted Hughes, *Crow* (1970)		
Tom Stoppard, *Jumpers* (1972)		Britain joins the EEC (European Economic Community, or Common Market) (1973)
V. S. Naipaul, *A Bend in the River* (1979)		Margaret Thatcher leads the Conservative Party to victory in the 1979 general election, becoming Britain's first woman prime minister and shifting the country's social and political agenda sharply to the right
Bruce Chatwin, *On the Black Hill* (1982)		Falklands War (1982)
Angela Carter, *Nights at the Circus* (1984)		A bitter miners' strike (1984) and a popular revolt against the Poll Tax (1989–90) polarize social allegiances in Britain
Seamus Heaney, *Seeing Things* (1991)		Gulf War (1991)
Andrew Motion, *Selected Poems 1976–1997* (1998)		Good Friday Agreement offers the hope of peace in Northern Ireland (1998)
Ian McEwan, *Atonement* (2001)		The 9/11 terrorist attack (11 September 2001) on the New York World Trade Center leads to the so-called War on Terror
Monica Ali, *Brick Lane* (2003)		War in Afghanistan (2002) War in Iraq (2003)

LITERATURE	DATE	LIFESTYLE
Early Middle English Literature Geoffrey of Monmouth, Marie de France, Layamon, Romances, Medieval Lyrics	**Twelfth– thirteenth centuries**	Founding of **Oxford** (twelfth century) and **Cambridge** (thirteenth century) universities
Middle English Literature Mystery Plays, Mandeville, Gawain poet, Langland, Chaucer, Gower, Julian of Norwich	**Fourteenth century**	**Clothes** reflect the influence of early Renaissance Italy. From about the mid-century, there is more emphasis on display – tights become fashionable for men, women's necklines get lower **Inns** begin to offer accommodation, freeing travelers from reliance on the hospitality of monasteries or great houses **Claret** is imported from the Bordeaux region of France, but ale and cider remain the most common alcoholic drinks
Hoccleve Lydgate Malory **The Scottish Chaucerians** (late fifteenth/early sixteenth centuries: Henryson, Douglas, Dunbar)	**Fifteenth century**	The **codpiece** is introduced in response to the fashion for shorter tunics **Forks** for eating are introduced from Italy but do not come into general use until the seventeenth century
Early Tudor Literature Skelton, More, Wyatt, Surrey	**1500–49**	The **harpsichord** is introduced and retains a central role in English music-making for over two centuries **Jewelry** is increasingly used for personal adornment The painter **Hans Holbein** settles in England in 1532
Sir Thomas Hoby, *The Boke of the Courtier* (1561, English translation of Castiglione) **Arthur Golding**, English translation of Ovid's *Metamorphoses* (Bks I–IV, 1565)	**1550–99**	The **ruff**, introduced from Spain, is fashionable wear for both men and women **Potatoes**, **tomatoes**, and other new varieties of vegetable and flower are cultivated in England

130

LITERATURE	DATE	LIFESTYLE
Roger Ascham, *The Scholemaster* (posthumous, 1570) **Edmund Spenser**, *The Shepheardes Calender* (1579) **Thomas Kyd**, *The Spanish Tragedy* (ca. 1587) **Christopher Marlowe**, *Edward II* (ca. 1592) **Thomas Nashe**, *The Unfortunate Traveller* (1594) **Francis Bacon**, *Essays* (first edition, 1597) **William Shakespeare**, *As You Like It* (ca. 1598)	**1550–99**	**Tea** is introduced but enjoys little popularity until after the Restoration The first permanent **public theaters** are built **Breeches** come into use for men towards the end of the century **Music:** Thomas Tallis (ca. 1505–85), William Byrd (ca. 1543–1623) **Painting:** Nicholas Hilliard (1547–1619)
George Chapman, *Bussy d'Ambois* (written ca. 1604) **Ben Jonson**, *Volpone* (1605–6) **John Donne**, *Holy Sonnets* (ca. 1609–ca. 1611) **Francis Beaumont** and **John Fletcher**, *The Maid's Tragedy* (1610–11) **Walter Ralegh**, *History of the World* (1614) **Thomas Middleton**, *A Game at Chess* (1624) **George Herbert**, *The Temple* (posthumous, 1633) **John Milton**, *Comus* (1634) **Thomas Browne**, *Religio Medici* (written ca. 1635, pub. 1642) **Edmund Waller**, *Poems* (1645) **Abraham Cowley**, *The Mistress* (poems) (1647)	**1600–59**	**Smoking** gains in popularity, following the introduction of tobacco in the previous century Rise in the production of **luxury goods** in London before the Civil War – clocks, spectacles, silks, etc. **Spirits** are drunk more widely, under the general name of aquavitae Puritans close the **theaters** (1642) **Music:** John Dowland (1563–1626), Thomas Campion (1567–1620), Orlando Gibbons (1583–1625) **Painting:** Anthony Van Dyck (1599–1641) **Architecture:** Inigo Jones (1573–1652)
John Evelyn, *Diary* (covers much of the century) **Samuel Butler**, *Hudibras* (Pt I, 1663)	**1660–99**	**Actresses** appear for the first time on the public stage (1660) **Coffee houses** become centers for news and gossip

LITERATURE	DATE	LIFESTYLE
John Bunyan, *Grace Abounding to the Chief of Sinners* (1666) **George Etherege**, *She Wou'd If She Cou'd* (1668) **John Milton**, *Samson Agonistes* (1671) **John Wilmot, earl of Rochester**, "A Satyr against Reason and Mankind" (ca. 1675) **William Wycherley**, *The Plain Dealer* (1676) **John Dryden**, *All for Love* (1677) **William Congreve**, *The Double Dealer* (1693)	**1660–99**	**Wigs** become fashionable for men and remain so until the late eighteenth century **Glass mirrors**, now produced in London, become increasingly common **Oranges**, imported from Portugal, become a popular fruit **Cheap sugar** from the West Indies increases the popularity of **tarts and puddings** **Wine** begins to be bottled in advance rather than taken from the wooden cask just before serving **Wallpaper** begins to replace tapestries in the houses of the rich, but whitewashed walls remain the norm First **street-lamps** in London **Fox-hunting** develops as a sport Huguenot refugees establish **carpet-weaving** in Wilton **Music:** Henry Purcell (1659–95) **Painting:** Peter Lely (1618–80) **Architecture:** Christopher Wren (1632–1723)
Jonathan Swift, *A Tale of a Tub* (1704) **Joseph Addison**, *Cato* (1713) **Daniel Defoe**, *Moll Flanders* (1722) **James Thomson**, *The Seasons* (1726–30) **Alexander Pope**, *An Essay on Man* (1733–4) **Samuel Johnson**, *London: A Poem* (1738) **Henry Fielding**, *Joseph Andrews* (1742)	**1700–49**	**Gin** is widely consumed until the Gin Act (1751) curbs its sale Among the upper classes, **port** becomes increasingly popular New **hospitals** (e.g., Guy's, Westminster, St. George's, Middlesex) are opened in London **Theatre Licensing Act** (1737) imposes crippling **censorship** The **Grand Tour** becomes a regular feature of upper-class education **Tea-drinking** increases among all classes, accompanied by a decline in the popularity of coffee and a growth in the consumption of sugar **Music:** George Frederick Handel (1685–1759)

LITERATURE	DATE	LIFESTYLE
Samuel Richardson, *Clarissa* (1747–8)	**1700–49**	**Painting:** William Hogarth (1697–1764) **Architecture:** John Vanbrugh (1664–1726), Nicholas Hawksmoor (1661–1736), William Kent (1685–1748)
Tobias Smollett, *The Adventures of Ferdinand Count Fathom* (1753) **Oliver Goldsmith**, *The Vicar of Wakefield* (1766) **Edward Gibbon**, *The Decline and Fall of the Roman Empire* (1776–88) **R. B. Sheridan**, *The School for Scandal* (1777) **William Cowper**, *The Task* (1785) **William Beckford**, *Vathek: An Arabian Tale* (1786) **William Blake**, *The Marriage of Heaven and Hell* (1790) **James Boswell**, *The Life of Samuel Johnson* (1791) **M. G. Lewis**, *The Monk* (1796) **Samuel Taylor Coleridge**, "Kubla Khan" (written ca. 1797)	**1750–99**	**Marriage Act** (1753) outlaws secret marriages **Horse racing** grows in popularity – the St. Leger, the Oaks, and the Derby are all established in this period The metal **water closet** comes into wider use from the 1770s **Plate glass** is introduced from France (1770s) The first English **pianos** are made The **mail coach** is introduced between London and Bristol (1784) *The Times* newspaper – renamed from the *London Universal Register* – is published (1788) **Pears' innovative transparent soap** is introduced (1789) **Painting:** Joshua Reynolds (1723–92), George Stubbs (1724–1806), Thomas Gainsborough (1727–88) **Architecture:** Robert Adam (1728–92)
George Crabbe, *Tales in Verse* (1812) **Jane Austen**, *Pride and Prejudice* (1813) **Lord Byron**, *Manfred* (1817) **Thomas de Quincey**, *The Confessions of an English Opium Eater* (1821) **Percy Bysshe Shelley**, *Adonais* (1821)	**1800–50**	**Trousers** replace breeches for men The **waltz** is introduced (ca. 1812) **Founding of the great literary/political periodicals** (*Edinburgh Review*, *Blackwood's Edinburgh Magazine*, *Westminster Review*, etc.) **Handbooks for tourists** in Europe are published by John Murray and later by Karl Baedeker First regular steam-powered **ferry service across the Channel** (1821)

LITERATURE	DATE	LIFESTYLE
Walter Scott, *Redgauntlet* (1824)	**1800–50**	**National Gallery** is founded (1824) The **RSPCA** (Royal Society for the Prevention of Cruelty to Animals) is founded (1824)
William Cobbett, *Rural Rides* (1830)		**Regular police force** is established (1829)
		Poor Law Amendment Act (1834) forces paupers into the workhouse
Thomas Carlyle, *The French Revolution* (1837)		**Public school** system is reformed by Thomas Arnold (headmaster of Rugby, 1828–42)
Alfred Tennyson, *Poems* (1842)		**Penny post** is introduced (1840) **Gas lighting** is introduced for streets and, later in the century, for buildings
Charles Dickens, *Martin Chuzzlewit* (1843–4)		Regular **steamship services** operate across **the Atlantic**
		Steel pens increasingly replace the quill
Robert Browning, *Dramatic Romances and Lyrics* (1845)		**Hansom cabs** come into use on the London streets **Anesthetics** (initially ether, then chloroform) are introduced for surgical operations in the 1840s
Emily Brontë, *Wuthering Heights* (1847) **W. M. Thackeray**, *Pendennis* (1848–50)		**Package tours** are initiated by Thomas Cook The **first chocolate bars** are made by the Cadbury and Fry companies
John Ruskin, *The Stones of Venice* (1851–3) **Charles Dickens**, *Hard Times* (1854)	**1850–99**	**Cigarettes** become popular (about half a century after cigars) in the wake of the Crimean War The **sewing machine**, developed in America by Singer, is imported into Britain
R. M. Ballantyne, *The Coral Island* (1857)		**Divorce** for adultery is legalized by the Matrimonial Causes Act (1857)
Alfred Tennyson, *Idylls of the King* (first parts, 1859)		**Mayhew's** *London Labour and the London Poor* is published (1861–2)
George Eliot, *Mill on the Floss* (1860) **John Henry Newman**, *Apologia Pro Vita Sua* (1864)		**Fresh milk**, transported by train from country to town, becomes increasingly popular among the middle classes

LITERATURE	DATE	LIFESTYLE
Walter Pater, *Studies in the History of the Renaissance* (1873) **Anthony Trollope**, *The Way We Live Now* (1874–5) **Gerard Manley Hopkins**, "The Wreck of the Deutschland" (1876) **Matthew Arnold**, *Selected Poems* (1878) **Dante Gabriel Rossetti**, *Ballads and Sonnets* (1881) **George Moore**, *A Modern Lover* (1883) **Robert Louis Stevenson**, *The Strange Case of Dr Jekyll and Mr Hyde* (1886) **Thomas Hardy**, *The Woodlanders* (1887) **Oscar Wilde**, *The Picture of Dorian Gray* (1890) **A. E. Housman**, *A Shropshire Lad* (1896)	**1850–99**	**Ceramic water closets** and enamelled cast iron bath tubs are developed in the 1870s The **Bank Holidays** Act (1871) **Modern refuse collection** and measures for **drainage** and a constant **water supply** are introduced by the Public Health Act (1875) **Trams**, first horse drawn and later electric, become a common form of city transport **Electric lighting** is installed in a number of private houses **Universal schooling** up to the age of 10 is introduced by the Education Act (1880) **Neckties** begin to replace cravats for men A number of household **electric appliances** (kettles, fires, toasters) appear towards the end of the century **Wrist watches** begin to be worn **NSPCC** (National Society for the Prevention of Cruelty to Children) is founded (1884) **Birth of the cinema** (1890s)
Rudyard Kipling, *Kim* (1901) **Henry James**, *The Ambassadors* (1903) **J. M. Barrie**, *Peter Pan* (1904) **G. K. Chesterton**, *The Man Who Was Thursday* (1908) **T. S. Eliot**, *Prufrock and Other Observations* (1917) **James Joyce**, *Ulysses* (1922) **Noël Coward**, *The Vortex* (1924) **P. G. Wodehouse**, *Carry on, Jeeves* (1925) **Robert Graves**, *Goodbye to All That* (1929)	**1900–49**	**Safety razors** are popularized by the American King C. Gillette Domestic **refrigerators** come into common use The **Town Planning Act** (1909) regulates future development in urban areas **BBC** begins radio broadcasts (1922) The **Jazz Age** reflects the postwar climate of the 1920s, encouraging cultural fashions that emphasize youth and emancipation

LITERATURE	DATE	LIFESTYLE
Stephen Spender, *Poems* (1933) **Evelyn Waugh**, *A Handful of Dust* (1934) **W. H. Auden** and **Louis MacNeice**, *Letters from Iceland* (1937) **Christopher Isherwood**, *Goodbye to Berlin* (1939) **Keith Douglas**, *Selected Poems* (1943) **Samuel Beckett**, *Watt* (completed, 1944) **Malcolm Lowry**, *Under the Volcano* (1947) **Graham Greene**, *The Heart of the Matter* (1948) **Christopher Fry**, *The Lady's not for Burning* (1948) **Elizabeth Bowen**, *The Heat of the Day* (1949)	**1900–49**	The **Age of Marriage Act** (1929) fixes the minimum age for marriage at 16 (previously it had been 12 for girls and 14 for boys) **30 mph speed limit** introduced for built-up areas (1935) **Grounds for divorce** are extended by the Matrimonial Causes Act (1937) Wartime **food rationing** is introduced (1940) **Free secondary schooling** for all is established by the Education Act (1944) Christian Dior's **"New Look"** (1947) introduces what will become the classic look of the 1950s woman **National Health Service** comes into operation (1948) The **Kinsey Report** (Alfred Kinsey's *Sexual Behavior in the Human Male*) is published (1948) **Immigrants** arrive from the West Indies (1948), to be followed by others from the Commonwealth in the 1950s and 1960s
Anthony Powell, *A Question of Upbringing* (1951) **Nicholas Monsarrat**, *The Cruel Sea* (1951) **Angus Wilson**, *Hemlock and After* (1952) **Ian Fleming**, *Casino Royale* (first of the James Bond series, 1953) **John Betjeman**, *Summoned by Bells* (1960)	**1950–2005**	**Festival of Britain** (1951) Britain's first three **National Parks** are designated (1951) **First jet airline service** is introduced by BOAC (British Overseas Airways Corporation) (1952) **Mount Everest** climbed by Edmund Hilary and Tenzing Norgay (1953) Trial of ***Lady Chatterley's Lover*** (1960)

LITERATURE	DATE	LIFESTYLE
Joe Orton, *Entertaining Mr Sloane* (1964)	**1950–2005**	**Supermarkets** are boosted by the abolition of resale price maintenance (1964)
Tom Stoppard, *Rosencrantz and Guildenstern are Dead* (1966)		More **liberal attitudes** to social issues such as censorship, abortion, and homosexuality are reflected in a range of legislation in the 1960s
Geoffrey Hill, *King Log* (1968)		New emphasis on **youth culture**, notably pop music and fashion
Germaine Greer, *The Female Eunuch* (1970)		**Expansion of air travel** and cheap package holidays in the 1970s encourage increased foreign travel
David Storey, *Pasmore* (1972)		
Beryl Bainbridge, *The Bottle Factory Outing* (1974)		Britain's first **McDonald's** opens in South London (1974)
Christopher Hampton, *Treats* (1976)		**Supersonic passenger flights** become available on Concorde (1976)
Salman Rushdie, *Shame* (1983)		By 1983, 98% of households in the UK own at least one **TV**
Hanif Kureishi, *The Buddha of Suburbia* (1990)		Launch of the **worldwide web** (1990) acts as a catalyst for rapid growth in the use of **personal computers**
Peter Porter, *Afterburner* (2004)		By 2003 **mobile phones** are owned or used by three quarters of the adult population of the UK

LITERATURE	DATE	SCIENCE AND TECHNOLOGY
Early Middle English Literature Geoffrey of Monmouth, Marie de France, Layamon, Romances, Medieval lyrics	**Twelfth– thirteenth centuries**	First **European universities** are founded First **medieval cathedrals** are made possible by architectural developments such as the pointed arch, the flying buttress, and the ribbed vault The **horse collar** multiplies the domestic and agricultural uses of the horse **Gunpowder** is brought to western Europe The **magnetic compass** (ca. 1200) and **navigational charts** (late thirteenth century) open up new possibilities of exploration
Middle English Literature Mystery Plays, Mandeville, Gawain poet, Langland, Chaucer, Gower, Julian of Norwich	**Fourteenth century**	**Blast furnaces** to smelt iron ore are introduced from Europe at the end of the century
Hoccleve, Lydgate, Malory	**Fifteenth century**	**Matchlock firearms** are introduced **Printing** with movable type is invented by Johannes Gutenberg in the mid-century The first **domestic clocks** are made
Scottish Chaucerians Henryson, Douglas, Dunbar **Early Tudor Literature** Skelton, More, Wyatt, Surrey	**1485–1549**	**Bartholomew Diaz** rounds the Cape of Good Hope (1488) **Columbus** reaches the New World (1492) **Vasco da Gama** sails round the Cape of Good Hope to India (1497–8) **John Cabot,** sent by Henry VII, explores the coast of North America (1497–8) **Magellan** sails into the Pacific (1520) **Copernicus** formulates his theory that the earth revolves around the sun (ca. 1530)

LITERATURE	DATE	SCIENCE AND TECHNOLOGY
Elizabethan Prose Ascham, Lyly, Sidney, Hooker, Nashe, Greene, Deloney **Elizabethan Poetry** Spenser, Ralegh, Sidney, Drayton, Marlowe, Shakespeare, Campion, Donne, Jonson **Elizabethan Drama** Kyd, Marlowe, Shakespeare, Chapman, Marston, Heywood, Dekker, Jonson	**1550–99**	**Mercator's** map of the world (1569) provides the basis for future cartography **Frobisher** attempts to find the **Northwest Passage** from the Atlantic to the Pacific (1570s) **Drake** circumnavigates the globe (1577–80) An early form of **flintlock weapon** is introduced, which will later supersede the old matchlock firearms
Jacobean Drama Shakespeare, Jonson, Chapman, Marston, Tourneur, Webster, Fletcher, Middleton, Massinger, Beaumont, Ford **Metaphysical Poetry** Donne, King, Herbert, Carew, Crashaw, Cowley, Marvell, Vaughan **Pre-Restoration Prose** Bacon, Andrewes, Burton, Browne, Hobbes **Cavalier Poetry** Suckling, Lovelace, Carew, Herrick, Waller	**1600–60**	**Hudson** explores Canada (ca. 1610) **Experimental science** is championed in the work of **Francis Bacon** **Telescope** is invented in the early seventeenth century and developed by **Galileo** **Harvey** publishes discovery of **circulation of the blood** (1628)
Restoration Poetry and Prose Milton, Marvell, Pepys, Rochester, Dryden, Bunyan, Behn **Restoration Drama** Dryden, Etherege, Wycherley, Vanbrugh, Congreve, Farquhar	**1660–99**	**Royal Society** is founded (1660) **Newton** and **Boyle** lay the foundations of modern physics and chemistry, respectively **Watches** are improved by the invention of the balance spring

LITERATURE	DATE	SCIENCE AND TECHNOLOGY
Augustan Literature Swift, Addison, Steele, Gay, Pope, Johnson **Rise of the Novel** Defoe, Richardson, Fielding, Smollett	**1700–49**	**Seed drill** invented by Jethro Tull (1701) **Mercury thermometer** invented by Gabriel Fahrenheit (1714) **Thomas Newcomen** develops the first commercially successful **steam engine** (much improved by James Watt in the 1760s) **Coal** becomes an increasingly important resource **Metal fillings** for teeth are developed to treat decay
Thomas Gray, "Elegy Written in a Country Churchyard" (1751) **Tobias Smollett**, *The Adventures of Peregrine Pickle* (1751) **Samuel Johnson**, *A Dictionary of the English Language* (1755) **Horace Walpole**, *The Castle of Otranto* (1764) **Laurence Sterne**, *A Sentimental Journey through France and Italy* (1768) **Oliver Goldsmith**, *The Deserted Village* (1770) **Frances (Fanny) Burney**, *Cecilia* (1782) **Ann Radcliffe**, *The Mysteries of Udolpho* (1794) **William Wordsworth** and **Samuel Taylor Coleridge**, *Lyrical Ballads* (1798)	**1750–99**	Experiments with **electricity** are conducted by Benjamin Franklin (ca. 1752) **Gregorian calendar** is introduced (1752) **British Museum** is founded (1753) **Linnaeus's *Species Plantarum*** (1753) systematizes the naming of flowering plants The manufacture of **high-quality pottery** is developed in Staffordshire (1760s) **Cotton industry** transformed by inventions that facilitate weaving **East Coast of Australia** is claimed for Britain by Captain Cook (1770) **Composition of air** is investigated by Priestley and Lavoisier (1770s) **Hot air balloon** is invented by the Montgolfier brothers (1782) **Vaccine for smallpox** is discovered by Edward Jenner (ca. 1796/8) Discovery of the **Rosetta stone** (1799), which later unlocks the mystery of Egyptian hieroglyphs

140

LITERATURE	DATE	SCIENCE AND TECHNOLOGY
Maria Edgeworth, *Castle Rackrent* (1800) **William Blake**, *Jerusalem* (ca. 1804–20) **Walter Scott**, *Marmion* (1808) **Jane Austen**, *Emma* (1816) **John Keats**, "The Eve of St. Agnes" (1820) **Lord Byron**, *Don Juan* (last two cantos, XV and XVI, 1824) **Edward Bulwer-Lytton,** *Last Days of Pompeii* (1834) **Thomas Carlyle**, *Chartism* (1839) **Benjamin Disraeli**, *Coningsby* (1844) **Anne Brontë**, *The Tenant of Wildfell Hall* (1848)	**1800–49**	**Electric battery** invented by Alessandro Volta (1800) **Steamboat** and **locomotive engine** both invented in the first decade of the century. Theory of evolution is foreshadowed in the work of **Jean-Baptiste Lamarck** (1809) **Safety lamp** for use in coal mines is invented by Humphry Davy (1815) **Road-building** is transformed by McAdam and Telford **First electrical generator** is invented by Michael Faraday (1831) **Steel plowshare** is developed (1830s) The **daguerrotype** (1839) marks an important step towards modern photography **First telegraph message** is sent by Samuel Morse (1844) The **"railway fever"** of the 1840s promotes rapid expansion of the network
Elizabeth Gaskell, *North and South* (1855) **Charles Dickens**, *A Tale of Two Cities* (1859) **Mrs Henry Wood**, *East Lynne* (1861) **Lewis Carroll**, *Alice's Adventures in Wonderland* (1865)	**1850–99**	**Steel production** is greatly increased by invention of the Bessemer process (1855) **Darwin** formulates the theory of evolution in *On the Origin of Species* (1859) The first usable **bicycle** is invented in France (1861) **Work on heredity** is published by Gregor Mendel (1865)

LITERATURE	DATE	SCIENCE AND TECHNOLOGY
Matthew Arnold, *Essays in Criticism* (1865) **Algernon Charles Swinburne**, *Poems and Ballads* (1866) **Wilkie Collins**, *The Moonstone* (1868) **Anthony Trollope**, *The Eustace Diamonds* (1873) **George Eliot**, *Daniel Deronda* (1876) **Henry James**, *The American* (1877) **George Meredith**, *The Egoist* (1879) **George Gissing**, *Workers in the Dawn* (1880) **H. Rider Haggard**, *King Solomon's Mines* (1885) **Rudyard Kipling**, *Barrack Room Ballads* (1892) **Thomas Hardy**, *Jude the Obscure* (1895) **H. G. Wells**, *War of the Worlds* (1898)	**1850–99**	**Antiseptic** precautions during surgery are introduced by Joseph Lister (ca. 1865) Invention of **dynamite** by Alfred Nobel (1866) **Typewriter** is patented in America (1868) **Germ theory** of infection is formulated by **Louis Pasteur**, leading to an expanded range of effective vaccines **Telephone** is invented by Alexander Graham Bell (1876) **Phonograph** (1877) and **electric lightbulb** (1879) invented by Thomas Edison George Eastman markets the **box camera** (1880) **Maxim gun** invented (1884) The **petrol-driven car** is developed (1880s) **Reinforced concrete** is invented (1892) **Radioactivity** is discovered by Henri Becquerel (1898), with further work by Pierre and Marie Curie
Joseph Conrad, *Lord Jim* (1900) **George Bernard Shaw**, *Man and Superman* (written 1903) **John Galsworthy**, *Strife* (1909) **Arnold Bennett**, *Clayhanger* (1910) **D. H. Lawrence**, *Sons and Lovers* (1913) **Ford Madox Ford**, *The Good Soldier* (1915)	**1900–49**	Electric **vacuum cleaner** is invented (1901) **First powered flight** is made by the Wright brothers (1903) **First flight across the Channel** is made by Louis Blériot (1909) **Structure of the atom** is established by Niels Bohr and Ernest Rutherford (1906–14) **Assembly line** manufacture is introduced by Henry Ford for the Model-T (1913) **Einstein's theories of relativity** (special, 1905; general, 1916)

142

LITERATURE	DATE	SCIENCE AND TECHNOLOGY
Ronald Firbank, *Valmouth* (1919) **Aldous Huxley**, *Crome Yellow* (1921) **Sean O'Casey**, *The Plough and the Stars* (1926) **Radclyffe Hall**, *The Well of Loneliness* (1928) **Evelyn Waugh**, *Vile Bodies* (1930) **Graham Greene**, *England Made Me* (1935) **W. H. Auden**, *Selected Poems* (1938) **George Orwell**, *Animal Farm* (1945)	**1900–49**	First **non-stop flight across the Atlantic** is made by Alcock and Brown (1919) First **birth control clinic** is opened by Marie Stopes in London (1921) **Television** is invented by John Logie Baird (1926) **Penicillin** is discovered by Alexander Fleming (1928) Frank Whittle registers a patent for the **turbojet engine** (1930) The **ballpoint pen** is invented by the Hungarian Laszlo Biro (1935) **Nylon** is invented (1938) **Nuclear fission** is discovered (1938), leading to the development of the **atomic bomb** (1945)
L. P. Hartley, *The Go-Between* (1953) **Harold Pinter**, *The Caretaker* (1960) **Muriel Spark,** *The Prime of Miss Jean Brodie* (1961) **Elizabeth Jennings**, *Collected Poems* (1967) **John Fowles**, *The French Lieutenant's Woman* (1969) **Malcolm Bradbury**, *The History Man* (1975) **William Golding**, *Darkness Visible* (1979) **Len Deighton**, *Berlin Game* (1983) **Ian McEwan**, *The Innocent* (1990) **David Hare**, *Amy's View* (1997) **Don Paterson**, *Landing Light* (2003)	**1950–2005**	**DNA** is discovered (1953) **Contraceptive pill** is developed (ca. 1960) **First human in space**: the Russian Yuri Gagarin orbits the earth (1961) **Heart transplant** operation is carried out successfully by Christian Barnard (1967) **First human on the moon** (1969) **Personal computer** is developed (1975) First **test-tube baby** (1979) **AIDS** virus is identified (1983) **Worldwide web** is launched (1990) A **cloned sheep** is born (1997) **Human Genome Project** is completed (2003)

LITERATURE	DATE	ENGLISH LANGUAGE
	First century AD	**Use of Latin** introduced to Celtic-speaking Britain by the Romans
	Fifth century	**Decline of Latin** after the departure of Roman troops in 410 A variety of **Germanic dialects** are introduced by invading Jutes, Saxons, and Angles from Denmark and the Low Countries; **Old English** eventually emerges from the mixture
Caedmon	Sixth–seventh centuries	**Latin becomes the language of learning** after the arrival of Roman missionaries in 597. Its influence on Old English increases as Christianity spreads through the country
Bede, *Historia Ecclesiastica Gentis Anglorum* (731) *Dream of the Rood* (? eighth century) *Beowulf* (? eighth century) Cynewulf (late eighth/early ninth century) *Battle of Maldon* Aelfric	Eighth–tenth centuries	Old English absorbs a range of **Scandinavian words** in the wake of the Viking raids which begin in 787
Wulfstan	Eleventh century	**French becomes the language of the upper classes** for the two centuries following the Norman conquest in 1066
Early Middle English Literature (Geoffrey of Monmouth, Marie de France, Layamon, Romances, Medieval lyrics)	Twelfth–thirteenth centuries	**Many Old English words die out** during the period of Middle English (from the mid-twelfth century to the end of the fifteenth century) and are replaced by French or Latin alternatives **Changes in grammar** over the same period turn English from an inflected language into the more or less uninflected language we speak today

LITERATURE	DATE	ENGLISH LANGUAGE
	Twelfth–thirteenth centuries	**French declines in importance** following the loss of Normandy by King John in 1204–5 **Many French words** come into the language from the middle of the thirteenth century (especially in areas such as government, law, the church, military affairs, learning, the arts, fashion, and food), as more of the French-speaking upper classes begin to speak English By the end of the century **English is widely spoken** by all classes
Middle English Literature (Mystery Plays, Mandeville, Gawain poet, Langland, Chaucer, Gower, Julian of Norwich)	**Fourteenth century**	The **Black Death** in 1348–9 increases the economic power of surviving members of the laboring classes and therefore the importance of their language **English is used in schools** From 1362, **legal proceedings are** (theoretically, at least) **conducted in English**
Hoccleve Lydgate **The Scottish Chaucerians** (late fifteenth/early sixteenth century: Henryson, Douglas, Dunbar)	**Fifteenth century**	During the first half of the century, **English displaces both French and Latin** to become the principal written language **London English becomes the prevailing dialect** in the second half of the century and is accepted as standard. The process of standardization is aided by the development of printing. The **"Great Vowel Shift"** (a major change in the way long vowels are pronounced) brings pronunciation much closer to modern English

LITERATURE	DATE	ENGLISH LANGUAGE
Early Tudor Literature (Skelton, More, Wyatt, Surrey) **The Elizabethans** (Spenser, Sidney, Marlowe, Shakespeare, Nashe, Donne) **The Elizabethans**	**Sixteenth century**	**English stakes its claim against Latin** as a language suitable for **learned discourse**. In doing so, it borrows from Latin increasingly complex sentence structures Imported **Latin and Greek words**, dubbed **inkhorn terms** by their opponents, are introduced to fill gaps in the language and to enlarge English vocabulary **Borrowings from French, Italian, and Spanish**, brought back by Renaissance travelers, contribute to a rapid expansion of English vocabulary **Translations of classical texts** into English by Renaissance scholars become common, particularly in the second half of the century Aided by the Reformation, English has by the end of the century established itself as the **language of scholarship and intellectual debate**
Shakespeare, Jonson Jacobean Dramatists Metaphysical Poets Stuart Prose Writers Cavalier Poets Restoration Poetry, Prose, and Drama	**Seventeenth century**	Progress towards the **standardization of English spelling** is made in the first half of the century After the Restoration, the influence of the **Royal Society** contributes to an increasing emphasis on **clarity** and **precision** in the use of language
Augustan Literature (Swift, Addison, Steele, Gay, Pope, Johnson)	**Eighteenth century**	Contemporary **desire to standardize and fix the language** is reflected in Swift's *A Proposal for Correcting, Improving, and Ascertaining the English Tongue* (1712), suggesting what is in effect an academy on the lines of the *Académie française*

LITERATURE	DATE	ENGLISH LANGUAGE
Rise of the Novel (Defoe, Richardson, Fielding, Sterne, Smollett)	**Eighteenth century**	The first attempt at a comprehensive **English dictionary** is published in 1721
		Samuel Johnson's *A Dictionary of the English Language* (1755)
Gothic Fiction (Walpole, Beckford, Radcliffe, Lewis)		Several **books on grammar** are published, including works by Joseph Priestley and Noah Webster
Early Romantics (Blake, Wordsworth, and Coleridge)		**Use of English spreads in North America, India, and Australia**, prompting new coinages to meet unfamiliar circumstances
		New words enter the language through contact with colonial populations and with Spanish and Portuguese colonizers in Central and South America
Romantics (Wordsworth, Coleridge, Byron, Shelley, Keats)	**Nineteenth century**	Noah Webster's *American Dictionary of the English Language*, which will have a huge influence on both spelling and pronunciation in America, is published in 1828
Victorian Poetry (Tennyson, the Brownings, Arnold, the Rossettis, Swinburne)		**Shorthand** is popularized by the publication of Isaac Pitman's *Stenographic Soundhand* (1837)
Victorian Novel (Gaskell, Thackeray, Dickens, Trollope, the Brontës, Eliot)		**Colonial possessions** in Africa and Asia continue to enrich the language with a trickle of borrowings, as do the usual contacts with European countries
Late Victorians (Hardy, James, Wilde, Gissing, Kipling, Wells)		Developments in **science and technology** further enlarge the vocabulary

LITERATURE	DATE	ENGLISH LANGUAGE
Modernism **Literature of World War I** **Political Writing of the 1930s** Postwar writing reflects the widening cultural base of English literature. **Sam Selvon, George Lamming, V. S. Naipaul, Ruth Prawer Jhabvala, Buchi Emecheta, Salman Rushdie, Timothy Mo, Kazuo Ishiguro, Linton Kwesi Johnson, Ben Okri, and Hanif Kureishi** are just a few names among many	**Twentieth century**	The final section of ***The New English Dictionary on Historical Principles***, also known as the the ***Oxford English Dictionary***, is published in 1928. Work on it had begun in the mid-nineteenth century and was continued under the supervision of James A. H. Murray Throughout the century the language continues to grow and change, thanks to an **influx of words inspired by science, technology, business, war, travel, empire, and the immigrations that followed the end of empire** Popular interest in the language is reflected in a number of successful books on the subject, including A. C. Baugh and Thomas Cable, *A History of the English Language* (revised edn., 2002), Simon Elmes, *The Routes of English* (2000–1), Melvyn Bragg, *The Adventure of English 500 AD–2000* (2003), David Crystal, *The Stories of English* (2004)

The **background information** below is primarily historical, but I've sometimes given as much space to popular legend as to historical fact. A literature student is more likely to come across a casual reference to Alfred burning the cakes – in Lawrence's *Sons and Lovers*, for example – than to his victory at the battle of Edington.

This is essentially a reference section, but it's arranged by period to make the option of browsing more attractive. The entries here are not a substitute for the background books you'll be expected to study; they're intended simply to provide some bearings. If you read them through, you should end up with enough information to keep you afloat. A couple of lines on the Counter-Reformation won't tell you all you need to know, but they will at least make sure you have an idea what it is.

Each subsection is prefaced by a very brief outline of the period to give a rough framework for the entries that follow.

THE ROMAN CONQUEST TO THE WARS OF THE ROSES

In AD 43 the invading legions of the Emperor Claudius crossed the Channel. For over three centuries England would remain under Roman rule. When the legions withdrew in 410, the former province was ill-equipped to defend itself. Picts and Scots swarmed across **Hadrian's*** (p. 86) now unguarded wall; within half a century successive waves of Saxons, Angles, and Jutes were setting sail from northern Europe. Out of the resulting mixture of natives, ex-colonists, and invaders emerged the patchwork that was Anglo-Saxon England.

The spread of Christianity during the seventh century was followed by a brief cultural flowering associated with figures such as **Bede*** and **Alcuin**. Then, towards the end of the eighth century, came the **Vikings**.* Thanks largely to **Alfred the Great**,* these new invaders were eventually forced to settle in the area of eastern and northern England known as **Danelaw**.

The death of King Edward the Confessor in 1066 opened the way to the **Norman Conquest*** that brought Anglo-Saxon England to an end. For the next two centuries French was the language of the ruling class, and French culture dominated English life. It was only in the thirteenth century that a revival of the native language and culture began to take hold. By the second half of the fourteenth century, England's embroilment in the **Hundred Years War***

with France had reinforced the need to affirm an independent English identity. It was during these years that medieval England produced its greatest literature in the works of Chaucer, Langland, and the Gawain poet.

The Hundred Years War was quickly followed by the **Wars of the Roses**.* This struggle for the throne between the Houses of York and Lancaster ended only with the accession of Henry VII in 1485 and the establishment of the Tudor dynasty. Just nine years earlier **William Caxton*** had set up England's first printing press.

ALFRED THE GREAT (849–99) King of Wessex from 871 to 899. Alfred's crucial achievement was to secure the immediate future of Anglo-Saxon England by checking the Danish invaders. After defeating them at the **battle of Edington** (Ethandun) in 878, he contained them by a mixture of diplomacy and careful defensive measures. Dedicated to the promotion of learning, Alfred himself helped to translate **Bede*** and **Boethius**.* A popular legend tells how, while harassing the Danes in the period before Edington, he took refuge incognito with a peasant woman who told him to look after the cakes she was baking. Preoccupied with affairs of state, Alfred allowed them to burn and was fiercely scolded for his negligence. See DANISH INVASIONS.

AQUINAS, SAINT THOMAS (ca. 1225–74) A Dominican monk from Naples, Aquinas (nicknamed *Doctor Angelicus*, the Angelic Doctor) became the most influential Christian theologian and scholastic philosopher of the Middle Ages. His two greatest works were his *Summa contra gentiles* (1259–64) and the unfinished *Summa theologica*, begun in 1266. The basis of Thomism was his conviction that Christian faith is compatible with human reason.

ARTHURIAN LEGEND If the figure of **King Arthur** has any historical basis, he probably ruled in the west country sometime in the sixth century. The son of Uther Pendragon, he proved his title to the kingship by being the only person able to withdraw the sword **Excalibur** from the rock in which it had been fixed by **Merlin**, the magician who later became his counselor. The legends that grew up around Arthur center on his court at **Camelot** and the group of knights who had a place at the **Round Table** – so designed to avoid quarrels over precedence. The ultimate chivalric quest was to find the **Holy Grail**,* but numerous adventures were undertaken along the way. After early triumphs, Arthur's own story took a somber turn when his wife **Guinevere** became the lover of **Lancelot of the Lake**, the most accomplished of all the knights. While Arthur was fighting Lancelot in Brittany, his nephew and regent **Mordred** seized the kingdom and abducted Guinevere. Arthur returned to England and in the final battle killed Mordred but was himself mortally wounded. Having ordered **Sir**

Bedivere to fling Excalibur into the water, from which the hand of the **Lady of the Lake** arose to receive it, he was borne in a barge to **Avalon** (the Celtic paradise), leaving behind a rumor that he will one day return to rule again. Various, sometimes conflicting, legends emerge from the body of Arthurian romances. The following are among other figures who play an important part:

Galahad: Son of Lancelot and Elaine, Sir Galahad was the model of a chivalrous knight. He alone was pure enough to occupy the *Siege Perilous*, the empty seat at the Round Table reserved for the knight who could complete the quest for the Holy Grail.

Gawain: Arthur's nephew, a courteous and courageous knight who figures in a number of romances, including *Sir Gawain and the Green Knight*. He supported Arthur against Lancelot but was killed at Dover when they returned to face Mordred.

Morgan le Fay: Arthur's half-sister, an enchantress and, in some legends, a malign figure who seeks his downfall.

Perceval: The knight who, along with Galahad and **Bors**, is finally granted a sight of the Holy Grail.

Tristan (Tristram): Nephew of King Mark of Cornwall and heir to the legendary kingdom of **Lyonesse** between Land's End and the Scilly Isles, which later disappeared beneath the sea. Tristan was sent to fetch the king's intended bride, Iseult, from Ireland. On the way back, the two unwittingly drank a love potion and fell hopelessly in love, with tragic consequences.

AUGUSTINE OF CANTERBURY, SAINT

Sent by Pope Gregory to bring Christianity to England, Augustine landed in Kent in 597. According to the legend, Gregory had decided on the conversion of England after seeing some fair-haired youths in the Roman slave market. On being told they were Angles, he is said to have replied, "Not Angles, but angels (*Non Angli, sed angeli*) – if they but had the word of God." Augustine's mission was successful. Having converted King Ethelbert, he went on to become the first archbishop of Canterbury. Before his death in 604, he had established the administrative basis of the church in

From **Alfred Tennyson, "Morte d'Arthur," lines 1–12**

So all day long the noise of battle rolled
Among the mountains by the winter sea;
Until King Arthur's table, man by man,
Had fallen in Lyonesse about their Lord,
King Arthur: then, because his wound was deep,
The bold Sir Bedivere uplifted him,
Sir Bedivere, the last of all his knights,
And bore him to a chapel nigh the field,
A broken chancel with a broken cross,
That stood on a dark strait of barren land.
On one side lay the ocean, and on one
Lay a great water, and the moon was full.

England. Sixty years later, the **Synod of Whitby** (664) determined England's adoption of Roman rather than Celtic Christianity.

AUGUSTINE OF HIPPO, SAINT (354–430) Born in what is now Algeria, Augustine became, after some youthful indiscretions that included fathering an illegitimate child, one of the greatest of the early Christian Fathers. Among his works are the 22-volume *De Civitate Dei* (*The City of God*) and his spiritual autobiography, *The Confessions*. He is particularly important for his insistence on the doctrine of Original Sin, in opposition to the teaching of **Pelagius**.* In 396 he became bishop of Hippo (present-day Annaba).

BACON, ROGER (ca. 1220–ca. 1292) English monk, scholar, philosopher, and scientist, known as *Doctor Mirabilis* for his prodigious range of learning. An early champion of experimental science, he was the first European to describe the manufacture of gunpowder, invented some three centuries earlier in China.

BAYEUX TAPESTRY A tapestry (231 feet long × 19.5 inches wide), probably woven by women of Canterbury in the 1070s, depicting the story of the Norman Conquest. Its political aim was to legitimize William of Normandy's claim to the English throne.

BECKET, SAINT THOMAS (? 1118–70) A trusted companion of Henry II, he was appointed chancellor by the king and then archbishop of Canterbury. His strong defense of church rights brought him into conflict with Henry. On December 29, 1170 four of the king's knights murdered him in Canterbury Cathedral. He was canonized three years later.

BEDE (ca. 673–735) English priest and historian based at the monastery at Jarrow, and known as the Venerable Bede. His great work, still a vital source for early English history, is the *Historia Ecclesiastica Gentis Anglorum* (*Ecclesiastical History of the English People*), completed in 731. He was canonized in 1899.

BENEDICTINE RULE The regulations governing monastic life drawn up by St. Benedict of Nursia in the sixth century and introduced into England by St. Wilfrid in the following century. They imposed vows of poverty, chastity, and obedience, while stressing the importance of study and manual work. The **Cistercian** order was founded in the eleventh century as a more austere offshoot of the Benedictines.

BLACK DEATH A catastrophic outbreak of plague – primarily bubonic but also pneumonic – that spread from the Far East, reaching England in 1348. It killed about a third of the population, with far-reaching economic, social, and psychological consequences.

BOADICEA See BOUDICCA.

BOCCACCIO, GIOVANNI (1313–75) Italian writer. His *Decameron*, a collection of 100 tales told by a group of young people who have escaped to the countryside from plague-stricken Florence, had a wide influence on medieval and Renaissance literature. Among those who feature in the stories is **Griselda**, a model of patience who reappears in several medieval texts.

BOUDICCA (or **Boadicea**, d. AD 61) Queen of the Iceni tribe in what is now Norfolk. On the death of her husband in AD 60, the Romans seized her property and behaved with great cruelty to her and her daughters. She raised a rebellion, sacking the towns of Colchester, St. Albans, and London, and massacring Romans and their sympathizers. Finally defeated by the Roman governor **Paulinus**, she committed suicide.

BRUT (or **Brutus**) Legendary founder of Britain. According to the story, he was a descendant of **Aeneas*** (see p. 68) who was banished from Rome and sailed with his Trojan followers to England, where he defeated the resident giants and established a new kingdom.

CADE, JACK In 1450 he led a Kentish rebellion against the high-taxing administration of Henry VI. After initial successes he was defeated and killed.

CANUTE (or **Cnut**) Danish king who invaded England, secured the crown, and reigned from 1016 to 1035. A successful ruler, he lives in popular memory chiefly for the legend that he once chastened a group of sycophantic courtiers, who'd claimed that even the waves would obey his command, by having his throne placed in the path of the advancing tide and then vainly ordering the sea to turn back.

CAXTON, WILLIAM (ca. 1422–91) The first English printer. Originally a cloth merchant, he learnt printing in Cologne and later set up a press in Bruges where in 1475 he produced the first book printed in English. He returned to England in 1476 and established a press in Westminster. Among the early volumes he printed was Chaucer's *Canterbury Tales* (printed 1478).

COCKAIGNE (or **Cockayne**), **LAND OF** A mythical kingdom of idleness and luxury, referred to in medieval legend. It is sometimes identified with the Fortunate Isles, which were believed in classical times to be the paradise of the blessed, situated beyond the Pillars of Hercules.

COINAGE British coinage can be traced back to the time of Offa, king of Mercia in the eighth century. He introduced the **silver penny**, of which there were 240 to a pound of silver. The system of 240 pennies to the pound survived until the British coinage was decimalized in 1971. These are some of the pre-decimalization coins often referred to in earlier literature but now withdrawn:

Farthing: a quarter of a penny. It was originally introduced as a silver coin in the thirteenth century.

Groat: fourpenny piece introduced in the late thirteenth century but discontinued by Elizabeth I.

Noble: gold coin worth 6 shillings and 8 pence (i.e., a third of a pound), introduced in the fourteenth century. Its value was later increased to 10 shillings (i.e., half a pound).

Angel: gold coin worth 6 shillings and 8 pence (i.e., a third of a pound), introduced in the fifteenth century to replace the noble when the latter was revalued.

Sovereign: gold coin worth 20 shillings (i.e., 1 pound) introduced by Henry VII in the late fifteenth century.

Shilling (originally called a teston or testoon): silver coin worth 12 pence introduced by Henry VII at the beginning of the sixteenth century. (The value of the Saxon *scilling* had been fixed at 12 pence by William I in the eleventh century.)

Sixpence: the silver sixpence and **threepence** were introduced in the sixteenth century.

Crown: a coin, initially gold then silver, worth 5 shillings, introduced by Henry VIII in the sixteenth century, along with the **half-crown**.

Penny and **half-penny**: copper coins introduced in 1672.

Guinea: gold coin worth 20 shillings when it was introduced just after the Restoration but whose value was increased to 21 shillings early in the eighteenth century.

Florin: silver coin worth 2 shillings, introduced in the mid-nineteenth century.

Banknotes made their first appearance in the early eighteenth century.

CRUSADES A series of military expeditions undertaken by the countries of western Europe to restore the Holy Land to Christian rule. In the two centuries from 1095, when **Pope Urban II** preached the First Crusade, to 1291, when the loss of Acre signaled the end of a Christian presence in the Holy Land, there were eight crusades. Apart from the first of them, which resulted in the capture of Jerusalem (retaken by **Saladin** in 1187), they achieved little beyond diverting the violence of the military class on to foreign soil.

DANISH INVASIONS The first Viking incursions towards the end of the eighth century were followed in the ninth century by larger-scale invasions that culminated in the arrival of the "Great Army" in 865. King Alfred's victory at **Edington** (878) in Wiltshire made it possible to restrict the invaders to an area of northern and eastern England known as **Danelaw**, within which Danish laws and customs prevailed. Alfred's successors maintained the boundaries for a time, but by the late tenth century the threat of raids from the Danelaw forced **Ethelred the Unready** to buy the Vikings off with huge sums of money (**Danegeld**) raised from taxation. In 1016 the Danish king **Canute*** defeated Ethelred's successor **Edmund "Ironside"** to become king of England.

DANTE ALIGHIERI (1265–1321) Florentine poet, author of the *Vita Nuova* and the *Divina Commedia* (*Divine Comedy*). As a young man he fell in love with the woman referred to in these two poems as **Beatrice**. She died in 1290 and became for Dante an image of the ideal. The last 20 years of his life were spent as an exile from Florence after he became involved in the political struggle between the Guelphs and the Ghibellines, the two parties that supported respectively the pope and emperor. Dante's *Divina Commedia*, in which he narrates his journey through Hell (the Inferno), Purgatory and finally, guided by Beatrice, Paradise, is probably the single most influential work in medieval European literature.

> **Dante Alighieri, the opening lines of the *Divina Commedia*, "Inferno," Canto 1**
>
> Nel mezzo del cammin di nostra vita
> mi ritrovai per una selva oscura,
> che la diritta via era smarrita.
>
> (In the middle of the journey of our life I came to myself in a dark wood where the straight way was lost.)

DE MONTFORT, SIMON (ca. 1208–65). Earl of Leicester and brother-in-law of King Henry III. He headed a group of barons who forced the king to accept an advisory committee – in effect, a ruling council – under the so-called **Provisions of Oxford** (1258). When Henry reneged on this agreement, de Montfort moved to open rebellion, defeating the king at the **battle of Lewes**

(1264). As ruler of the country, he summoned what is often considered the first English parliament, since it included representatives of the commons as well as the nobility. Deserted by a number of the barons, de Montfort was defeated and killed by the king's son, the future Edward I, at the battle of Evesham (1265).

DOMESDAY BOOK The survey ordered by **William I** to determine the extent of his lands and the tax revenue due from them. Carried out shire by shire in 1086, it provides a detailed account of land ownership and use, recorded in two volumes now in the Public Record Office. London, Winchester, and parts of northern England were omitted from the survey. The name it acquired, likening it to the Day of Judgment, is an awestruck acknowledgment of the scale of this exercise in counting, measuring, and assessing.

FRIARS Members of religious orders, bound by vows but not living in a monastery. Notable preachers, they were expected to live by begging, and hence called mendicants. Of the ten mendicant orders, the four principal ones, all founded in the thirteenth century, were the **Franciscans**, the **Dominicans**, the **Carmelites**, and the **Augustinians** (or **Austins**). The first three were known from the color of their habits as, respectively, **Grey Friars**, **Black Friars**, and **White Friars**. The normal clergy frequently looked on friars with suspicion as both spiritual and economic rivals. See MONKS.

GALEN (ca. AD 129–ca. 200) Greek physician whose theories dominated medieval medicine. See HUMOURS.

GARTER, ORDER OF THE Order of knighthood founded by Edward III in 1348. According to the legend, he was dancing with the Countess of Salisbury when her blue garter fell to the floor. The king retrieved it and put it on his own leg with the words *Honi soit qui mal y pense* ("Shame on him who thinks evil of it" – more often rendered "Evil be to him who evil thinks"). This became the motto of the order.

GEOFFREY OF MONMOUTH (d. 1155) Medieval cleric and chronicler who was the author of the *Historia Regum Britanniae* (*History of the Kings of Britain*). Geoffrey's chronicle is of little historical value, but as a source of myth and legend – about **Brut**,* **King Arthur**,* **King Lear**, **Cymbeline**, and others – it had an important influence on later writers.

GODIVA, LADY Wife of an eleventh century earl of Mercia. The story goes that he agreed to remit a tax on the people of Coventry if she would ride naked through the streets at midday, which she did. Alone among the grateful inhabitants, the tailor **Peeping Tom** looked out at her – for which he was struck blind.

GRAIL See HOLY GRAIL.

HENGIST and HORSA The two brothers said to have led the first Anglo-Saxon invasion of England in the middle of the fifth century.

HEREWARD THE WAKE An eleventh-century rebel who won a place in English folklore as the focus of Anglo-Saxon resistance to Norman rule. His revolt against William the Conqueror came to an end when he was besieged on the Isle of Ely, but Hereward himself escaped capture.

HOLY GRAIL The chalice from which Jesus drank at the Last Supper and in which Joseph of Arimathea was said to have caught some of his blood at the crucifixion. It became the supreme object of quest for the Arthurian knights. In the end, Galahad, Perceval, and Bors were allowed to find it. See ARTHUR.

HOLY LAND Ancient Palestine, roughly the area between the Mediterranean and the River Jordan. The sites of pilgrimage were those associated with the life of Jesus.

HUMOURS According to the theory which **Galen*** developed from **Hippocrates*** (see p. 90), human beings were composed of four humours: black bile, blood, yellow bile, and phlegm. These corresponded to the four elements of which all matter was supposedly made up: earth (black bile), air (blood), fire (yellow bile), and water (phlegm); and also to four character types: **melancholic** (black bile), **sanguine** (blood), **choleric** (yellow bile), and **phlegmatic** (phlegm). The individual's personality was determined by the mix of these four humours. Ideally, none would dominate, and it was the business of the physician to achieve a proper balance within the patient. This theory, frequently referred to in contemporary literature, was central to the practice of medieval and Renaissance medicine.

HUNDRED YEARS WAR (1337–1453) The basis of the war was the English monarch's claim to the throne of France and a large area of French territory. This long conflict, punctuated by periods of uneasy peace, went first in favor of England then of France before repeating the same cycle across another half century. The English won some much celebrated victories, notably under

Edward III at the battle of **Crécy** (1346); under his son the Black Prince at the battle of **Poitiers** (1356); and under Henry V at **Agincourt** (1415). But from 1429, when **Joan of Arc** inspired the French army to raise the siege of Orléans, the tide turned decisively. By the time the French brought the war to an end by winning the battle of **Castillon** in 1453, Calais alone remained in English hands.

JAMES I OF SCOTLAND (1394–1437) King of Scotland from 1406 until his murder in 1437, he imposed his sovereignty on the Scottish lords with iron determination. For the literary student he is notable as the probable author of *The Kingis Quair*, a poem supposedly inspired by his experience of falling in love while a prisoner of the English.

LOLLARDS Followers of **John Wycliffe**,* most of whom were drawn from the poorer classes. Their heterodox religious views and critical attitude to the clergy provoked the hostility of those in power. In 1414 the Lollard leader **Sir John Oldcastle** led an unsuccessful uprising which finished them as a political force. Nonetheless, their movement played a significant part in preparing the ground for the **Reformation*** (p. 177). The name *Lollards*, a satirical reference to their habits of prayer, was derived from the Dutch word for someone who mumbles.

> **The *Magna Carta*, Clause 39**
>
> No freeman shall be taken or imprisoned or disseised or outlawed or exiled or in any way destroyed, nor will we go against him nor send against him, except by the lawful judgment of his peers or by the law of the land.

MAGNA CARTA The "Great Charter" reluctantly granted by King John at his meeting with the barons at Runnymede on June 15, 1215. The driving force behind it was **Stephen Langton**, archbishop of Canterbury, who saw the opportunity to capitalize on growing dissatisfaction with John's arbitrary and ill-judged exercise of power. Though its main beneficiaries at the time were the church and the barons, the Magna Carta later came to be regarded as the cornerstone of English civil liberties. Among its 63 clauses were provisions to limit the monarch's powers of taxation, to protect the freedom of the church, and, crucially, to guarantee individual property rights and freedom from unlawful imprisonment.

MONKS Members of a religious community withdrawn from secular life. The principal monasteries in Britain were at **Iona**, **Lindisfarne** (Holy Island), and **Jarrow**. Throughout the early Middle Ages they were the main centers of learning in England and a focus of civilization, but their wealth made them a target for the Vikings. From the thirteenth century the rise of the mendicant orders (see FRIARS) led to a waning of their spiritual influence that facilitated the **Dissolution of the Monasteries*** (p. 168) under Henry VIII.

NORMAN CONQUEST In 1066, following the death of King Edward the Confessor, **William of Normandy** (William the Conqueror) invaded England in support of his claim to the English throne. He was opposed by **Harold Godwinson**, who, in spite of earlier promises to William, had declared himself king. The two met at the **battle of Hastings**, where Harold was defeated and killed, pierced through the eye by an arrow. The subsequent imposition of Norman rule changed for ever the language and culture of England.

NORSE MYTHOLOGY The Viking invasions of the ninth century brought with them the influence of Norse mythology. Among the central figures were **Odin** (or Woden/Wotan), the supreme god; his son **Thor**, god of thunder; **Freya**, the goddess of love; **Loki**, the spirit of evil; and the **Valkyries**, warrior maidens who chose those heroes marked for death in battle and conducted them to the banqueting hall of **Valhalla**. Here they feasted with Odin until **Ragnarok**, the last great battle between the gods and the forces of evil. Another son of Odin was **Balder** (or Baldur), god of light and beauty. His mother had secured an oath from all things on earth that they would not injure him, but she overlooked the mistletoe, and it was by a branch of mistletoe that, through the machinations of Loki, he was killed.

OCCAM, WILLIAM OF (died ca. 1349) Franciscan philosopher known today for his dictum, *Entia non sunt multiplicanda* ("Entities should not be multiplied") – i.e., all unnecessary facts and assumptions should be excluded from the analysis of the matter in question. This is referred to as **Occam's razor**.

PEASANTS' REVOLT A popular uprising of peasants and artisans in 1381, of which the immediate cause was a new **Poll Tax**.* The main body of rebels was drawn from Essex and Kent. Under the leadership of **Wat Tyler** they marched on London, destroyed John of Gaunt's palace, and murdered the chancellor and the archbishop of Canterbury, along with numerous foreigners, lawyers, and other undesirables. Wat Tyler himself was killed by the mayor of London, while the other rebels were successfully fobbed off with promises from the young **King Richard II**, who went out in person to meet them. Among those prominent in the revolt, most of whom were hunted down and executed, was the priest **John Ball**.

PELAGIUS The monk who in the late fourth century originated the heresy that came to be known as Pelagianism. Concluding that the belief in inherent human sinfulness was partly responsible for the moral laxity he saw around him in Rome, he insisted on the basic goodness of human nature, the need actively to choose good over evil, and the possibility of salvation by good works. He was condemned for heresy and excommunicated. Foremost among his accusers was **Augustine*** of Hippo, who strenuously reaffirmed the doctrines of Original Sin and salvation by grace.

PETRARCH (Francesco Petrarca, 1304–74) Italian poet whose work – in particular the *Canzoniere*, addressed to **Laura**, his idealized beloved – greatly influenced the development of European lyric poetry. His enthusiasm for the writers of classical antiquity anticipated and inspired the Humanist scholars of the **Renaissance*** (p. 177).

PILLORY A device introduced in the mid-thirteenth century to punish criminals. It consisted of a wooden frame with holes for the neck and wrists. The offender was exposed in a public place and pelted with anything to hand by onlookers, an ordeal which could sometimes be fatal. The pillory was abolished in Britain in the nineteenth century.

POLL TAX A tax levied on each individual (poll = *head*). Introduced in the early thirteenth century to support the Crusades, it was used with increasing frequency in the later fourteenth century, becoming a major cause of the **Peasants' Revolt**.* Thereafter it fell out of favor until briefly revived in the late twentieth century.

PRINCES IN THE TOWER The uncrowned Edward V (young son of Edward IV) and his brother Richard. The two boys were consigned to the Tower of London by their uncle Richard of Gloucester, ostensibly for their own safety. They disappeared, probably murdered on the instructions of Gloucester, who then took the throne as Richard III.

ROBERT THE BRUCE (1274–1329) King of Scotland, 1306–29. His crushing defeat of Edward II at the **battle of Bannockburn** in 1314 did much to secure Scotland's freedom from English rule. Popular legend tells how once, on the run from the English, he was given new heart by watching the tireless persistence of a spider as it wove its web.

ROLAND According to the legend, Roland was the commander of **Charlemagne's** rearguard when it was ambushed by Basques in the gorge of Roncesvalles in 778 as a result of the treachery of **Ganelon**. In his pride Roland refused to sound the horn for help until it was too late, despite the urging of his companion **Oliver**. By the time Charlemagne got back to them, Roland was dead and the rearguard massacred.

ROSES, WARS OF THE (1455–85) A period of intermittent warfare for the crown of England between the Houses of Lancaster and York, both of which claimed the throne by descent from Edward III. Its name was derived from the red and white roses taken as badges of allegiance by the Lancastrians and Yorkists respectively. The conflict came to an end in 1485, when **Henry Tudor** defeated the Yorkist Richard III at the battle of **Bosworth**, and succeeded to the throne as Henry VII. The Tudor rose, with red and white petals, was intended to symbolize the union of the two warring houses. Lingering Yorkist opposition nonetheless surfaced in the unsuccessful insurrections that gathered around two impostors, **Lambert Simnel** (1487) and **Perkin Warbeck** (1498), who claimed to be heirs to the throne.

SEVEN DEADLY SINS The cardinal sins established by the early Christian church and frequently represented in medieval art and literature: pride, covetousness, lust, envy, gluttony, anger, and sloth.

STOCKS An instrument of punishment in use from the Middle Ages to the nineteenth century. It consisted of a wooden frame with holes to secure the legs of petty criminals, who were obliged to sit there for a specified time enduring public shame.

TEMPLARS The Knights Templar or, in full, the Poor Knights of Christ and of the Temple of Solomon, were a military order founded in the early twelfth century to protect pilgrims to the **Holy Land**.* Over the next two centuries the order amassed vast wealth and considerable political influence. The Templars were brutally suppressed in the early years of the fourteenth century at the instigation of the French king, **Philippe le Bel**, who wanted their gold and mistrusted their power. Such of their property as did not go to the state was made over to their rivals the **Hospitallers** (Knights of the Order of the Hospital of St. John of Jerusalem, later known as the Knights of Malta), whose order survives to the present.

TITHES The tenth part of an individual's income (money or produce), paid for the upkeep of the church and its clergy. In England the payment of tithes became compulsory in the tenth century. Although the concept was modified at different times, tithing was not abolished until 1936.

TROUBADOURS Lyric poets in twelfth- and thirteenth-century southern France who were also musicians and performers. Their development of the conventions of **courtly love**, which elevated the lady into an ideal figure to whom the lovesick lord must sue for mercy, had an enormous influence on the literature of medieval Europe.

VIKINGS See DANISH INVASIONS.

VILLEINS In the Middle Ages villeins were unfree peasants who held land from the lord of the manor. In exchange for it they provided labor on his untenanted land (known as **demesne land**). They were also subject to numerous restrictions, such as the obligation to grind their corn at the lord's mill. The system began to unravel as a consequence of the labor shortages that followed the **Black Death**.*

WANDERING JEW A medieval legend with numerous variants tells of a Jew who taunted Jesus on his way to Calvary, to whom Jesus responded, "Tarry till I come again," or some such words, condemning him to wander the earth until the Day of Judgment.

WATLING STREET An important Roman road, originally running northwest from London through St. Albans (Verulamium) to Wroxeter, and later extended to Chester. Its name derives from the Anglo-Saxon name for Verulamium.

WYCLIFFE, JOHN (ca. 1330–84) Church reformer. His criticism of the papacy and attacks on the doctrine of transubstantiation (the belief that the bread and wine taken at the Eucharist actually become the body and blood of Christ) make him a forerunner of the **Reformation**.* Even more important in this context was his concern to translate the Bible into English, thereby providing any literate person with a source of authority that could challenge the church.

YEOMAN Originally a servant in a noble (or the royal) household. From the early fifteenth century the term referred to a small farmer who cultivated his own land.

162

When Henry VII fought his way to the throne in 1485, England was still emerging from the Middle Ages. By the time Elizabeth I, the last Tudor monarch, died in 1603, it was on the brink of the Modern Age. At the heart of this transition was the progress of the European **Reformation**.* In England it dates from Henry VIII's break with the Church of Rome in the 1530s. For the next century and a half political history was shaped by religious controversy.

In 1553 the new Church of England that had been evolving under Henry VIII and Edward VI was abruptly outlawed by Queen Mary, who reimposed Roman Catholicism with a harshness that earned her the nickname **Bloody Mary**. Five years later she was succeeded by Elizabeth, who pushed the pendulum back towards Protestantism. The Protestant conspiracies that had been hatched against Mary were replaced by Catholic conspiracies against Elizabeth. On the international stage, fiercely Catholic Spain had become England's most formidable enemy. In 1588 it dispatched the Spanish **Armada**.*

Against this background of religious upheaval the Tudors succeeded in turning England into a world power. The navy which Henry VIII had built up played a major role both in protecting England's borders and in asserting its claim to the wealth that was being discovered in the New World, following the voyages of Christopher Columbus, Vasco da Gama, Ferdinand Magellan, and others. Meanwhile, **Renaissance*** Europe provided an energizing stream of intellectual and artistic activity that had a far-reaching influence on English culture.

The Stuart King James VI of Scotland came to the English throne as James I in 1603. His fervent belief in the **Divine Right*** of kings was shared by his son and successor Charles I, whose autocratic ways, supported by archbishop **Laud*** and the earl of **Strafford**,* fueled an increasingly bitter conflict with Parliament that led ultimately to the **Civil War**. The eventual victory of Parliament, due in large measure to the New Model Army formed by **Thomas Fairfax*** and **Oliver Cromwell**,* was sealed by the execution of Charles I in 1649 and the establishment of a Republican government in the form of the **Commonwealth**.* The **Protectorate**,* which replaced it in 1653, was unable to survive Cromwell's death. Within 18 months the way was open to the **Restoration**.*

ABSOLUTISM See DIVINE RIGHT OF KINGS.

ALCHEMY A pseudo-science whose main goal was the discovery of the so-called **philosopher's stone**, thought to be capable of transmuting base metals such as copper or lead into gold. Related to this was the search for the **elixir of life**, which would confer immortality, and for the **panacea**, which would cure all sickness. Translations of Arab texts in the Middle Ages introduced alchemy into Europe, where it maintained a degree of respectability until the rise of modern science in the seventeenth century.

ARMADA, SPANISH The fleet commanded by the duke of Medina-Sidonia that Phillip II of Spain sent to invade England in 1588. The Spaniards were defeated by an English fleet under the command of **Lord Howard** of Effingham and **Sir Francis Drake**.* Buffeted by gales, the Spanish ships suffered further losses on the return journey. Of over 130 that set out, fewer than 80 got back to Spain.

Queen Elizabeth's address to the troops at Tilbury, 1588

Let tyrants fear; I have always so behaved myself that, under God, I have placed my chiefest strength and safeguard in the loyal hearts and good will of my subjects. And therefore I am come amongst you at this time, not as for my recreation or sport, but being resolved, in the midst and heat of the battle, to live or die amongst you all; to lay down, for my God, and for my kingdom, and for my people, my honor and my blood, even the dust. I know I have but the body of a weak and feeble woman; but I have the heart of a king, and of a king of England, too . . .

ARMINIANISM The movement that developed from the ideas of the Dutch Protestant theologian Jacobus Arminius (1560–1609), who opposed Calvin's rigid insistence on predestination and asserted the importance of human free will.

BABINGTON PLOT (1586) A Roman Catholic conspiracy, headed by Anthony Babington, to assassinate Elizabeth I and place **Mary Stuart**,* Queen of Scots, on the throne. It was discovered by spies of **Sir Francis Walsingham**,* and Babington and his associates were executed. An exchange of letters implicating Mary Queen of Scots in the conspiracy was one of the factors that led to her trial and execution the following year.

BACON, FRANCIS (1561–1626) Lawyer and philosopher who rose to become James I's lord chancellor but was brought down by charges of bribery and corruption. The celebrated *Essays* (1597, 1625) were only one product of a wide-ranging Renaissance mind. His classification of the sciences and his account of inductive reasoning were of lasting importance. By a wintry misfortune it was his commitment to experimental science that brought on his death. Having stopped his carriage one day to stuff a chicken with snow to see if this would preserve it, he caught a chill and died.

BEDLAM The Bethlehem Royal Hospital. Founded in the mid-thirteenth century, it later became England's first asylum for the insane. Its name was subsequently used as a generic term for any mental asylum and hence for any sort of frantic uproar.

BOOK OF COMMON PRAYER The liturgy of the Church of England, for which **Thomas Cranmer*** was primarily responsible. Church services were simplified and for the first time rendered in English rather than Latin. After the first Prayer Book in 1549, a more Protestant version was produced in 1552, and this, with slight modifications, was imposed for general use by Elizabeth I's Act of Uniformity in 1559. (The standard version until the late twentieth century was that of 1662.)

From **The Order for the Burial of the Dead, Book of Common Prayer (1662)**

Man that is born of a woman hath but a short time to live, and is full of misery. He cometh up, and is cut down, like a flower; he fleeth as it were a shadow, and never continueth in one stay.

In the midst of life we are in death: of whom may we seek for succour, but of thee, O Lord, who for our sins art justly displeased? . . .

Forasmuch as it hath pleased Almighty God of his great mercy to take unto himself the soul of our dear *brother* here departed, we therefore commit *his* body to the ground; earth to earth, ashes to ashes, dust to dust; in sure and certain hope of the resurrection to eternal life, through our Lord Jesus Christ; who shall change our vile body, that it may be like unto his glorious body, according to the mighty working, whereby he is able to subdue all things to himself.

BURBAGE, RICHARD (ca. 1567–1617) Celebrated actor who was a contemporary and associate of Shakespeare. He was the first to play many of Shakespeare's greatest roles, including Hamlet, Othello, Macbeth, and Lear. His father, **James Burbage**, was a joiner as well as an actor and built the first English playhouse some ten years after Richard's birth.

CALVIN, JOHN (1509–64) French-born Protestant reformer whose *Institutio Christianae Religionis* (*Institutes of the Christian Religion*) (first edn. 1536) laid the groundwork for the religious and social system he set up as ruler of Geneva from 1541 until his death. The basis of Calvinism is the belief that human beings, steeped in sin, are predestined either to damnation or, in the case of the elect, to salvation. Through their own actions they can never win salvation, which is available only through divine grace. His doctrines have had a profound influence on religious belief in Europe – notably Scotland, the Netherlands, and Switzerland – and also in the USA.

CASTIGLIONE, BALDASSARE (1478–1529) Italian diplomat and writer who served at the court of Urbino. In *Il Cortegiano* (1528) he describes the qualities that go to make up the ideal courtier, emphasizing the sense of effortless grace (*sprezzatura*) that should inform his words and actions. Translated into English in 1561 by Sir Thomas Hoby, *The Courtier* became an important Renaissance text.

CAVALIERS AND ROUNDHEADS The names given to the opposing parties in the **English Civil War***: the royalist supporters of the king, and the parliamentarians. Whereas the cavaliers favored flamboyant court dress and long hair, the roundheads (so called for the short haircuts of the apprentices who demonstrated against the king in 1641) dressed with deliberate sobriety.

CERVANTES, MIGUEL DE (1547–1616) Spanish author of *Don Quixote* (Part I, 1605; Part II, 1615). Cervantes fought at the battle of **Lepanto*** (1571) and was later captured by pirates and sold into slavery in Algiers, where he remained for five years until the ransom could be raised. His story of the deluded knight errant **Don Quixote**, mounted on the decrepit **Rosinante**, and attended by his down-to-earth squire **Sancho Panza**, has had an incalculable influence on the development of the European novel.

CIVIL WAR, ENGLISH (1642–51) The conflict between Charles I and Parliament, which led to the execution of Charles (January 30, 1649) and the declaration of the **Commonwealth**.* Sparked by Charles's refusal to accept the reforms demanded by the **Long Parliament**,* its first phase began with the battle of **Edgehill** (1642) and was brought to an end by the battle of **Naseby** (1645), where Thomas Fairfax's **New Model Army** and Oliver Cromwell's regiment of cavalry (the **Ironsides**) won a decisive victory. Subsequent royalist uprisings engineered by Charles in the second phase of the war were unsuccessful. In 1650 his son was crowned Charles II in Scotland but was forced to flee to France after the battle of **Worcester** (1651), hiding in an oak tree *en route*, to escape the pursuit of Parliamentary soldiers.

COMMONWEALTH Sometimes used of the whole of the **Interregnum*** (1649–60), the term applies more specifically to the period of Republican government from the execution of Charles I in 1649 to the establishment of the **Protectorate*** under Oliver Cromwell in 1653.

COPERNICUS, NICOLAUS (1473–1543) Polish astronomer who developed the hypothesis that the earth goes round the sun rather than vice versa. His theories, published in *De Revolutionibus Orbium Coelestium* (*On the Revolution of the Celestial Spheres*) in 1543, meant the overthrow of Ptolemaic cosmology (see p. 106), which had put the earth at the center of the universe. Similar ideas had been canvassed in earlier centuries, but it was only with Copernicus that they began to acquire an irresistible scientific force. The replacement of a geocentric by a heliocentric system had revolutionary implications that affected almost every aspect of human thought.

COUNTER-REFORMATION A revival movement in the Roman Catholic Church designed to combat the spread of the Protestant **Reformation*** and to address abuses within the church. Central to this project were the decrees of the **Council of Trent** (1545–63), which set out to clarify doctrine and institute measures of reform. To assist the pursuit of heresy, the **Inquisition*** was brought from Spain into other European countries. Much of the Counter-Reformation, including its missionary work, was spearheaded by the **Jesuits**.*

CRANMER, THOMAS (1489–1556) Archbishop of Canterbury and one of the architects of the English **Reformation**.* Having recommended himself to Henry VIII by helping to extricate him from several unwanted marriages, he became under Edward VI the driving force behind the Protestant Prayer Book and the **Thirty-Nine Articles**.* When the accession of Mary in 1553 brought a return to Roman Catholicism, he was tried for heresy and burned at the stake. After initially recanting, he withdrew his recantations and

> **From An Account of Thomas Cranmer's death, written by an anonymous spectator**
>
> Fire being now put to him, he stretched out his right hand, and thrust it into the flame, and held it there a good space, before the fire came to any other part of his body; where his hand was seen of every man sensibly burning, crying with a loud voice, "This hand hath offended." As soon as the fire got up, he was very soon dead, never stirring or crying all the while.

in a celebrated gesture thrust into the fire his right hand, which had signed them, so that it should be the first part of him to be consumed by the flames.

CROMWELL, OLIVER (1599–1658) English soldier and statesman who was a Puritan MP in the **Long Parliament*** before distinguishing himself as a general in the **Civil War**.* He helped to create the **New Model Army** and was second in command to its chief, **Sir Thomas Fairfax**.* After the execution of Charles I, Cromwell directed the ruthless subjugation of Ireland and was responsible for the massacres of civilians at Drogheda and Wexford. From December 1653 he took the office of Lord Protector and in effect ruled England until his death. The office was inherited by his son, but the political structure Cromwell had created began to crumble almost at once.

CROMWELL, THOMAS (ca. 1485–1540) Starting as a protégé of **Cardinal Wolsey**,* he quickly rose to become Henry VIII's chancellor and closest adviser. He was instrumental in bringing about the English church's break with Rome, superintended the **Dissolution of the Monasteries**,* and organized a range of administrative reforms. His central role in sorting out Henry's various marital problems ended badly when he persuaded the king to marry the unattractive Anne of Cleves. Henry found this hard to forgive and had him executed on a spurious charge of treason.

DIGGERS A radical group that attempted from 1649 to 1650 to cultivate common land. Headed by **Gerard Winstanley**, they enjoyed a good deal of popular support, but their communist project unsettled both the Commonwealth government and the local landowners. Harassed by mobs and the machinery of the law, the pacifist Diggers were forced to disband.

DISSOLUTION OF THE MONASTERIES The suppression of the English monasteries, orchestrated for Henry VIII by **Thomas Cromwell*** between 1536 and 1540. It brought vast lands to the crown, most of which were sold off to the nobility and gentry, giving a much needed boost to Henry's treasury. The dissolution spelt the end of any significant monastic influence on English life and the destruction of many of the old buildings.

DIVINE RIGHT OF KINGS The doctrine, strongly affirmed by James I, that the authority of the king comes from God and is therefore absolute, unchallengeable by either subjects or Parliament.

DRAKE, FRANCIS (ca. 1540–96) English explorer and admiral. After early success as a buccaneer on the Spanish Main, he became the first Englishman to sail round the world (1577–80), for which he was knighted by Queen Elizabeth aboard his ship the *Golden Hind*. In 1587 he led a raid on the harbor at Cadiz, where he was said to have "singed the king of Spain's beard" by destroying a number of Spanish ships. The following year he helped to defeat the **Armada**,* earning fame for his *sang froid* when he declared that he would finish his game of bowls before going off to battle.

ERASMUS, DESIDERIUS (ca. 1466–1536) Humanist scholar and writer, born in Rotterdam. A man of skeptical intelligence, he promoted the historical study of religious writings and acted as a catalyst for the **Reformation**,* though he himself refused to take sides in the conflict between Martin Luther and the papacy. He was a friend of Thomas More, at whose house he wrote one of his best known works, *Encomium moriae* (*Praise of Folly*).

ERASTIANISM The doctrine that the state should have authority over the church. It took its name from the Swiss theologian Thomas Erastus (1624–83), an opponent of Calvinism.

ESSEX, ROBERT DEVEREUX, 2ND EARL OF (1567–1601) English soldier and courtier, one-time favorite of Elizabeth I. He earned credit fighting the Spanish but was disgraced after his failure to put down a rebellion in Ireland. In 1601 he led an unsuccessful revolt against the crown and was executed.

FAIRFAX, THOMAS (1612–71) Commander of the Parliamentary forces during the **English Civil War**.* Fairfax was largely responsible for the creation of the **New Model Army**, whose discipline and professionalism were a decisive factor in the defeat of the royalists. Opposed to the execution of Charles I, he was among those who facilitated the **Restoration**.*

FIELD OF THE CLOTH OF GOLD The site near Calais of an extravagantly opulent meeting between Henry VIII and François I of France in 1520. In spite of the sumptuous decorations and lavish entertainment – among other novelties, a gilt fountain spouted wine – there was little to show for the encounter. Before long, Henry had entered a pact against François with Charles V, the Holy Roman Emperor.

FLINTLOCK WEAPONS A form of weapon in which the charge is lit by a spark from a flint. This was a significant improvement on the old **matchlock guns**, which used a burning fuse that made them hopelessly unreliable in the wet. Flintlock weapons became common in the seventeenth century.

FLODDEN, BATTLE OF (1513) Battle in which the invading Scots were crushed by an English force under the command of Thomas Howard, earl of Surrey. The Scottish King James IV was killed in the battle.

FOXE's *BOOK OF MARTYRS* The popular title of John Foxe's *Actes and Monuments* (1563), which was widely read for its graphic account of Christian martyrdoms – in particular, those of English Protestants.

***From* John Foxe, *Acts and Monuments* (1563): the martyrdom of William Hunter**

Then William rose and went to the stake and stood upright to it. Then came a bailiff and made fast the chain about William. Then said Browne [the Justice], "Here is not wood enough to burn a leg of him." Then said William, "Pray for me while ye see me alive, good people, and I will pray for you." "Now," quoth Browne, "pray for thee? I will pray no more for thee than for a dog." William answered, "Mr. Browne, now you have that which you sought for, and I pray God it be not layed to your charge in the last day." Then said William, "son of God, shine upon me"; and immediately the sun in the element shone out of a dark cloud so full in his face that he was constrained to look another way; whereat the people mused, because it was so dark a little time before. The William took up a faggot of broom and embraced it in his arms . . . "Then," quoth the priest, "how thou burnest here, so shalt thou burn in hell."

GALILEO GALILEI (1564–1642) Italian mathematician, physicist, and astronomer. By using a modified version of the newly invented telescope to study the skies, he was able to confirm the theories of Copernicus and in 1632 published his conclusions in *Dialogue on the Two Great World Systems- Ptolemaic and Copernican*. He was prosecuted by the Inquisition and forced to recant, spending his last years under house arrest. According to legend, he murmured after the recantation, in which he had accepted that the earth was a fixed body at the center of the universe, *"Eppur si muove"* ("And yet it does move").

GREY, LADY JANE (1537–54) Great-granddaughter of Henry VII, she was proclaimed queen in 1553 on the death of Edward VI. She reigned for nine days before popular support for Mary forced her to abdicate. A pawn in the political game of her relations, she was executed for treason the following year at the age of 16.

GUNPOWDER PLOT A Roman Catholic conspiracy, led by **Robert Catesby**, to blow up James I and the Houses of Parliament on November 5, 1605. An informant gave away the plot, and **Guy Fawkes**, one of the conspirators, was discovered with barrels of gunpowder in a cellar of the Palace of Westminster.

GUSTAVUS II ADOLPHUS (1594–1632) King of Sweden, whose intervention in the **Thirty Years War*** assured the survival of Germany as a Protestant nation and earned him the nickname "Lion of the North."

HARVEY, WILLIAM (1578–1657) Personal physician to James I and Charles I whose work on anatomy led him to the discovery of the circulation of the blood. His findings were published in 1628.

HOBBES, THOMAS (1588–1679) English political philosopher. In his greatest work, *Leviathan* (1651), he argued that man's innate selfishness required an absolute sovereign as the only way of ensuring order and security.

From Thomas Hobbes, *Leviathan*, Part I, Ch. 13

Hereby it is manifest, that during the time men live without a common power to keep them all in awe, they are in that condition which is called war; and such a war, as is of every man, against every man . . .

In such condition, there is no place for industry; because the fruit thereof is uncertain: and consequently no culture of the earth; no navigation, nor use of the commodities that may be imported by sea; no commodious building; no instruments of moving, and removing such things as require much force; no knowledge of the face of the earth; no account of time; no arts; no letters; no society; and which is worst of all, continual fear, and danger of violent death; and the life of man, solitary, poor, nasty, brutish, and short.

HOLINSHED, RAPHAEL (died ca. 1580) English chronicler and translator who was responsible for the publication of *Chronicles of England, Scotlande, and Irelande* (1577), which were used as a source by Shakespeare and other Elizabethan dramatists.

HOOKER, RICHARD (ca. 1554–1600) Theologian. His principal work, *Of the Laws of Ecclesiastical Politie*, made him one of the architects of Anglican theology.

HUMANISM The term given to the cultural movement that was the basis of the **Renaissance*** in Europe. Among its key elements were the rediscovery of classical Greek and Roman texts, a new focus on the arts and sciences as opposed to purely theological concerns, and a belief in the high potential of human nature and of the individual human being. See PETRARCH (p. 160).

INQUISITION Launched in the late twelfth century as a tribunal to combat heresy, the Inquisition became a permanent Catholic institution in 1231. After a period in abeyance during the fourteenth and fifteenth centuries, it was revived with great severity in Spain in 1478 and was later extended to Italy and elsewhere in the struggle against Protestantism. Its secrecy, its use of torture, and its wide-ranging powers made it a feared and hated symbol of Roman Catholic oppression.

INTERREGNUM (1649–60) The period between the reigns of Charles I and Charles II.

JESUITS Members of the Society of Jesus, a Roman Catholic order founded by **Ignatius Loyola** in 1534. They played an important part in the **Counter-Reformation*** and were implicated in plots against both Elizabeth I and James I. Prominent as educators and missionaries, they were highly disciplined, trained in disputation, and well qualified to move at ease in the corridors of power.

JONES, INIGO (1573–1652) English architect much influenced by the classical style of **Andrea Palladio**.* His greatest achievement was the Banqueting Hall, Whitehall (1619–22), but he also worked on theatrical designs for masques and plays.

KEPLER, JOHANNES (1571–1630) German astronomer. Having studied under the Danish astronomer **Tycho Brahe** (1546–1601), he went on to formulate the three principles known as Kepler's laws of planetary motion and to develop an improved version of Galileo's telescope.

KNOX, JOHN (ca. 1514–72) Scottish Protestant reformer and a leading figure in shaping the Presbyterian Church of Scotland. After fleeing to the Continent during the reign of Queen Mary, he came under the influence of Calvin. Among his more notorious works was his *First Blast of the Trumpet against the Monstrous Regiment of Women* (1558), a tract aimed primarily at Mary, Queen of Scots and Mary Tudor.

LATIMER, HUGH Protestant reformer and bishop who was martyred in October 1555. Convicted of heresy during Queen Mary's persecutions, he was burned at the stake in Oxford along with fellow-reformer **Nicholas Ridley**. His words at the stake have won him a special place in Protestant history: *"Be of good comfort, Master Ridley, and play the man. We shall this day light such a candle, by God's grace, in England as I trust shall never be put out."*

LAUD, WILLIAM (1573–1645) Archbishop of Canterbury under Charles I. His determination to impose religious uniformity, based on the **Book of Common Prayer**,* set him at odds with the Puritans and led to his impeachment and execution during the **Civil War**.*

LEPANTO (1571) The great sea-battle in which the forces of Catholic Europe, led by Don John of Austria, destroyed the Turkish fleet and broke the Ottoman empire's hold on the Mediterranean.

LEVELLERS A radical group that came into being in 1645 and drew much of its support from the Parliamentary army. Apart from demanding the abolition of rank (hence their name), the Levellers wanted republican government with adult male suffrage, religious toleration, and a variety of social reforms. Cromwell's rejection of this program was answered by mutinies in the army that led him to suppress the movement in 1649.

LONG PARLIAMENT Summoned by Charles I in 1640 to raise money for his war against the Scots, it quickly asserted an independence that culminated in the passing of the **Grand Remonstrance** (1641), a fierce denunciation of the king's authoritarian rule and the undue influence of the bishops. The rejection of this by Charles increased momentum towards the civil war that broke out a few months later. By the end of the war, power was in the hands of the army, and in 1648 Colonel Pride expelled all the more moderate members of the Long Parliament in what became known as **Pride's Purge**, leaving only a hardcore of 60 to serve in the so-called **Rump Parliament**. This was forcefully dismissed by Cromwell in 1653 to make way for the Protectorate. The Long Parliament was reinstated in 1659 but dissolved itself in the following year to be replaced by the Convention Parliament, which arranged the **Restoration**.*

LUTHER, MARTIN (1483–1546) An Augustinian monk and priest who became the founder of Protestantism and initiator of the **Reformation**.* Luther was dismayed by the corruption of the Roman Catholic Church, and particularly by its practice of selling **Indulgences** (dispensations from punishment in Purgatory). In 1517 he expressed his criticisms in **95 theses** that he nailed to the door of the castle church at Wittenberg. He saw himself as a reformer rather than a schismatic, but this act set in train the events that led to the Reformation. At the core of Lutheranism is his insistence that salvation is a divine gift and can be attained by faith alone.

MACHIAVELLI, NICCOLO (1469–1527) Florentine diplomat and writer. His greatest work, *Il Principe* (*The Prince*), was written in 1513. Partly inspired by his observations of **Cesare Borgia**, it propounds the view, based on Machiavelli's fairly pessimistic assessment of human nature, that the political end justifies the means, even when the means are brutal or devious. A relatively upright man himself, he became a byword for amoral political cunning.

From **Niccolò Machiavelli,** *Il Principe* **(***The Prince***) (written 1513), Chapter 17**

Nevertheless a prince ought to inspire fear in such a way that, if he does not win love, he avoids hatred; because he can endure very well being feared whilst he is not hated, which will always be as long as he abstains from the property of his citizens and subjects and from their women. But when it is necessary for him to proceed against the life of someone, he must do it on proper justification and for manifest cause, but above all things he must keep his hands off the property of others, because men more quickly forget the death of their father than the loss of their patrimony.

MARPRELATE TRACTS Puritan pamphlets attacking the Anglican bishops, published 1587–9 under the pseudonym Martin Marprelate ("mar a prelate").

MARY STUART, QUEEN OF SCOTS (1542–87) Daughter of James V of Scotland and Mary of Guise, she was brought up a Catholic in France and married the dauphin, later François II. Following his early death in 1560, she returned to Scotland where her reign was blighted by an unpopular marriage to her vicious cousin Lord Darnley, by whom she became mother of the future James VI of Scotland (James I of England). According to the suspect evidence of the **Casket Letters**, she then began an affair with the earl of Bothwell. A rebellion of the Scottish nobility forced her to flee to England, where she was imprisoned by Elizabeth I, who was nervous of her appeal to dissident Roman Catholics. A number of Catholic plots to place her on the English throne confirmed Elizabeth's fears. In 1587 Mary, Queen of Scots was beheaded at Fotheringhay Castle.

MONTAIGNE, MICHEL EYQUEM DE (1533–92) French writer who coined the term "essay" (French *essai* = attempt) and initiated the genre in its modern form. His enquiring, tolerant, skeptical *Essais* (1580 and 1588) were translated into English by John Florio in 1603.

MORE, SIR THOMAS (1477–1535) Scholar and lawyer who rose to become lord chancellor after the fall of **Wolsey**.* His opposition to Henry VIII's religious policies and his refusal to take the **Oath of Supremacy** (which would have meant acknowledging the king rather than the pope as supreme head of the English church) led to his trial and execution. He was a close friend of Erasmus, and the author of *Utopia* (1516).

NOSTRADAMUS (Michel de Notredame, 1503–66) French physician and astrologer who won the favor of Catherine de Médicis and Charles IX of France. His *Centuries* (1555), a book of artfully obscure prophecies in rhyming quatrains, arranged in groups of a hundred, made him celebrated as a seer.

PALLADIO, ANDREA (1508–80) Italian architect whose classical designs, based on the theories of the Roman architect **Vitruvius** (first century BC), were hugely influential. **Palladianism** – marked by a concern with order, symmetry, and harmony – was embraced by **Inigo Jones*** and later enjoyed a renewed vogue in early eighteenth-century England.

PARACELSUS (1493–1541) Outstanding Swiss physician who rejected traditional medical practice based on the theories of **Galen*** and anticipated several aspects of modern medicine.

PILGRIM FATHERS The 102 colonists (of whom only 35 were actually Puritan Separatists) who sailed from Plymouth in the *Mayflower* in 1620 and founded the first permanent colony in New England.

PILGRIMAGE OF GRACE (1536–7) The name given to uprisings in Lincolnshire and Yorkshire against Henry VIII. Inspired by opposition to his religious reforms, notably the **Dissolution of the Monasteries**,* the rebels took York but were dispersed by false promises and later crushed.

PRESBYTERIANISM A form of Protestantism, based on the teachings of **Calvin**,* in which government is by presbyters (elders) rather than by bishops. It was adopted by the Church of Scotland.

PROTECTORATE (1653–9) The government established by Oliver Cromwell, with himself as Lord Protector. After his death in 1658 it continued for a few months under his son Richard.

PRYNNE, WILLIAM (1600–69) Puritan pamphleteer who became a focus of hostilities between Parliament and the king. Shorn of his ears and branded on both cheeks for what he had written, he had the satisfaction of helping to send his enemy archbishop **Laud*** to the scaffold. Unwilling to accept the legitimacy of the Commonwealth government, he was eventually among those who voted for the **Restoration**.*

PURITANS Extreme Protestants of the sixteenth and seventeenth centuries. Essentially Calvinist in their theology, they wanted to root out all traces of Roman Catholicism. Their austere morality strongly colored the conduct of social life during the **Interregnum**.*

QUATTROCENTO (Italian = *four hundred*) The Italian term for the fifteenth century, often used in talking of Renaissance art. Less frequently, *trecento* (fourteenth century), *cinquecento* (sixteenth century), and *seicento* (seventeenth century) are also encountered. They can be used as either adjectives or nouns.

RABELAIS, FRANÇOIS (ca. 1494–1553) Priest, scholar, doctor, and author of *Pantagruel* (1532) and *Gargantua* (1534). The exuberant, outrageous, scatological character of these masterpieces, which chronicle the adventures of the giant Gargantua and his son Pantagruel, gave us the word *Rabelaisian*.

RALEGH, SIR WALTER (? 1554–1618) Courtier, poet, explorer, historian. He was a favorite of Queen Elizabeth I, celebrated for gallantly throwing his cloak over a puddle that was in her path. His efforts to found a colony in Virginia were unsuccessful, but popular legend credits him with introducing tobacco and the potato to England. Under James I he was imprisoned for treason and later, after a failed expedition to find Eldorado, executed.

REFORMATION A religious movement in sixteenth-century Europe which aimed to reform the Roman Catholic Church but led in the end to the establishment of independent Protestant churches. Its start is traditionally reckoned as October 31, 1517, the date on which **Martin Luther*** is said to have nailed up his 95 theses against the sale of Indulgences. In England the break with Rome was precipitated in the 1530s by Henry VIII's determination to secure a divorce from Catherine of Aragon in order to marry Anne Boleyn. The process of establishing a Protestant Church of England was completed under Edward VI and Elizabeth I. A turning point in European history, the Reformation has an importance measured not just in religious terms but also in the social and political consequences it had for English life.

RENAISSANCE From the French word for rebirth, the term refers to a cultural movement that began in fourteenth-century Italy and lasted in western Europe into the early seventeenth century. Invigorating both the arts and the sciences, it was marked by a revival of interest in classical culture, a spirit of intellectual and physical adventure, and an emphasis on the range and dignity of human achievement. See HUMANISM.

RIDOLFI PLOT A plot, instigated by the Italian banker Roberto Ridolfi, to murder Elizabeth I and place Mary, Queen of Scots on the English throne. It was discovered in 1571 while Ridolfi himself was out of the country.

SAVONAROLA, GIROLAMO (1452–98) A Dominican friar whose ferocious denunciations of social frivolity and political corruption led to the temporary expulsion from Florence of the ruling Medici family and made him a byword for fanatical religious austerity. His attacks on the papacy led to his excommunication and finally to his death at the stake for heresy.

SHIP MONEY A tax levied on coastal towns and counties to maintain the navy. Under Charles I its use was expanded to the point where it became a focus for opposition to the king.

STAR CHAMBER, COURT OF THE A court of law that originally sat in the Star Chamber at Westminster Palace. Primarily a court of appeal, it became under **Cardinal Wolsey*** a means of bypassing common law to bring fractious nobles to heel. Its abuse by Charles I to enforce royal and episcopal authority made it extremely unpopular, leading to its abolition by the **Long Parliament.***

STRAFFORD, THOMAS WENTWORTH, 1ST EARL OF (1593–1641) English statesman. After initially opposing Charles I, he became his most trusted adviser. As one of the chief agents of the king's authoritarian policies, he attracted widespread hostility. He was impeached by the **Long Parliament*** and executed.

SUPREMACY, ACTS OF The Act of Supremacy in 1534 made Henry VIII supreme head of the Church of England, independent of the pope. Following the brief reintroduction of Roman Catholicism by Queen Mary (1553–8), the Protestant Church of England was finally established by a new Act of Supremacy (1559) under Elizabeth I. See REFORMATION.

THIRTY YEARS WAR (1618–48) A savage European war between the Protestant princes of the north and the Holy Roman Empire. It had a decisive influence on the political map of seventeenth- and eighteenth-century Europe, weakening the power of the Holy Roman Empire and leaving Germany independent but devastated.

THIRTY-NINE ARTICLES (1563) The articles of faith which, along with the Book of Common Prayer, define the doctrine of the Church of England. Developed from Thomas Cranmer's earlier 42 articles, they establish the distinction between Anglican beliefs and those of the Roman Catholics on one side, and of the more extreme Protestant sects on the other.

TYBURN A stream crossing the west end of London which gave its name to the site of the public gallows that stood near present-day Marble Arch from medieval times until 1783, when it was moved to Newgate. Tyburn tree was a popular term for the gallows.

VILLIERS, GEORGE, 1ST DUKE OF BUCKINGHAM Powerful favorite of both James I and Charles I. His son, the 2nd Duke of Buckingham, was an intimate of Charles II and a member of the inner circle of advisers known, from the initials of its members, as the **cabal**.

WALSINGHAM, SIR FRANCIS (1532–90) Secretary of state to Elizabeth I. He established the network of spies that formed the basis of an early intelligence service.

WOLSEY, CARDINAL THOMAS (ca. 1475–1530) Son of an Ipswich butcher, he became a trusted adviser of Henry VIII, enjoying a spectacular rise within both church and state. At the height of his power, as lord chancellor of England, he was second only to the king, overseeing both domestic and foreign policy. But his high taxes and ostentatious lifestyle made enemies. After failing to secure a papal annulment of Henry's marriage to Catherine of Aragon, he fell from grace and was charged with treason. He died on his way to face trial.

Following the **Restoration*** in 1660, Charles II had to maintain a delicate balance between competing religious and political forces. At the same time he needed to wring money out of a Parliament suspicious of his dissipated lifestyle and Catholic sympathies. Trade wars with the Dutch and the successive afflictions of the **Great Plague*** and the **Fire of London*** added to the troubles of the 1660s. It was nonetheless an age of social exuberance and scientific discovery, the latter reflected in the work of **Newton*** and **Boyle** as well as in the founding of the **Royal Society*** and the **Royal Observatory**.

After Charles's death the crown passed to his brother James, whose overbearing rule and open Catholicism provoked implacable opposition. In 1688 the **Glorious Revolution*** replaced him with the Protestant William of Orange, who became joint sovereign with his wife Mary. James meanwhile fled to France before raising a force in Ireland that was defeated by William at the **battle of the Boyne** in 1690. Thereafter his supporters and descendants plotted a Jacobite return to power that issued in two unsuccessful rebellions in 1715 and 1745.

The revolution of 1688 served to reaffirm the importance of Parliament, whose two main political groupings came to be known as **Whigs*** and **Tories**.* The more prominent role of government ministers, particularly under the Hanoverians, led over the next half century to the emergence of the office of prime minister.

At the beginning of the eighteenth century William's determination to check the expansionist ambitions of Louis XIV took England into the **War of the Spanish Succession**,* celebrated in popular memory for the duke of Marlborough's victories over the French.

In 1714 the English throne passed to the Hanoverian King George I, marking the start of the **Georgian age**.* It was a period that saw the unfolding of the **agricultural revolution*** and the beginnings of the **Industrial Revolution**.* Meanwhile, the age of empire was dawning: India and Canada were two major colonial prizes won in the **Seven Years War*** (1756–63). Despite the loss of the American colonies in 1783, Britain's course as an imperial power was set.

ADAM, ROBERT (1728–92) One of a family of Scottish architects, he is remembered especially for his elegant interiors in a style developed from Palladianism but enlivened by Byzantine and Italian Baroque influences.

AGRICULTURAL (OR AGRARIAN) REVOLUTION Name given to the changes in agriculture that took place during the eighteenth and early nineteenth centuries to feed an expanding population. These included the **enclosure*** of land, the **improvement of breeding techniques**, the **rotation of crops** (corn alternating with fodder crops like turnip and clover to avoid the need for a fallow year), and the **introduction of new technology** such as the seed drill invented by **Jethro Tull** at the beginning of the eighteenth century. Among those famous for promoting the new practices were **Thomas Coke** of Holkham and **Charles "Turnip" Townshend**.

AMERICAN REVOLUTION (1775–83) Resentment of British colonial rule, and in particular British taxation, had already surfaced in the years before the war, notably at the **Boston "Tea Party"** (1773), when rebellious Americans, dressed as Mohawks, had boarded the East India Company's ships and tipped chests of tea into the harbor. The **American War of Independence** broke out in April 1775 with skirmishes at Lexington and Concord in Massachusetts. Fifteen months later, on July 4, 1776, the **Declaration of Independence** was issued. The surrender of General Cornwallis at Yorktown in October 1781 signaled the defeat of British forces, and in 1783 American independence was formally recognized by the **treaty of Versailles**.

ANCIEN RÉGIME The term used to refer to the pre-Revolutionary French system of government.

BERKELEY, GEORGE (1685–1753) Irish philosopher who became bishop of Cloyne. It was his contention that the material world exists only insofar as it can be perceived. Samuel Johnson famously dismissed this theory by stamping on a large stone and saying, "I refute it *thus*."

BILL OF RIGHTS (1) The 1689 Act of Parliament which embodied the **Declaration of Rights**, setting out the justification for the **Glorious Revolution*** that had brought William and Mary to the throne in place of James II. It claimed supremacy for Parliament, enjoining free elections and parliamentary freedom of speech. (2) The first ten amendments, ratified in 1791, to the **American Constitution**. The most famous are the **first amendment**, guaranteeing freedom of speech, press, and religion; the **second**, guaranteeing the right to bear arms; and the **fifth**, guaranteeing the right to due process of law, including the right not to bear witness against oneself.

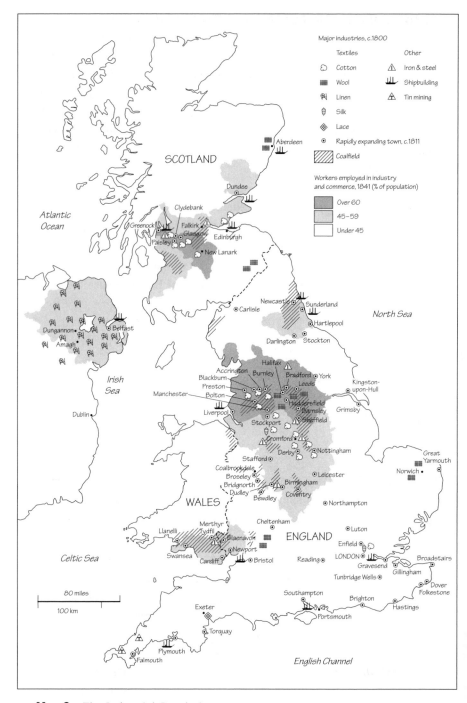

Map 3 The Industrial Revolution

BLACK HOLE OF CALCUTTA A cell, 18ft. × 15ft., in which 146 British soldiers were alleged to have been locked up on the night of June 20, 1756 by the nawab of Bengal, **Siraj-ud-Dawlah**, who had attacked Calcutta in support of the French at the start of the **Seven Years War**.* According to the story told by the commander of the East India Company's garrison, only some 23 of the soldiers survived the appalling conditions. The incident caused public outrage in Britain, though later research suggests that the number of those imprisoned was greatly exaggerated.

BLOODY ASSIZES The west country assizes that meted out justice under Judge George Jeffreys after **Monmouth's rebellion*** in 1685. The notoriously harsh sentences resulted in execution or transportation for hundreds of Monmouth's supporters.

BRIDEWELL Originally a palace, it became in the sixteenth century a workhouse where vagrants and petty criminals were subjected to whipping and forced labor. Public galleries allowed this to become a fashionable spectacle in the seventeenth and eighteenth centuries. Bridewell was closed in the mid-nineteenth century.

BROWN, LANCELOT (CAPABILITY) (1715–83) Landscape gardener. In contrast to the continental fashion for carefully ordered, geometrical layouts, Brown strove for an effect of nature in his gardens, as, for example, in the park at Blenheim. Known also as an architect, he became the foremost "improver" of his time, nicknamed "Capability" from his habit of remarking that a property had "capabilities."

BURKE, EDMUND (1729–97) MP and political philosopher whose advocacy of responsible aristocratic government had an important influence on the development of Conservative philosophy. Partially sympathetic to the American Revolution, he opposed that of the French, setting out his views in *Reflections on the Revolution in France* (1790). Apart from his political writings, he made a notable contribution to aesthetic theory in *A Philosophical Enquiry into the Origin of Our Ideas of the Sublime and Beautiful* (1757).

CALENDAR Until the mid-eighteenth century Britain continued to use the **Julian calendar** (introduced by Julius Caesar), even though Roman Catholic countries had been using Pope Gregory XIII's more accurate alternative since the late sixteenth century. The British Parliament finally adopted the **Gregorian**

calendar in 1752, rearranging the dates for that year so that September 2 was immediately followed by September 14. Popular anxiety about this move, which seemed to steal the intervening period from people's lives, was expressed in the cry *"Give us back our eleven days."*

CARRIAGES Private horse-drawn coaches were in use in England from the middle of the sixteenth century. The first public **stagecoaches** came into service about a hundred years later. From the mid-eighteenth century, road improvements led to a proliferation of different kinds of carriage, many of which are referred to in contemporary literature. These are the most common varieties used in England:

Brougham: A four-wheeled closed carriage, drawn by a single horse, with a raised seat for the driver. Named after the nineteenth-century lord chancellor, Henry Brougham, it could be a smart private carriage or, later and less comfortably, a hired carriage popularly known as a "growler."

Cabriolet: A form of chaise fashionable in the eighteenth century. The name was later shortened to cab and used of carriages that plied for hire.

Calash: An open carriage with two or four wheels and facing passenger seats.

Chaise: A light carriage for one or two people. It had a folding hood and was drawn by a single horse. Distinct from this, the **post chaise** was a four-wheeled carriage for public hire that traveled rapidly between staging posts, where the horses were changed. It was introduced in the 1660s.

Curricle: An open two-wheeled carriage drawn by a pair of horses abreast.

Gig: An open two-wheeled carriage drawn by a single horse.

Hackney carriage: A four-wheeled coach for six passengers, drawn by two horses and plying for hire. It appeared in England in the early seventeenth century.

Hansom cab: A two-wheeled closed carriage for two, named after its designer, Joseph Hansom. The driver was on a raised seat behind the cab, with the reins passing over the roof to a single horse. Introduced in the 1830s, it became the most popular London cab.

Landau: A heavy four-wheeled carriage invented in Germany in the mid-eighteenth century. Its upper half was in two folding parts that met together in the middle. Drawn by four horses, it was primarily a vehicle for grand occasions.

Mail coach: A specially adapted stagecoach introduced in the late eighteenth century as a quicker alternative to the post-boys, who had previously transported mail on horseback.

Phaeton: An open four-wheeled vehicle, drawn by a variable number of horses and driven by the owner. It was especially popular in Regency England.

Trap: A two-wheeled carriage, similar to the gig, with a storage box under the seat.

Victoria: An elegant four-wheeled, doorless carriage for two people, named after Queen Victoria.

CHIPPENDALE, THOMAS (ca. 1718–79) English cabinetmaker and furniture designer. Along with **George Hepplewhite** (d. 1786) and **Thomas Sheraton** (1751–1806), he had an important influence on eighteenth-century taste in furniture.

CLARENDON CODE A series of Parliamentary Acts, including the 1662 **Act of Uniformity**, that were passed between 1661 and 1665 to strengthen the position of the Anglican Church and clamp down on **Nonconformists**.* Though the measures took their name from the earl of Clarendon, Charles II's lord chancellor, he himself had little enthusiasm for them.

COOK, CAPTAIN JAMES (1728–79) British navigator who explored the Pacific, leading an expedition to Tahiti in 1768 to observe the transit of Venus across the sun. He also charted New Zealand and eastern Australia. The enlightened dietary regime he imposed, high in vitamin C, practically eliminated scurvy among his crew. He was killed in a fracas with Hawaiian islanders.

DEISM A current of religious thought in the seventeenth and eighteenth centuries that accepted the existence of a Supreme Being or Creator but rejected the notion of divine intervention in human affairs. Hostile to revealed and organized religion, the Deists advocated a natural religion, based on reason. Their beliefs influenced not just England, France, and Germany, but also, by the end of the eighteenth century, America.

DISSENTERS See NONCONFORMISTS.

EAST INDIA COMPANY A commercial company originally formed to take advantage of the spice trade, and granted a royal charter in 1600. Driven out of the East Indies by the Dutch, it began to focus its activities on India. A century later, following the victory of its employee **Robert Clive** at the **battle of Plassey** (1757), which secured mastery of Bengal, the East India Company became the effective government of British India. In spite of a reduction in its powers in the late eighteenth century, the company survived until 1873.

EMPIRICISM The philosophical belief, hostile to both rationalism and metaphysics, that all knowledge is based on experience derived from the senses. Associated in Britain with **John Locke**,* **George Berkeley**,* and **David Hume**,* it has been a powerful force in modern western philosophy.

ENCLOSURE The process of enclosing communal open land so that it can be more efficiently farmed by individual owners. It began in the Middle Ages and became more widespread in the sixteenth century, when it sparked social unrest among those who saw their traditional rights to farm common land disappearing. The **agricultural revolution*** brought in new systems of farming that demanded further enclosure, and by the early nineteenth century, after a number of Enclosure Acts, the process was more or less complete.

ENCYCLOPÉDIE (1751–72) The 28-volume (17 of articles, 11 of illustrations) *Dictionnaire raisonné des sciences, des arts et des métiers* whose production was supervised by Diderot and d'Alembert. Later expanded to 35 volumes, it attracted contributions from many of the principal writers and intellectuals of the time (see ENLIGHTENMENT), whose ideas were already pointing the way towards the French Revolution. With its skepticism, its tolerance, and its commitment to scientific method and rational enquiry, the *Encyclopédie* became the great manifesto of the European Enlightenment.

ENLIGHTENMENT An eighteenth-century European intellectual movement that grew out of the work in the previous century of scientists and philosophers such as Descartes, Pascal, **Newton**,* and **Locke**.* Led by the group of French writers and thinkers known as *philosophes* – among them Montesquieu, **Voltaire**,* **Rousseau**,* and Diderot – it challenged traditional authority and religious orthodoxy in the name of reason, philosophical enquiry, and empirical investigation. The principles of the Enlightenment are most clearly embodied in the achievement of the ***Encyclopédie***.*

FIRE OF LONDON (1666) The fire that broke out at a baker's in Pudding Lane in the early hours of September 2 and raged for three days, causing only a dozen or so deaths but destroying four fifths of the city, including the medieval St. Paul's Cathedral.

FLEET PRISON A London prison that acquired notoriety for the so-called "Fleet marriages" – impromptu ceremonies performed there clandestinely by venal clergymen or hirelings masquerading as priests. The 1753 **Marriage Act*** put a stop to them.

FOX, CHARLES JAMES (1749–1806) Whig politician and Britain's first foreign secretary. An inveterate gambler, he was also a consistent champion of liberty, who played a notable part in abolishing the slave trade. His opposition to George III ensured that he was never long in government, but he stands out as perhaps the most colorful and engaging politician of the age.

GLORIOUS REVOLUTION (also known as the **Bloodless Revolution**) The term given to the events of 1688–9 that led to the overthrow of James II and the accession to the throne of his daughter Mary and her husband William of Orange. James's unconstitutional and pro-Catholic rule had excited strong opposition. On William's arrival in England, he fled to France without a fight. William and Mary accepted the **Declaration of Rights** (see BILL OF RIGHTS) and were enthroned as joint sovereigns.

GORDON RIOTS (1780) Six days of violent anti-Catholic rioting in London that caused much destruction and left between 300 and 500 dead. The riots were instigated by Lord George Gordon, agitating for the repeal of the 1778 **Catholic Relief Act**, which had restored a number of civil rights to Roman Catholics.

GRAND TOUR The European journey that was used by the aristocracy as a way of completing their sons' education. It generally lasted two or three years during which the traveler, accompanied by a tutor (referred to as a "bear leader"), was expected to visit at least France, Italy, Switzerland, Germany, and the Netherlands, learning languages, meeting people of note, developing skills of connoisseurship and social address, collecting antiquities, and sowing wild oats. The practice began in the seventeenth century, enjoyed its heyday in the eighteenth, when it extended to some members of the gentry, and more or less died away after the French Revolution.

> **Alexander Pope, *The Dunciad*, Bk. 4, lines 311–16 (The Grand Tourist)**
>
> . . . he saunter'd Europe round,
> And gather'd ev'ry Vice on Christian ground;
> Saw ev'ry Court, heard ev'ry King declare
> His royal Sense, of Op'ra's or the Fair;
> The Stews and Palace equally explor'd,
> Intrigu'd with glory, and with spirit whor'd;

GREAT PLAGUE (1665) The last great outbreak of bubonic plague in Britain. In the course of 1665 it killed some 70,000 people in London.

> **From Samuel Pepys, *Diary*, June 7, 1665**
>
> This day, much against my will, I did in Drury Lane see two or three houses marked with a red cross upon the doors, and "Lord have mercy upon us" writ there – which was a sad sight to me, being the first of that kind that to my remembrance I ever saw. It put me into an ill conception of myself and my smell, so that I was forced to buy some roll-tobacco to smell to and chaw – which took away the apprehension.

GRUB STREET A London street near Moorfields which in the eighteenth century was inhabited by writers who turned their pens to anything that would earn them a living. Its name was changed in the nineteenth century to Milton Street, but the term has retained its association with literary hack-work.

HANOVERIANS The sovereigns belonging to the House of Hanover, which ruled Britain from 1714 to 1901. In this context, the adjective "Hanoverian" usually refers to the eighteenth century rather than to the whole period. See SETTLEMENT, ACT OF.

HEARTH TAX A tax of 2 shillings on every fireplace, levied in England from 1662. Deeply unpopular, it was abandoned in 1689.

HOGARTH, WILLIAM (1697–1764) English painter and engraver. In works like *Gin Lane* and his series *A Rake's Progress* and *Marriage à la Mode* he provided a sharp satirical perspective on aspects of eighteenth-century social life.

HUGUENOTS French Protestants. Following Louis XIV's revocation in 1685 of the **Edict of Nantes** (which had guaranteed their freedom of worship), many of them emigrated to neighboring Protestant countries, including England, bringing with them valuable skills as craftsmen, manufacturers, and entrepreneurs.

HUME, DAVID (1711–76) Scottish philosopher whose *Treatise of Human Nature* (1739–40), though much less popular at the time than his *History of England* (1754–62), became a cornerstone of British empiricist philosophy. See EMPIRICISM.

INDUSTRIAL REVOLUTION Term used to describe the process, beginning in the mid-eighteenth century, that transformed Britain into an industrial nation. Its catalysts were a number of key inventions that revolutionized the production of textiles, taking it out of the home and into purpose-built factories. Among these were the spinning jenny, invented by **James Hargreaves** in ca. 1765 to increase the speed of spinning; the water frame, patented by **Richard Arkwright** in 1769 to take advantage of water power for spinning; and the mule, invented by **Samuel Crompton** in 1779 as an improved cross between these two machines (hence the name). The development of an efficient steam engine by **James Watt** in 1769 marked a crucial stage in the revolution, heralding a shift in focus from rivers to coalmines, as water power gave way to steam. Improvements in transport and communications were effected first by the extension of the canal system and developments in road building, and later by the spread of railways.

JACOBITE A supporter of the deposed Stuart King James II and his descendants. After the death of James II in exile, there were two Jacobite rebellions against the Hanoverian monarchy, both of which failed. In 1715 James's son James Edward Stuart (known as the Old Pretender) mounted an invasion of Scotland, and in 1745 James Edward's son Charles Edward Stuart (known as **Bonnie Prince Charlie**, or the Young Pretender) did likewise. The crushing of this last rebellion at the **battle of Culloden** in 1746 put an end to Jacobite hopes. The terms JACOBEAN (p. 242) and JACOBIN (p. 209) are altogether distinct. See also PRETENDERS.

JENKINS'S EAR, WAR OF A war between Britain and Spain that began in 1739 and was absorbed into the **War of the Austrian Succession** (1740–8). The immediate cause of war was the claim by Captain Robert Jenkins that in 1731 Spanish coastguards had boarded his ship in the West Indies and cut off

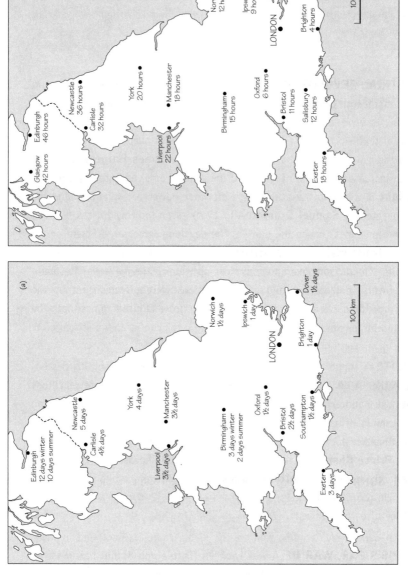

Map 4 (a) Coach journey times from London c. 1750; (b) Coach journey times from London in the 1830s

Source: Pope, Rex, *Atlas of British Social and Economic History since c. 1700* (London: Routledge, 1990).

his ear. Seven years later he produced the ear in the House of Commons and whipped up a frenzy of public indignation that forced the prime minister, **Robert Walpole**, to take action. The war was more about commercial rivalry than Jenkins's ear, but it became symbolic of imperial Britain's readiness to defend her subjects against the insolence of foreign powers. In military terms, it was notable chiefly for the disastrous naval attack on Cartagena (1741) that Tobias Smollett witnessed as a surgeon's mate and recorded in *Roderick Random* (1748).

From Tobias Smollett, *Roderick Random*, Chapter 33 (the botched attack on Cartagena)

Such was the economy in some ships, that, rather than be at the trouble of interring the dead, their commanders ordered their men to throw the bodies overboard, many without either ballast or winding-sheet; so that numbers of human carcasses floated in the harbour, until they were devoured by sharks and carrion crows; which afforded no agreeable spectacle to those who survived.

LATITUDINARIANS Name given in the seventeenth century to Anglican churchmen who did not take up a dogmatic position on the controversies about church government and ritual that separated the **High Church** enthusiasts for ceremony and clerical hierarchy from their **Low Church** opponents. The Latitudinarian emphasis on rationality, doctrinal tolerance, and practical piety became increasingly influential in the eighteenth century.

LICENSING ACT An act, initially passed in 1662 and later extended, that required all publications to be licensed. It was a measure designed to ensure the censorship of any writings considered seditious or contrary to the teachings of the Church of England.

LOCKE, JOHN (1632–1704) English philosopher whose *Essay Concerning Human Understanding* (1690) made him the father of British empiricism. In the same year his *Two Treatises on Government* (1690) set out the principles of liberal democracy, arguing against the divine right of kings and in favor of a form of social contract under which it is the ruler's duty to preserve the civil rights and liberties of citizens. *Some Thoughts Concerning Education* (1693) was Locke's influential contribution to contemporary debates on child rearing.

MANSFIELD RULING (1772) A legal judgment by Lord Mansfield (William Murray, 1st earl of Mansfield) that a runaway slave could not be taken out of the country by force to be sold into slavery abroad. It is often claimed, inaccurately, that this had the effect of making slavery illegal in England.

MARRIAGE ACT (1753) Introduced by Lord Hardwicke, it was designed to prevent the increasing scandal of runaway or enforced marriages, celebrated in secret and often by mock clergymen. Under its provisions, marriages required the publication of banns or the obtaining of a special license and could only be celebrated in an Anglican church. See FLEET PRISON.

METHODISM See NONCONFORMISTS.

MONMOUTH'S REBELLION (1685) An uprising against James II led by the Protestant James Scott, duke of Monmouth, who claimed the throne as the illegitimate son of Charles II. The rebellion was swiftly crushed at the **battle of Sedgemoor**, and Monmouth himself was captured and beheaded. See BLOODY ASSIZES.

NEWGATE A London prison from the Middle Ages to the late nineteenth century. Standing on what is now the site of the Central Criminal Court (the Old Bailey), it was destroyed and rebuilt a number of times before becoming, from 1783, the place of execution in succession to Tyburn.

NEWTON, ISAAC (1642–1727) Physicist and mathematician. Britain's greatest scientist, he discovered the law of gravitation, invented calculus, identified white light as a mixture of colored lights, and propounded his three laws of motion. Legend has it that he was inspired to the discovery of gravity by the sight of an apple falling from a tree. His major work, and the foundation of modern science, was the *Philosophiae Naturalis Principia Mathematica* (*Mathematical Principles of Natural Philosophy*), published in 1687 and usually referred to as the *Principia*.

NONCONFORMISTS British Protestants who do not accept the doctrines or conform to the rituals of the Church of England. After the **Act of Uniformity** in 1662 the Nonconformists, also known as **Dissenters**, were liable to legal penalties, though the situation improved after the 1689 **Toleration Act**. Among the principal Nonconformist groups are the following:

Baptists: A group founded in the early seventeenth century who believe in adult baptism by immersion.

Congregationalists: A group established in 1580, and known in the seventeenth century as Independents. They adopt a form of devolved church government in which local congregations are autonomous.

Methodists: Name given to the group founded by **John Wesley** (1703–91) in about 1730. Wesley began his itinerant preaching in 1738, putting a strong emphasis on the possibility of personal salvation. Early Methodists included his brother Charles, who wrote some of the movement's most rousing hymns, and the preacher George Whitefield. The appeal of Methodism was particularly strong among the new industrial working classes.

Presbyterians: (See p. 176) As members of the Church of Scotland, they regard Anglicans rather than themselves as the Nonconformists.

Plymouth Brethren: A hardline group established in Plymouth in 1831 who tread a particularly austere path through a sinful world.

Quakers: Founded by George Fox in the late 1640s, and known as the Society of Friends, they were persecuted for their rejection of many aspects of conventional social and religious life. In 1681 William Penn founded a colony of Quaker refugees in Pennsylvania. Notable pacifists, they were at the forefront of campaigns for the abolition of slavery and the reform of prisons.

Unitarians: A group that rejects the Trinity and the divinity of Christ, stressing rational faith and the essential goodness of human nature. Originating in the sixteenth century, they became more influential in the eighteenth, absorbing a number of other Nonconformist groups.

NONJURORS Those Anglican clergy (some 400 of them, including eight bishops) who refused to take an oath of allegiance to William and Mary after the **Glorious Revolution*** and were deprived of their livings.

PAINE, THOMAS (1737–1809) Writer and political theorist whose *Rights of Man* (1791) presented a wide-ranging defense of the French Revolution in response to **Burke's*** *Reflections*. Paine's earlier pamphlet *Common Sense* (1776) had been a rallying cry for the American revolutionaries and a key influence on the **Declaration of Independence**.

Thomas Paine, the opening lines of *Common Sense* (1776)

Some writers have so confounded society with government, as to leave little or no distinction between them; whereas they are not only different, but have different origins. Society is produced by our wants and government by our wickedness; the former promotes our happiness *positively* by uniting our affections, the latter *negatively* by restraining our vices. The one encourages intercourse, the other creates distinctions. The first is a patron, the last a punisher.

Society in every state is a blessing, but government, even in its best state, is but a necessary evil; in its worst state an intolerable one: . . . Government, like dress, is the badge of lost innocence; the palaces of kings are built upon the ruins of the bowers of paradise.

PERRAULT, CHARLES (1628–1703) French poet who published an important collection of fairy tales in 1697 subtitled *Contes de ma mère l'Oye* (*Tales of Mother Goose*). Among others, it included the following stories:

Blue Beard: A rich man, distinguished by his blue beard, marries a young woman in an eastern country. When called away on business, he leaves her with the keys of the house, instructing her not to enter one particular room. She disobeys and finds inside it the bodies of all his previous wives. Moreover, the key to the room is now magically stained with blood, enabling Bluebeard to deduce on his return what has happened. She begs for a brief reprieve before he murders her, and her brothers arrive just in time to kill him and rescue her.

Cinderella: Forced by her stepmother and spiteful stepsisters to do the household chores and sit at the edge of the hearth among the cinders (hence her name), Cinderella watches sadly as her stepsisters go off to a ball. Her fairy godmother then comes on the scene and sends her off to the ball in a fine coach transformed from a pumpkin. But she must be back by midnight, when the magic will end. At the ball she captivates the Prince and on the stroke of midnight rushes away just in time, leaving behind one of her glass slippers. The Prince searches for the person it fits. To the dismay of her stepsisters, Cinderella alone can wear it, and he marries her.

Red Riding Hood: Little Red Riding Hood is sent to take food to her sick grandmother but falls into conversation on the way with a wolf who finds out where she's going. He runs ahead, eats the grandmother and takes her place in bed. Having successfully tricked little Red Riding Hood, he eats her up as well.

Sleeping Beauty: A princess is condemned by a spiteful fairy to prick herself with a spindle and die, but she escapes this fate by the intervention of another fairy who makes her fall asleep for a hundred years, to be woken at the end of that time by a prince.

PITT, WILLIAM, THE ELDER, 1ST EARL OF CHATHAM (1708–78) English statesman, known as the Great Commoner. His direction of Britain's policy in the **Seven Years War*** laid the foundations of the country's imperial power.

PITT, WILLIAM, THE YOUNGER (1759–1806) Son of William Pitt the Elder, he became, at the age of 24, Britain's youngest ever prime minister and later led the country during the period of the Revolutionary and Napoleonic wars with France. (In 1799 he was responsible for introducing income tax, presented as a temporary measure to support the war effort.) His chief political opponent was the Whig **Charles James Fox**.*

POPISH PLOT (1678) A supposed conspiracy to assassinate Charles II and reestablish Roman Catholicism by setting his brother James on the throne. Invented by **Titus Oates** and Israel Tongue, this fictitious plot had the desired effect of exciting a wave of anti-Catholicism. Its apparent discovery led to many unjust executions and the exclusion of Roman Catholics from Parliament.

PORTEOUS RIOTS (1736) Responding to an aggressive demonstration against the execution of a smuggler in Edinburgh, Captain John Porteous ordered the city guard to fire into the crowd, causing several deaths. For this he was tried and sentenced to death. When he was subsequently granted a reprieve, an armed mob broke into the prison, seized him, and hanged him. The episode was given an added political edge by Jacobite sympathies among the rioters as well as among those high-ranking Scots who supported them. It was later used by Walter Scott in his novel *Heart of Midlothian* (1818).

PRETENDERS, OLD AND YOUNG So called because they were pretenders (i.e., claimants) to the English throne. The Old Pretender was James Edward

Stuart, James II's son; the Young Pretender, known as **Bonnie Prince Charlie**, was the Old Pretender's son, Charles Edward Stuart. The Stuart pretender in exile was sometimes referred to by Jacobites as "the King over the water." See JACOBITE.

PRIESTLEY, JOSEPH (1733–1804) Presbyterian minister and British chemist who was one of the discoverers of oxygen. A supporter of the French Revolution, he was forced by mob violence and public hostility to emigrate to America in 1794.

QUAKERS See NONCONFORMISTS.

RESTORATION The term refers specifically to the restoration of the monarchy in 1660 after the collapse of the Protectorate, but it is also used more generally, in talking about English culture, to designate the three or four decades that followed.

ROTATION OF CROPS See AGRICULTURAL REVOLUTION.

ROTTEN BOROUGHS AND POCKET BOROUGHS Terms used in the early nineteenth century to refer to parliamentary constituencies with so few electors that they were "in the pocket" of a single individual or family with the power to dictate who should be elected. The effect of this, until it was partially remedied by the 1832 **Reform Act**, was to give the landowning classes in control of these boroughs disproportionate influence in Parliament, to the disadvantage of the growing population in industrial areas.

ROUSSEAU, JEAN-JACQUES (1712–78) French writer and social philosopher, born in Geneva, to whom we owe the popular concept of the "noble savage" (though the term itself goes back to Dryden's *The Conquest of Granada*). Rousseau's belief in the essential goodness of human nature, uncorrupted by society, was vastly influential. Three of his works, in particular, had a direct impact on aspects of late eighteenth-century culture: his novel *Julie, ou la Nouvelle Héloïse* (1761), on the development of Romanticism; his analysis of the relationship between the individual and society in *Du Contrat social* (1762), on revolutionary politics; the theory of education he set out in *Émile* (1762), on prevailing attitudes to childhood. His posthumous *Confessions* (1782 and 1789) opened the way for modern autobiographical writing.

ROYAL ACADEMY An institution founded in 1768 for the promotion of painting, sculpture, and architecture. Among its founder members were the British artists **Sir Joshua Reynolds** (1723–92), who became its first president, and **Thomas Gainsborough** (1727–88).

ROYAL SOCIETY Britain's oldest and most important scientific society. Founded in 1660 on the back of earlier informal meetings among a group of scientists, it was granted a royal charter in 1662. Among its early members were the chemist **Robert Boyle**, formulator of Boyle's law on gases; the physicist **Robert Hooke**; **Christopher Wren**, the architect of St. Paul's Cathedral; **Isaac Newton***; and the diarist **Samuel Pepys**.

SCOTTISH ENLIGHTENMENT Name given to the flowering of culture in eighteenth-century Scotland. It included such diverse figures as **Robert Adam**,* **David Hume**,* **Adam Smith**,* and **James Watt**.*

SETTLEMENT, ACT OF (1701) The Act of Parliament designed to ensure Protestant succession to the English throne. It stipulated that if William III and his sister-in-law Anne, next in line to the throne, should both die without heir, the crown should go to James I's granddaughter Sophia, Electress of Hanover, and to her Protestant descendants. In the event, Sophia died in 1714, the same year as Queen Anne, and her son succeeded to the throne as George I.

SEVEN YEARS WAR (1756–63) A European war whose central elements were Austria's wish to recover Silesia from Prussia, and France's conflict with England (Prussia's ally) over colonial interests. The English victories of **Clive** in India and **Wolfe*** in North America established the basis of Britain's empire and made it the main European colonial power. Early in the war, Admiral **John Byng**, having failed to prevent the French from taking Minorca, was court-martialed and shot – "*pour encourager les autres,*" as Voltaire sardonically put it. See EAST INDIA COMPANY.

SHAFTESBURY, ANTHONY ASHLEY COOPER, 3RD EARL OF (1671–1713) English politician and philosopher, grandson of the Restoration statesman who was satirized as Achitophel in Dryden's *Absalom and Achitophel*. His *Characteristicks of Men, Manners, Opinions, Times* (1711) made an influential contribution to contemporary debates on morality, aesthetics, and religion.

SMITH, ADAM (1723–90) Scottish economist whose *Inquiry into the Nature and Causes of the Wealth of Nations* (1776) became the manifesto of the free-trade movement. It had an important influence on the *laissez-faire* economic policies of the nineteenth century, which sought to leave market forces unfettered by government interference.

> **From Adam Smith, *An Enquiry into the Nature and Causes of the Wealth of Nations* (1776), Chapter 5**
>
> Every man is rich or poor according to the degree in which he can afford to enjoy the necessaries, conveniences, and amusements of human life. But after the division of labour has once thoroughly taken place, it is but a very small part of these with which a man's own labour can supply him. The far greater part of them he must derive from the labour of other people, and he must be rich or poor according to the quantity of that labour which he can command, or which he can afford to purchase.

SOUTH SEA BUBBLE (1720) The stock boom in the South Sea Company, which had been set up in 1711 to trade with Spanish America. A frenzy of speculative investment in 1720 dangerously inflated the value of its shares. When the bubble burst, many were ruined and the subsequent scandal implicated government ministers and the king.

SPANISH SUCCESSION, WAR OF THE (1701–14) A European war triggered by the death of Charles II of Spain in 1700. Britain's main concern was to check the expansionist ambitions of Louis XIV, whose grandson Philip had claimed the Spanish throne. In a series of brilliant victories at Blenheim (1704), Ramillies (1706), Oudenarde (1708), and Malplaquet (1709), the duke of Marlborough and his European allies defeated the French, enabling Britain, in spite of later reverses, to make an advantageous peace under the Treaty of Utrecht (1713).

TEST ACTS (1673, 1678, 1681) Various Acts of Parliament in England and Scotland designed to ensure that Nonconformists and Roman Catholics could not hold public office or enter Parliament.

TOLERATION ACT (1689) Act of Parliament, passed in the wake of the **Glorious Revolution**,* to allow **Nonconformists*** freedom of worship.

TORIES See WHIGS AND TORIES.

TRANSPORTATION System of transporting criminals to colonial territories overseas. They were forced to work there as laborers, often virtual slaves, for a period of years, or sometimes for life. From the seventeenth century until the **American Revolution*** the usual destination was America or the West Indies. Thereafter, the convict ships went to Australia – initially to Botany Bay in New South Wales. The practice was abandoned in 1868.

TURNPIKES Gates or spiked barriers across a road, which could only be passed on payment of a toll. The first turnpike roads in England were introduced by Act of Parliament in 1663. The revenue generated enabled the roads to be maintained to a higher standard than before, allowing the development of faster and more efficient coach services. By the end of the eighteenth century there were over 20,000 miles of turnpike road in Britain, but the coming of railways in the following century contributed to their decline.

UNIFORMITY, ACTS OF A number of Acts were passed in the sixteenth century to impose the use of various editions of the **Book of Common Prayer** (see p. 165). The Act of 1662, part of the **Clarendon Code**,* was more draconian in its penalties. Some 2,000 clergymen who refused to accept it lost their livings.

UNION, ACTS OF Acts of Union in 1536 and 1542 had linked England and Wales. The 1707 Act of Union united England and Scotland to form Great Britain, though James I had already taken the title "king of Great Britain" back in 1604. In 1800 a further Act of Union incorporated Ireland, creating the United Kingdom on 1 January 1801.

UNITARIANS See NONCONFORMISTS.

VANBRUGH, SIR JOHN (1664–1726) Writer and architect. After a career as a fashionable Restoration playwright, he designed some of England's most successful baroque buildings, including Castle Howard and Blenheim Palace.

VOLTAIRE (François-Marie Arouet, 1694–1778) Recognized during his lifetime as Europe's greatest man of letters, Voltaire was a writer on history, science, and philosophy as well as being the author of several dramas. His most popular work today is the satirical moral fable *Candide* (1759), with its naive hero and his incorrigibly optimistic tutor, **Dr. Pangloss**, who remains convinced through every misfortune that "*all is for the best in the best of possible worlds.*"

To the end of his long career Voltaire continued to put the case for reason and humanity against the claims of authority, prejudice, and blind emotion.

WALPOLE, ROBERT (1676–1745) Regarded as Britain's first prime minister (1721–42), Walpole dominated political life under George I and II. A Whig politician, he was in later years opposed by the Tory statesman William Pitt the Elder. The restrictions he put on theatrical performances in his 1737 **Licensing Act** had the effect of stifling the development of English drama. Among his sons was the writer Horace Walpole.

WATT, JAMES (1736–1819) Scottish engineer and inventor. His improved version of the steam engine, developed in the 1760s, played a major part in the Industrial Revolution.

WEDGWOOD, JOSIAH (1730–95) British potter who opened a factory in Staffordshire in the mid-eighteenth century. The popularity of his unglazed stoneware, decorated with classical motifs, spread across Europe.

WHIGS and TORIES The two main political groupings that emerged in late seventeenth-century England. The Whigs were largely responsible for the **Glorious Revolution*** and remained politically dominant through much of the eighteenth century. Hampered by their association with Jacobitism, the Tories only returned from the political wilderness in the 1780s under the leadership of **William Pitt the Younger**.* Half a century later, under **Robert Peel**, they became the Conservatives, while the Whigs developed into the Liberal Party under **Gladstone*** during the 1860s.

WILKES, JOHN (1727–97) Radical politician and journalist whose turbulent career established him as a champion of individual liberty. As a young man he belonged to the notorious **Hellfire Club** that met in the ruins of St. Mary's Abbey at Medmenham, supposedly for Satanic orgies. Later he became an MP but was arrested and subsequently expelled from the House after issue no. 45 of his weekly paper the ***North Briton*** accused the government of lying in the king's speech. In spite of being repeatedly outlawed and expelled, he continued to be reelected on a tide of popular support and was finally allowed to take his seat as an MP.

WINDOW TAX A tax levied on the number of windows in each house. Introduced in the late seventeenth century to replace the hearth tax, it became increasingly onerous during the Revolutionary wars against France in the 1790s. People responded to it by boarding up their windows, and the tax was finally abolished in the mid-nineteenth century.

WOLFE, JAMES (1727–59) British soldier best known for his victory over the French in Quebec during the **Seven Years War**.* He led his forces up the Heights of Abraham to defeat the French general **Montcalm** but was mortally wounded in the final assault. His victory paved the way for British control of Canada.

The late eighteenth and early nineteenth centuries were the period of **Romanticism**.* In both political and cultural terms the dominant event was the **French Revolution**,* which began in 1789 and sent shock-waves throughout Europe. Before long, the initial enthusiasm of many observers had turned to disillusionment. Fear that sedition might spread across the Channel led to increasing political oppression during the 1790s. From 1792 to 1815 England was intermittently at war with France, first against the Revolutionary armies, then against **Napoleon**. The naval victory of **Trafalgar** (1805) secured England against invasion, and in 1815 the battle of **Waterloo** brought Napoleon's career to an end. Meanwhile, George III had gone mad (probably a result of porphyria), and from 1811–20 his son ruled as Prince Regent.

The industrialization of Britain through the nineteenth century saw a movement of population away from rural areas to London and the new industrial centers of the midlands and north. These urban agglomerations produced enormous wealth but also spawned conditions of appalling squalor and misery for many of their inhabitants. Attempts to respond to this changing social landscape resulted in a range of legislation such as the **Reform Acts**,* **Education Acts**,* **Factory Acts**,* and **Poor Laws**.*

Overseas, Britain was increasing its possessions, particularly in Africa. One way or another most of its military conflicts in the nineteenth century were related to questions of empire: the **Crimean War**,* the **Indian Mutiny**,* the **Afghan*** and **Zulu*** wars, and finally the **Boer Wars**.*

At home, the **Evangelical*** movement did much to influence the moral climate of Victoria's reign (1837–1901). Religious controversy, a continuing thread in the cultural life of the time, was intensified by the publication in 1859 of **Darwin's*** theory of evolution. By the end of the century, science and technology had changed the texture of everyday life. Railways, anesthetic gas, electric lighting, photography, bicycles, cars, and telephones were just a few of the inventions that marked the progress of the Victorian age.

AFGHAN WARS In the nineteenth century Afghanistan became a focal point in the struggle between Britain and Russia for influence in central Asia. The **first Afghan War** (1839–42), which began with a move to install an emir favorable to British interests, led to the slaughter of the British garrison as they retreated in 1842 from Kabul to India under a promise of safe-conduct. The **second Afghan War** (1878–80), remembered chiefly for General Roberts's epic march to relieve a British force besieged in Kandahar, was again fought to defuse the threat of a Russian invasion of India. In 1919 an Afghan invasion of western India set off the **third Afghan War**, which ended with a treaty that gave Afghanistan independence. See GREAT GAME.

ANGLO-CATHOLICISM A movement in the Church of England that grew out of the **Oxford Movement**.* It stressed the importance of Catholic tradition and ritual within Anglicanism.

ART NOUVEAU An ornate decorative style that favored long curving lines and sinuous forms. It was fashionable in the 1890s and the first decade of the twentieth century. The drawings of Aubrey Beardsley and the designs of Hector Guimard for the Paris métro are characteristic examples.

BOER WARS Wars between the Boers (Dutch settlers in South Africa, also known as **Afrikaners**) and the British. In the first of them (1880–1) the Transvaal gained independence under **Paul Kruger**. The second (1899–1902), and more brutal, was essentially a move by Britain to regain control of the Transvaal and its huge gold reserves. Tensions had already been aggravated by the **Jameson Raid** – an abortive attempt to invade the Transvaal four years earlier – but it was Kruger's denial of political rights to the British immigrants (Uitlanders) that provided the immediate pretext for war. In spite of early victories which enabled them to lay siege to **Mafeking** and **Ladysmith**, the outnumbered Boers were finally defeated. The war was marked by one of the first uses of **concentration camps**, in which the British general **Lord Kitchener** rounded up the Boer women and children rendered homeless by his scorched earth policy. Some 20,000 of them died.

BOXER RISING (1900) A nationalist rebellion against the western presence in China. The Boxers (so called because they belonged to a secret society known as the Fists of Righteous Harmony) marched on Peking (Beijing) and besieged the foreign legations. The uprising was suppressed by an international coalition.

BROAD CHURCH The moderates in the nineteenth-century Church of England who occupied the middle ground between the **Anglo-Catholics*** (High Church) on one side and the Protestant **Evangelicals*** (Low Church) on the other.

CATHOLIC EMANCIPATION ACT (1829) The Act allowed Roman Catholics, who had previously been liable to civil penalties for their faith, to enter Parliament and to hold most public offices. Further legislation in 1871 more or less completed the process of emancipation by enabling them to attend university.

CATO STREET CONSPIRACY (1820) A plot to assassinate members of the British cabinet and overturn the government. The conspirators were arrested in Cato Street and later hanged.

CHARTISM A working-class movement for political reform, born out of economic misery and named after the ''People's Charter'' drawn up in 1838. The Charter, which had 1.2 million signatures, made six demands: (1) universal male suffrage; (2) annual elections; (3) voting by ballot; (4) equal electoral districts; (5) abolition of the property qualification for MPs; (6) payment of MPs. In 1839 Parliament rejected the Charter out of hand. Two subsequent petitions in 1842 and 1848 were similarly dismissed.

CLAPHAM SECT A group of prominent **Evangelicals**,* nicknamed the Saints, who were active from about 1785 to 1830. They led the campaign against slavery and promoted missionary work. The most famous of them was **William Wilberforce**.*

CORN LAWS Laws enacted from the Middle Ages onwards to protect British agriculture by regulating the import and export of grain. In the early nineteenth century, legislation setting the price that home-grown corn had to reach before any could be imported from abroad provoked widespread resistance on the grounds that it kept the price of bread artificially high, to the advantage of landowners and the disadvantage of everyone else. The **Anti-Corn-Law League** was founded, leading in 1846 to the repeal of the Corn Laws by the Conservative prime minister **Sir Robert Peel**.

CRIMEAN WAR (1854–6) War fought mainly on the Crimean peninsula between Russia on one side and Turkey (the Ottoman empire), Britain, France, and Sardinia-Piedmont on the other. Britain's primary concern was to check Russian expansion in Europe. The focus of the war was the year-long siege of Sebastopol, punctuated by the battles of Alma, Balaclava – the occasion of the celebrated **charge of the Light Brigade** – and Inkerman. The Russians withdrew from Sebastopol in September 1855, leaving the way open for peace. Many of the casualties of the war were due to disease spread by the frightful conditions that **Florence Nightingale** set out to remedy.

DARWIN, CHARLES ROBERT (1809–82) British naturalist who developed the theory of evolution by natural selection, i.e., by the survival of those species, and characteristics within species, that are best adapted to their environment. The concept of evolution had been canvassed as far back as **Lucretius** in the first century BC, and more recently by the French naturalist **Jean-Baptiste Lamarck** (1744–1829), but it was Darwin's voyage to South America and the Pacific aboard the *Beagle* (1831–6) that provided convincing evidence. His observations led in 1859 to the publication of ***On the Origin of Species by Means of Natural Selection***. To many Victorians, Darwin's ideas were an assault on the foundations of religious faith – a concern highlighted by the debate at Oxford between Darwin's supporter T. H. Huxley and Bishop Samuel Wilberforce. The gradual acceptance of evolutionary theory had a profound effect on the temper of late nineteenth-century Britain.

DISRAELI, BENJAMIN (1804–81) Prime minister and novelist. As a Conservative MP in the 1840s he joined the **Young England** group, which was critical of the party leader Sir Robert Peel. Later, he served twice as prime minister (1868 and 1874–80) and led the opposition to **Gladstone's** first ministry (1868–74). His friendship with Queen Victoria reflected his position at the head of a Conservative Party that balanced a commitment to social reform with a growing sense of itself as the party of the British establishment. See also p. 239.

EDUCATION ACTS The Elementary Education Act (1870) laid the foundations of the modern British educational system by establishing School Boards – in effect, local education authorities – that were charged with setting up elementary schools in areas where none was available. A second Education Act (1880) made attendance at school compulsory up to the age of 10.

EVANGELICALS Members of a Low Church movement within the Anglican Communion that emphasized the authority of the Bible and the doctrine of salvation by faith. Their earnest conviction, social concern, and reforming zeal made them an influential force in both church and society from the late eighteenth century through much of the Victorian period.

FABIAN SOCIETY An organization founded in 1884 to bring about the gradual spread of socialism in Britain. It was named after the Roman general Fabius Maximus (d. 203 BC), whose cautious tactics (hence his nickname *Cunctator*, the Delayer) had helped to defeat Hannibal (see p. 86). Among early Fabians were **George Bernard Shaw**, **Sidney and Beatrice Webb**, **Annie Besant**, and **H. G. Wells**.

FACTORY ACTS A series of laws passed from the early nineteenth century onwards to protect workers. The first Factory Acts (1802 and 1819) limited the number of working hours for children in cotton mills and set the age at which they could be employed (9 years old), but it was not until **Lord Shaftesbury's** wider-ranging legislation of 1833 that factory inspectors were appointed to enforce such measures. Later Acts, particularly in the 1840s and 1850s, put more general limits on the hours of work and the age of employees.

Ernest Dowson, "Dregs" (1899)

The fire is out, and spent the warmth thereof,
(This is the end of every song man sings!)
The golden wine is drunk, the dregs remain,
Bitter as wormwood and as salt as pain;
And health and hope have gone the way of love
Into the drear oblivion of lost things.
Ghosts go along with us until the end;
This was a mistress, this, perhaps, a friend.
With pale, indifferent eyes, we sit and wait
For the dropt curtain and the closing gate:
This is the end of all the songs man sings.

FIN-DE-SIÈCLE (French = *end of century*) A term referring to the spirit of weary decadence supposedly engendered by the end of the century. It is applied particularly to the cultural atmosphere of late nineteenth-century France and England.

FRENCH REVOLUTION (1789–99) The social upheaval that overturned the Bourbon monarchy, demolished the feudal structures of French society, and sent tremors of Romantic enthusiasm and conservative horror across Europe. Premonitory rumblings had been heard for some time, but its start is traditionally dated from the storming of the Bastille fortress on July 14, 1789. Among early revolutionary voices were those of the great orator **Mirabeau** and the radical journalist **Jean-Paul Marat**, who was murdered in his bath by **Charlotte Corday**. The progress of the revolution led to the execution of **Louis XVI** in January 1793 and the emergence of political leaders such as **Georges Jacques Danton** and **Maximilien Robespierre**. It was the latter, known as the "Incorruptible," who presided over the "Reign of Terror" that sent thousands to the guillotine. The *coup d'état* of 1799 by which **Napoleon** established the Consulate can be taken to mark the end of the Revolution. See JACOBINS.

FRENCH REVOLUTIONARY AND NAPOLEONIC WARS (1792–1815) Wars with France that had their origins in the Revolution and continued in response to Napoleon's plans for European domination. Popular memory of them is focused on the naval victory of **Lord Nelson*** at **Trafalgar** (1805), which put an end to Napoleon's hopes of invading England, and the successes of Arthur Wellesley (future **duke of Wellington**) both in the Peninsular War (1808–14) in Portugal and Spain, and in the final defeat of Napoleon at **Waterloo** (1815).

GLADSTONE, WILLIAM EWART (1809–98) Prime minister. Having entered Parliament as a Tory, he later became a Liberal and served four times as prime minister (1868–74, 1880–5, 1886, 1892–4). An opponent of Disraeli's imperialism, he sponsored a number of measures of social and Parliamentary reform, including the 1870 **Education Act*** and the introduction of secret ballots. His efforts to introduce a **Home Rule** bill, which would have repealed the 1801 **Act of Union*** and given Ireland a parliament responsible for its own domestic affairs, were unsuccessful and led to his resignation in 1894.

GOETHE, JOHANN WOLFGANG VON (1749–1832) One of the great figures of European culture. The extraordinary range of his accomplishments is reflected in his work as a statesman, scientist, painter, educationalist, translator, and above all in his contribution to world literature. His early auto-biographical novel *The Sorrows of Young Werther* (1774) took Europe by storm and became a powerful influence on the development of the **Romantic Movement**. Later works included the drama *Iphigenia on Tauris* (1787), which reflected the classical interests inspired by his stay in Italy, the novel *Wilhelm Meister's Apprenticeship* (1795–6), and his masterpiece, the poetic drama *Faust* (1808).

GORDON, CHARLES GEORGE (1833–85) British general, known as Chinese Gordon for his role in suppressing the Taiping rebellion against the Qing (Manchu) dynasty in 1864. His death in Khartoum after defending the city against a ten-month siege by Sudanese rebels under the leadership of the **Mahdi** made him a national hero. The failure to get a relief force to him in time severely damaged Gladstone's government.

GREAT EXHIBITION (1851) Exhibition of industrial products from Britain and Europe that was planned by **Prince Albert** and held in the newly erected **Crystal Palace** in Hyde Park. It proved an extremely successful showcase for Victorian Britain's industrial dominance.

GREAT GAME Term first used of the nineteenth-century struggle for supremacy in Central Asia between the British and Russian empires. It is applied more specifically to the undercover activities of government agents in this context and is sometimes used loosely of the espionage world in general.

HEGEL, GEORG WILHELM FRIEDRICH (1770–1831) German philosopher. His unifying philosophy, based on a dialectical scheme that moves from thesis to antithesis and on to a higher synthesis, has influenced diverse political and philosophical groups. His principal works were *The Phenomenology of Mind* (1807), *Encyclopedia of the Philosophical Sciences* (1817), and *The Philosophy of Right* (1821).

IMPRESSIONISM A revolutionary movement in French painting that greatly influenced the development of modern art. Reacting against the historical dramas of Romantic art and the photographic realism of contemporary academic art, a number of painters – among them, Monet, Pissarro, Sisley, and Renoir – began to choose commonplace scenes and to experiment with ways of catching the transient effects of light. They held their first exhibition in 1874 and were dubbed Impressionists by a derisive journalist, alluding to the title of a painting by Monet, *Impression, soleil levant*. The revolution brought about by the eight Impressionist exhibitions between 1774 and 1886 affected not just art but also literature and music.

INDIAN MUTINY (1857–8) A revolt of Indian sepoys (native soldiers employed by the East India Company) in northern and central India that spiralled into a full-scale rebellion against British rule. The mutineers captured Delhi and besieged **Lucknow** and **Cawnpore** before British reinforcements arrived to suppress the mutiny with horrible ferocity. The administration of

India was afterwards transferred from the East India Company to the British government.

JACK THE RIPPER Notorious murderer who targeted prostitutes in the Whitechapel area of London, killing and mutilating at least seven of them between early August and early November 1888. His identity has never been established, but he left an enduring mark on the national consciousness.

JACOBINS The radical party that seized power in the National Assembly from the more moderate **Girondins** during the **French Revolution**.* They took their name from the Dominican convent in which their club had installed itself in 1789. It was the Jacobins, with **Danton** and **Robespierre** prominent among them, who inaugurated the Terror. In England the term was used of political radicals who were sympathetic to the Revolution, and has since come to be used of any revolutionary extremist.

JENNER, EDWARD (1749–1823) English physician who introduced **vaccination against smallpox**. In 1796 he discovered that a person inoculated with cowpox was immune from smallpox. (This was both more reliable and less dangerous than the method of inoculation with the disease itself that **Lady Mary Wortley Montagu** (1689–1762) had brought back from Turkey earlier in the century.) For the rest of his life Jenner worked to promote the procedure, for which he himself coined the term *vaccination* (Latin, *vacca* = cow).

LUDDITES Initially these were Nottingham textile workers who in 1811 destroyed new machinery they thought threatened their traditional livelihood. The movement, named after its supposed originator Ned Ludd, spread north and west in the following year. It was violently suppressed by the authorities but enjoyed a brief resurgence a few years later.

LYELL, SIR CHARLES (1797–1875) Scottish geologist whose work did much to establish that the formation of the earth's crust took place over huge spans of geological time. His *Principles of Geology* (1830–3) had an important influence on Darwin's theory of evolution.

MACAULAY, THOMAS BABINGTON (1800–59) English historian, politician, and poet. His immensely successful five-volume *History of England* (1849–61), which dealt primarily with the **Glorious Revolution*** (see p. 187) and its aftermath, was a seminal example of what came to be known as the **Whig**

interpretation of British history. This perspective, which tends to shape events into a story of progress towards current prosperity under the blessings of a constitutional monarchy, was later adopted by Macaulay's nephew and great-nephew, George Otto Trevelyan and George Macaulay Trevelyan.

MALTHUS, THOMAS ROBERT (1766–1834) English economist whose *Essay on the Principle of Population* (1798, expanded 1803) argued that the growth in population, if unchecked, will always outstrip the increase in food production and thereby thwart hopes of social improvement. His views had considerable impact on nineteenth-century social policy.

> *From* Thomas Malthus, *An Essay on the Principle of Population as it Affects the Future Improvements of Society* (1798), Chapter 1
>
> Population, when unchecked, increases in a geometrical ratio. Subsistence increases only in an arithmetical ratio. A slight acquaintance with numbers will shew the immensity of the first power in comparison of the second.
>
> By that law of our nature which makes food necessary to the life of man, the effects of these two unequal powers must be kept equal.
>
> This implies a strong and constantly operating check on population from the difficulty of subsistence. This difficulty must fall somewhere and must necessarily be severely felt by a large portion of mankind.

MARX, KARL (1818–83) German social philosopher, historian, and economist. In collaboration with **Friedrich Engels** (1820–95) he wrote the *Communist Manifesto* (1848), which set out the authors' view, strongly influenced by **Hegel**,* that social change is the result of a dialectical process driven by class struggle. The economic implications of this philosophy, later known as **dialectical materialism**, are explored in Marx's *Das Kapital* (1867–95).

MCADAM, JOHN LOUDON (1756–1836) Scottish engineer who invented the macadam road surface at the end of the eighteenth century. His method of raising the road to facilitate drainage and then covering it with crushed granite followed by light stones, all bound together with gravel or slag, greatly increased the speed and comfort of coach travel. Together with **Thomas Telford** (1757–1834), another civil engineer from Scotland, he transformed the British road network.

MILL, JOHN STUART (1806–73) Economist and philosopher, son of the historian and philosophical radical James Mill. As the author of *Principles of Economy* (1848), *On Liberty* (1859), *Utilitarianism* (1861), and *The Subjection of Women* (1869), he had an important influence on nineteenth-century thought, arguing cogently for individual rights and sexual equality.

> **From John Stuart Mill, *On Liberty* (1859), "Introductory"**
>
> The object of this Essay is to assert one very simple principle . . . That principle is, that the sole end for which mankind are warranted, individually or collectively, in interfering with the liberty of action of any of their number, is self-protection. That the only purpose for which power can be rightfully exercised over any member of a civilized community, against his will, is to prevent harm to others. His own good, either physical or moral, is not a sufficient warrant . . . The only part of the conduct of any one, for which he is amenable to society, is that which concerns others. In the part which merely concerns himself, his independence is, of right, absolute. Over himself, over his own body and mind, the individual is sovereign.

MUDIE'S CIRCULATING LIBRARY The most popular of Britain's nineteenth-century subscription libraries. Established in 1842 by Charles Edward Mudie, it came to wield considerable power, since its purchases could account for up to 75 percent of a book's sales. For half a century Mudie played an important part in guiding the scope and tone of the Victorian novel and also in maintaining its standard form of publication in three volumes, which conveniently enabled him to distribute a single work among three subscribers.

NABOB Anglicized version of the Urdu word for governor. It was used in the eighteenth and nineteenth centuries of Englishmen, like Jos Sedley in Thackeray's *Vanity Fair*, who had made fortunes in India.

NASH, JOHN (1752–1835) Outstanding Regency architect who worked for the future George IV to redesign areas of central London. He was responsible for the layout of Regent's Park and Regent Street, as well as for the oriental fantasy that became the Brighton Pavilion.

NELSON, HORATIO (1758–1805) British admiral who achieved heroic status in the Revolutionary and Napoleonic wars against France. In different engagements he lost the use of his right eye and also of his right arm, which had to be amputated above the elbow. During the battle of Copenhagen (1801) he famously ignored a signal to disengage by putting his telescope to the blind eye and claiming not to see it. His scandalous liaison with Emma Hamilton, wife of the British ambassador in Naples, added to his celebrity. Mortally wounded during the battle of **Trafalgar** (1805), he died aboard his flagship *Victory*.

OXFORD MOVEMENT A nineteenth-century religious movement within the Church of England that emphasized links with Catholic tradition and practice. It was launched by a sermon preached in 1833 by **John Keble** and became an influential counter-current to **Evangelicalism**.* Its ideas were spread in a series of 90 *Tracts for the Times* (1833–41) – many of them written by **John Henry Newman** – from which the movement acquired its alternative name, **Tractarianism**. After Newman was received into the Roman Catholic Church in 1845, the movement, sustained by Keble and **E. B. Pusey**, evolved into **Anglo-Catholicism**.*

PALEY's WATCH The phrase refers to the analogy drawn by the Anglican priest and theologian William Paley (1743–1805) between a watch, which pre-supposes the existence of a watchmaker, and the universe, which, he argued, similarly presupposes the existence of a Creator.

PETERLOO MASSACRE In the summer of 1819 troops were sent in to break up a mass meeting about Parliamentary reform that was being held in St. Peter's Fields, Manchester. They killed 11 people and injured many more. The episode was given the name "Peterloo massacre" in ironic reference to the battle of Waterloo.

PHOENIX PARK MURDERS The assassination in 1882 of the secretary of state for Ireland and his deputy. They were stabbed to death in Phoenix Park (Dublin) by Irish nationalists.

POLICE FORCE Modern policing dates from **Sir Robert Peel's** Metropolitan Police Act in 1829. Previously, the **Bow Street Runners**, founded by Henry Fielding and his half-brother in the mid-eighteenth century, had acted as paid thief-takers. Peel's Act introduced a regular force in London, which was extended to the provinces in the middle of the century.

POOR LAWS A number of laws were passed for the relief of the poor from the sixteenth century onwards. The **Speenhamland system**, established in the late eighteenth century and in general use for the first three decades of the nineteenth, supplemented laborers' wages from the parish rates according to the price of corn and the size of their family. This had the drawback of encouraging employers to keep wages artificially low. The **Poor Law Amendment Act** (1834) abolished it and instead forced the poor into workhouses, where conditions were designed to make almost anything else seem preferable. This is the origin of the Victorian workhouse.

POSTAGE A form of public postal service was in existence from the seventeenth century, but costs were calculated by distance and paid by the receiver. The modern system, including the use of postage stamps, was introduced by **Rowland Hill** in 1840 with the uniform **penny post**.

PRE-RAPHAELITE BROTHERHOOD A group formed in 1848 by **Dante Gabriel Rossetti**, **William Holman Hunt**, and **John Everett Millais** in reaction against the banality of establishment art. They turned to medieval themes and looked for inspiration among painters earlier than Raphael (d. 1520), who was regarded by many of their contemporaries as the pinnacle of western art. The group only lasted a few years, but, championed by **Ruskin**,* it had a considerable impact on nineteenth-century British art (and, to a lesser extent, literature), particularly on figures such as **Edward Burne-Jones** and **William Morris**.

PRIVATE OF THE BUFFS Private John Moyse of the Royal Kent Regiment (the Buffs) was captured in China in 1860 by a party of Tartars and subsequently beheaded for refusing to kowtow before the mandarin officer in command. He was celebrated as a type of rugged English heroism in the poem "The Private of the Buffs" by Sir Francis Hastings Doyle.

PUBLIC SCHOOLS The traditional British public school owes much of its ethos and organization to reforms carried out in the nineteenth century by **Thomas Arnold**, headmaster of Rugby School from 1828 to 1842. He took the rowdy, brutal institution that had developed out of the seventeenth-century grammar school and imbued it with a sense of moral earnestness inspired by ideals of

> *From* **Francis Hastings Doyle, "The Private of the Buffs"**
>
> Last night, among his fellow roughs,
> He jested, quaffed and swore;
> A drunken private of the Buffs,
> Who never looked before.
> To-day, beneath the foeman's frown,
> He stands in Elgin's place,
> Ambassador from Britain's crown,
> And type of all her race . . .
>
> Yes, honour calls! – with strength like steel
> He put the vision by;
> Let dusky Indians whine and kneel,
> An English lad must die.
> And thus, with eyes that would not shrink,
> With knee to man unbent,
> Unfaltering on its dreadful brink,
> To his red grave he went . . .

gentlemanly conduct and Christian responsibility. In practice, what resulted was a highly effective mechanism for defining and fostering the nation's administrative elite.

RAILWAYS In the eighteenth century railways were horse-drawn and used primarily for transporting coal short distances from the collieries. It was the development of the steam locomotive by **Richard Trevithick** at the turn of the century, leading in 1829 to **George Stephenson's *Rocket***, that laid the foundations of railway travel. The Stockton and Darlington railway opened in 1825, and in 1830 the Liverpool and Manchester Railway became the first line to carry passengers by steam engine. From then on, and particularly during the period of feverish speculation in the 1840s known as "**railway mania**," the rail network expanded rapidly across the country.

REFORM ACTS Three measures for electoral reform were passed in the nineteenth century, in 1832, 1867, and 1884. The 1832 Reform Act was the most controversial, extending the franchise, abolishing many of the **rotten and pocket boroughs*** (see p. 196), and providing more representation for the new industrial centers. The two subsequent Acts further extended the franchise, though it was 1918 before all adult males got the vote, and not until 1928 that women achieved full voting equality with men.

REGENCY (1811–20) The years during which the Prince of Wales (the future George IV) acted as regent for his mad father George III. It was a period characterized by its own styles of architecture, dress, and decoration.

ROMANTICISM A cultural movement that swept western Europe in the late eighteenth and early nineteenth centuries. Turning away from the values of order, reason, and restraint associated with **classicism**, it exalted the responses of the individual, putting a new emphasis on imagination, emotion, and spontaneity. A concern with the seductive complexities of the self and the beauties of the natural world are both characteristic of Romanticism. Its sympathies were revolutionary in political as well as cultural terms. Goethe, Schiller, Rousseau, Hugo, and Delacroix are among the figures associated with European Romanticism.

RUSKIN, JOHN (1819–1900) British art and social critic who had a commanding influence on Victorian cultural taste. A champion of **Turner**, and later of the **Pre-Raphaelites**,* he was also a leading enthusiast for the nineteenth-century revival of **Gothic architecture**. Among his works are *Modern Painters*

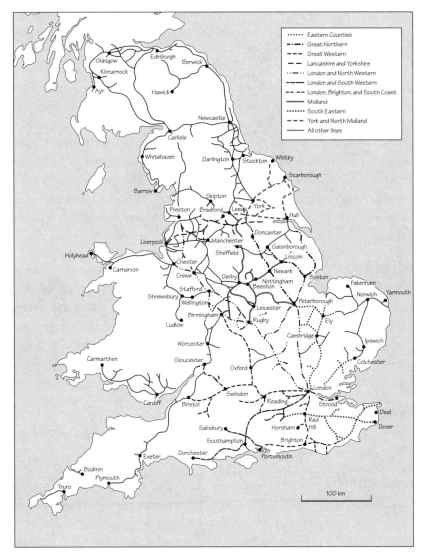

Map 5 (a) The railway system *c.* 1850; (b) The completed railway network
c. 1890
Source: Pope, Rex, *Atlas of British Social and Economic History since c.* 1700
(London: Routledge, 1990).

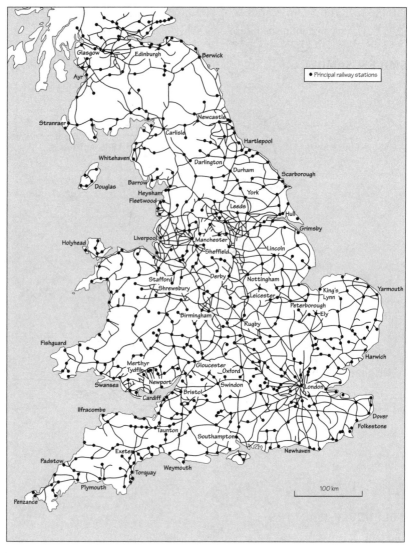

Map 5 (b)

(1843–60), *The Seven Lamps of Architecture* (1849), *The Stones of Venice* (1851–3), and his unfinished autobiography *Praeterita* (1885–9).

SMILES, SAMUEL (1812–1904) British writer, best remembered for *Self-Help* (1859), an enormously successful book which encapsulated Victorian belief in the virtue of work and the possibilities of self-betterment.

From **Samuel Smiles, *Self-Help* (1859), Preface to the 1886 edition**

The object of the book briefly is, to re-inculcate these old-fashioned but wholesome lessons – which perhaps cannot be too often urged, – that youth must work in order to enjoy, – that nothing creditable can be accomplished without application and diligence, – that the student must not be daunted by difficulties, but conquer them by patience and perseverance, – and that, above all, he must seek elevation of character, without which capacity is worthless and worldly success is naught.

SMITH, JOSEPH (1805–44) Founder of the **Mormon church**, which was based on the revelation to Smith of the sacred Book of Mormon. After his death, the Mormons established themselves in Salt Lake City, Utah, under the leadership of **Brigham Young**.

STAGECOACH The standard mode of public transport in Britain before the coming of the railways. In use from the mid-seventeenth century, the stage-coach enjoyed its heyday in the early nineteenth century, when improvements in the roads enabled it to offer a fast and efficient service that could take a passenger from London to Edinburgh in under 48 hours.

TOLPUDDLE MARTYRS Six Dorset farm laborers transported to Australia in 1834, essentially because they'd formed a trades union. They were pardoned, after pressure from the public, in 1836.

UTILITARIANISM An ethical doctrine that judges actions according to whether they produce happiness or the reverse. The best action is the one that produces the greatest happiness, and the least pain, for the greatest number of people. Foreshadowed in the philosophy of David Hume, it was expounded by Jeremy Bentham in *An Introduction to the Principles of Morals and Legislation* (1789). John Stuart Mill's *Utilitarianism* (1861) presents a modified version of Bentham's doctrine, which had a significant impact on nineteenth-century social thinking.

WILBERFORCE, WILLIAM (1759–1833) Leading parliamentary opponent of the slave trade. With other members of the **Clapham Sect*** he founded the **Society for the Abolition of the Slave Trade** in 1787. Twenty years later, in 1807, the trade was outlawed by Act of Parliament. Wilberforce went on to support a campaign for the abolition of slavery itself, which was finally successful a few weeks after his death.

WOLLSTONECRAFT, MARY (1759–97) Writer and teacher. Her brave attack on contemporary prejudice in *A Vindication of the Rights of Woman* (1792) made her a pioneer of the women's movement. Wife of the social philosopher **William Godwin**, she died shortly after the birth of their daughter, the future **Mary Shelley**.

From **Mary Wollstonecraft,** *A Vindication of the Rights of Women* **(1792), Chapter 3**

Women are everywhere in this deplorable state; for, in order to preserve their innocence, as ignorance is courteously termed, truth is hidden from them, and they are made to assume an artificial character before their faculties have acquired any strength. Taught from their infancy that beauty is woman's sceptre, the mind shapes itself to the body, and roaming round its gilt cage, only seeks to adore its prison. Men have various employments and pursuits which engage their attention, and give a character to the opening mind; but women, confined to one, and having their thoughts constantly directed to the most insignificant part of themselves, seldom extend their views beyond the triumph of the hour.

ZULU WAR As part of the imperial "scramble for Africa" the British invaded Zululand in January 1879. They were fiercely resisted by the Zulus and their king Cetshwayo, who won a bloody victory at the **battle of Isandlwana**. Within months, however, modern weaponry had tipped the balance in Britain's favor and the Zulus were defeated. The war is partly remembered for the heroism of a small group of defenders who held the supply station at **Rorke's Drift** against a large force of Zulus eager to follow up the victory at Isandlwana. The action resulted in the award of 11 Victoria Crosses.

Modernism, with its fractured images and calculated incoherence, was an apt response to the first two decades of the twentieth century, both to the legacy of intellectual upheaval inherited from the Victorians and to the cataclysmic violence of the new age. The devastating human cost of **World War I*** (1914–18) was separated by only 20 years from **World War II*** (1939–45). Between them came the economic depression of the 1930s and the concurrent rise of fascism. Though Britain played no official part in the **Spanish Civil War**,* the conflict nonetheless provided a focus for political tensions between left and right that had been growing through the decade.

The end of World War II saw the dawn of the atomic age and the emergence of America and Russia as the two dominant world powers. Political alignments quickly changed to produce a stand-off, dubbed the **Cold War**,* between the western powers and the communist countries of the eastern bloc.

In the postwar decades Britain gradually divested itself of its empire, though not without murderous local interludes such as the **Malayan emergency**, the **Mau Mau** revolt in Kenya, and the **EOKA** terrorist campaign in Cyprus. The 1956 **Suez crisis*** was regarded by many as the death knell of Britain's days as an imperial power. In 1973 the UK became a member of the European Economic Community (EEC).

Troubles in Northern Ireland between the Protestant majority and Catholic supporters of a united Ireland, spearheaded by the **IRA** (Irish Republican Army) and its political wing **Sinn Fein**, have been a major preoccupation since 1968. Elsewhere, the **Falklands War**,* the **Gulf War**,* the wars in **Afghanistan** and **Iraq**,* and the so-called "**War on Terror**"* have provided a background of continuing international conflict in which Britain has been more or less closely involved.

The social changes taking place against this background have been immense. In the years following World War I a new spirit of emancipation finally brought equal voting rights for women. The mood at the end of World War II gave impetus to a further range of social measures introduced by the 1945 Labour government, among them the launching of the **National Health Service**. The 1960s saw the beginnings of a cultural sea-change, reflected in the rise of feminism and the spread of more liberal attitudes to a variety of social and moral issues. At the same time the growth of car ownership and the rapid development of air travel opened the way to significant changes in lifestyle. Since then, the explosion of computer technology has transformed the tenor of daily life.

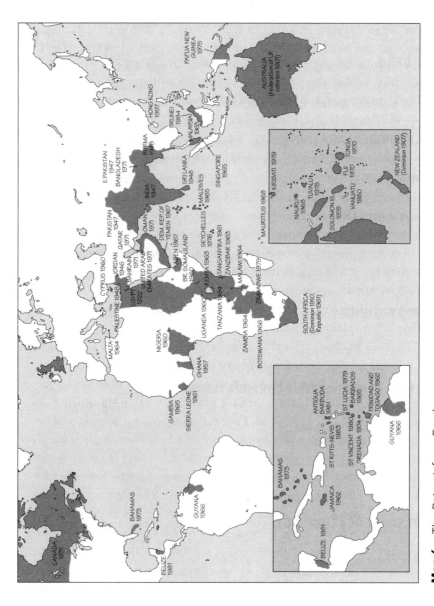

Map 6 The Retreat from Empire

Source: Cannon, John (ed.), *Oxford Companion to British History* (Oxford: Oxford University Press, 1997).

ABDICATION CRISIS (1936) The constitutional crisis precipitated by Edward VIII's determination to marry an American divorcée, Wallis Simpson. The combined opposition of Prime Minister **Stanley Baldwin** and other members of the British establishment, notably church leaders, forced him to abdicate before he was crowned. He was succeeded by George VI.

ART DECO A style of decorative art launched in the mid-1920s. Over the next decade its elegant streamlined forms, geometrical patterns, and bright colors revolutionized architecture and design in both Europe and America.

BALFOUR DECLARATION (1917) A statement of policy by the British foreign secretary Arthur Balfour, declaring the government's support for a Jewish homeland in Palestine.

BLACK AND TANS Name given to the auxiliary soldiers recruited by the British for the Royal Irish Constabulary in 1920–1. Dressed in dark green caps and khaki uniforms with black belts (hence their name), they acted to suppress the Irish republicans with a brutality that made them hated and feared.

BLOODY SUNDAY A grim landmark in the ongoing conflict between Catholics and Protestants in Northern Ireland. On January 30, 1972 British troops opened fire on Catholic protesters in Londonderry, killing 13 people.

BRITISH BROADCASTING CORPORATION The BBC was established as a public body under Royal Charter in 1927, with **John** (later **Lord**) **Reith** as its first director-general. It enjoyed a broadcasting monopoly that lasted until the introduction of commercial television in the early 1950s. Financed by a license fee, it is independent of Parliament and politically neutral, though its overseas broadcasts are paid for by the government.

BUTLER EDUCATION ACT (1944) The legislation introduced by the Conservative minister R. A. Butler to provide free compulsory education for all British children from the age of 5 to 15. The school leaving age was raised to 16 in 1972.

CAMBRIDGE SPIES Four Soviet agents recruited in the 1930s: **Guy Burgess**, **Donald Maclean**, **Kim Philby**, and the art historian **Anthony Blunt**, all of whom were drawn to communism while at Cambridge University. From positions of trust in the Foreign Office and the security services they were later able to pass valuable information to the Russians. When they were exposed (Burgess and Maclean in 1951, Philby in 1963, Blunt not until 1979), it became clear how much of their success had depended on the "old-boy network" that still dominated the upper reaches of British society. In 1991 John Cairncross (the "fifth man") was revealed as another member of the ring.

CAMPAIGN FOR NUCLEAR DISARMAMENT (CND) An organization formed in 1958 to campaign for the abandoning of nuclear weapons. It staged annual Easter marches from the government's atomic weapons research establishment at Aldermaston to Trafalgar Square in London. The waning threat of nuclear war in the 1960s led to a decline in its popularity, though it enjoyed a brief revival in the 1980s. In the heyday of the movement, the CND badge was a well-recognized symbol of left-wing allegiance, particularly among the young.

COLD WAR Name given to the hostile relations in the years following World War II between the Soviet Union and its eastern European allies on one side, and the USA and western Europe on the other. The Cold War was at its peak during the 1950s and early 1960s but did not come to an end until **Mikhail Gorbachev's** presidency of the USSR (1988–91). Throughout this period the threat of nuclear escalation prevented armed conflict, and it remained essentially an ideological war between communism and capitalism, fought by espionage, propaganda, and economic pressure. The term **iron curtain** was coined by Winston Churchill in 1946 for the divide between western and eastern Europe. A prominent symbol of the Cold War was the **Berlin Wall**, built in 1961 to separate East Berlin from the West and demolished in 1989. See CUBAN MISSILE CRISIS, MCCARTHYISM.

From **Winston Churchill's speech at Westminster College in Fulton, Missouri, March 5, 1946 ("Iron Curtain" speech)**

From Stettin in the Baltic to Trieste in the Adriatic an iron curtain has descended across the Continent. Behind that line lie all the capitals of the ancient states of Central and Eastern Europe. Warsaw, Berlin, Prague, Vienna, Budapest, Belgrade, Bucharest and Sofia; all these famous cities and the populations around them lie in what I must call the Soviet sphere, and all are subject, in one form or another, not only to Soviet influence but to a very high and in some cases increasing measure of control from Moscow.

CUBAN MISSILE CRISIS The single most dangerous episode of the **Cold War**,* when it looked for a time as though nuclear war was imminent. In 1962 the communist government of **Fidel Castro**, which had taken power in Cuba three years earlier, allowed the Soviet Union to install missile bases on the island, within striking distance of the USA. Faced with an ultimatum from American President **John F. Kennedy**, the Soviet leader **Nikita Khrushchev** agreed at the last moment to dismantle the bases.

CUBISM An artistic movement initiated by **Pablo Picasso** and **Georges Braque** in about 1907 that pioneered the development of abstract art. Influenced by the late paintings of **Cézanne**, it turned away from the naturalistic representation of external reality towards a conceptually driven art that aimed to represent the solidity of three-dimensional forms without creating the traditional illusion of the canvas as a three-dimensional space.

DADAISM A movement in art and literature which rejected the prevailing rationalist culture in order to create a nihilistic anti-art that exalted absurdity and unreason. Originating in Zurich in 1916 under the leadership of the poet **Tristan Tzara**, it later established itself in Paris where it influenced the future surrealists. Its most famous adherent was **Marcel Duchamp**, inventor of the "**ready-made**" – an everyday object arbitrarily assigned the status of a work of art.

DEPRESSION The period of economic depression, lasting through much of the 1930s, that followed the **Wall Street stock market crash** in 1929.

EASTER RISING Irish rebellion against British rule that started on Easter Monday 1916 with the aim of establishing an Irish Republic. Around 2,000 armed men took part, seizing the Dublin Post Office and other strategic buildings. There were many casualties in the subsequent street-fighting, but the rebellion failed to spread. After five days it was suppressed by the British army, and the leaders, including **Patrick Pearse** and **James Connolly**, were executed.

EXISTENTIALISM A philosophical movement that posits an absurd universe in which the individual must rely on personal acts of choice to define a relationship with a world that has no transcendent structure of meaning. Though its roots go back to the work of the nineteenth-century Danish philosopher **Søren Kierkegaard** (1813–55), twentieth-century existentialism owes most to the writings of the French philosopher **Jean-Paul Sartre** (1905–80), in particular to his *L'être et le néant* (1943, *Being and Nothingness*).

EXPRESSIONISM A movement in modern art and culture that includes a number of groups concerned with representing the internal reality of the emotions rather than the appearance of the external world. Its origins can be seen in some of the later works of **Van Gogh** and **Gauguin**, which anticipate the harsh lines, intense colors, and distorted figures that were characteristic of Expressionist groups such as the **Fauves** in France, and **Die Brücke** and **Der Blaue Reiter** in Germany. Similar preoccupations led to forms of Expressionism in literature, music, and the cinema in the first quarter of the twentieth century.

FALKLANDS WAR In 1982 Argentina invaded the British colony of the Falkland Islands. After fierce fighting, the task force sent to reclaim the islands defeated the Argentinians. The conflict was instrumental in securing Prime Minister **Margaret Thatcher's** reelection in the following year.

FESTIVAL OF BRITAIN An exhibition held in 1951 to mark the centenary of the Great Exhibition of 1851. It was intended to draw a line under the war-scarred decade of the 1940s and to showcase Britain's achievements in science and the arts. Its main focus was the South Bank site in London, for which the **Royal Festival Hall** was built.

FIRST WORLD WAR See WORLD WAR I.

FLAPPER Emancipated young woman of the 1920s, identified by her fashionable bobbed hair, uncorseted knee-length dresses, willingness to drink and smoke in public, and sexual independence.

FREUD, SIGMUND (1856–1939) Austrian psychiatrist who founded psychoanalysis. Though many of his specific claims have been challenged, his exploration of how unconscious forces, particularly sexual ones, affect our thought and behavior has changed the way we think about human nature. Among his pioneering studies were *The Interpretation of Dreams* (1899), *The Psychopathology of Everyday Life* (1904), *Totem and Taboo* (1913), and *Civilization and its Discontents* (1930).

FUTURISM An early twentieth-century movement in art and literature launched by the Italian poet **Filippo Marinetti's** Futurist manifesto, published in Paris in 1909. The movement glorified speed, technology, and the mechanization of the modern world. It did not survive World War I, but its enthusi-

224   SURVIVING HISTORY

asm for power and violence has been seen by some as prefiguring the cultural inclinations of fascism.

GENERAL STRIKE (1926) A national strike in Britain's key industries, called in support of miners threatened with a reduction in wages. It started on May 3 and lasted for nine days, until the Trades Union Congress, outmaneuvered by **Stanley Baldwin's** Conservative government, called it off. The following year, legislation was introduced to make general strikes illegal.

GOOD FRIDAY AGREEMENT (1998) An agreement brokered by the British and Irish governments to restore the Northern Irish Assembly and guarantee power-sharing between the Protestants and the Catholic minority in Northern Ireland. It proved little more enduring than earlier attempts to resolve the conflict but has remained the basis for hopes of a future settlement.

GULF WAR (1991) A military operation led by the USA and Britain to expel the Iraqi leader **Saddam Hussein** from **Kuwait**, which he had invaded in August 1990. The six-week campaign was successful but left Saddam still in power in Iraq. He was finally removed when the USA and Britain instigated a war against him in 2003.

HIROSHIMA The Japanese city about 400 miles southwest of Tokyo on which the first **atomic bomb** to be used in war was dropped on August 6, 1945. Justified by the USA on the grounds that it prevented the loss of life that would have followed a land invasion, the bomb destroyed the city and killed a total of some 130,000 people, well over a third of the population. Three days later a second atomic bomb was dropped on the city of **Nagasaki**. The surrender of the Japanese on August 14 brought World War II to an end.

HOLOCAUST The program of persecution and extermination of Jews carried out by the Nazis under **Adolf Hitler** between 1933 and 1945. Over 6 million Jews, about two thirds of European Jewry, were killed in concentration camps such as **Auschwitz**, **Treblinka**, **Belsen**, **Dachau**, and **Buchenwald**. Other groups, including Slavs and Gypsies, were also subject to programs of extermination by the Nazis.

HOME GUARD British volunteer defense force raised in 1940 to meet the threat of a German invasion. Disbanded in 1945, it numbered at its peak some 2 million armed men, drawn from those exempted from military service by their age or occupation.

HUNGER MARCHES A series of marches to London in the 1920s and 1930s by unemployed workers who hoped to draw attention to their plight. The most famous was the march in 1936 from **Jarrow**, a town in the northeast of England that had been particularly badly affected by the **Depression**.*

IRAQ WAR In 2003 a coalition army led by the USA and Britain invaded Iraq and toppled Saddam Hussein, leaving a power vacuum that competing interests struggled to fill. Unable to extricate themselves without discredit, the coalition forces had to remain in uneasy attendance. Iraq's supposed weapons of mass destruction, the ostensible reason for going to war, were never found.

JAZZ AGE A name given to the 1920s, particularly with reference to the sort of social milieu chronicled by **F. Scott Fitzgerald** – a world of **flappers**,* jazz, cocktails, fast living, and charleston dancing.

KOREAN WAR (1950–3) War between communist North Korea, supported by China, and non-communist South Korea, supported primarily by the United States. It began in 1950 when North Korea invaded the South across the **38th parallel**, established as the boundary between them after World War II. The conflict resulted in over 3 million deaths and ended in stalemate in 1953 with a recognition of the previously existing boundary.

LADY CHATTERLEY TRIAL In 1960 Penguin Books were prosecuted under the Obscene Publications Act for bringing out a paperback edition of **D. H. Lawrence's** *Lady Chatterley's Lover* (1928). The failure of this celebrated prosecution opened the door to a wide range of material previously regarded as unpublishable. It was a landmark in the history of censorship and a significant indication of changing social attitudes.

> *From* **Opening Address for the Prosecution in the trial of** *Lady Chatterley's Lover*, **October 20, 1960**
>
> You may think that one of the ways in which you can test this book, and test it from the most liberal outlook, is to ask yourselves the question, when you have read it through, would you approve of your young sons, young daughters – because girls can read as well as boys – reading this book. Is it a book that you would have lying around in your own house? Is it a book that you would even wish your wife or your servants to read?

MCCARTHYISM The anti-communist witchhunts orchestrated in the USA by Senator Joseph McCarthy in the early 1950s. As leader of a powerful senate committee, McCarthy promoted a climate of hysterical anti-communism that served his own political ends and ruined the careers of many people with left-wing sympathies. See COLD WAR.

MUNICH AGREEMENT A settlement agreed in 1938 by Britain, France, Italy, and Germany that allowed Germany to annex part of Czechoslovakia. In effect, Britain and France had sacrificed Czechoslovakia to avoid war with Hitler. It was the culmination of British Prime Minister **Neville Chamberlain's** policy of appeasement. He returned to England claiming to have won "peace with honor . . . peace in our time." How little the agreement meant to Hitler became apparent six months later when Germany invaded the rest of Czechoslovakia.

NATIONAL HEALTH SERVICE ACT (1946) The legislation that established the British National Health Service on the basis of recommendations made by the **Beveridge Report** in 1942. The Labour minister responsible for putting it into operation was **Aneurin Bevan**.

NATIONAL SERVICE A period of military service imposed on British men in the wake of World War II. When they reached 18, they were obliged to join the armed forces for 18 months (extended in 1950 to two years). This form of conscription was discontinued at the end of 1960.

NEW LOOK Name given to the style introduced by the dress designer **Christian Dior** in 1947. With its wide skirt, narrow waist, and accentuated bust and hips, it provided the classic western female outline of the 1950s.

NUREMBERG TRIALS (1945–6) The trials of 24 former Nazi leaders by an international military tribunal. Among those convicted and hanged were **Julius Streicher** and **Joachim von Ribbentrop**. **Hermann Goering** escaped the hangman by committing suicide. **Martin Bormann** was condemned to death in his absence. **Rudolf Hess** was condemned to life imprisonment, and **Albert Speer**, Hitler's chief architect, to 20 years.

PEARL HARBOR US naval base in Hawaii. It became notorious as the scene of a surprise Japanese air attack on December 7, 1941 which destroyed numerous ships and aircraft, killed over two thousand American personnel, and brought the United States into **World War II**.*

POLL TAX An ancient form of tax on each individual (poll = *head*) that was revived by **Margaret Thatcher's** Conservative government in 1989 to pay for local services. It led to widespread protests and was abandoned in 1991. See p. 160.

POSTIMPRESSIONISM Name first given by the critic **Roger Fry** to the art of a number of late nineteenth-century painters, forming no particular group, whose work developed out of Impressionism and in some cases reacted against it. Among them were **Cézanne**, **Van Gogh**, **Gauguin**, and **Toulouse-Lautrec**. Their art heralded several later movements such as **cubism**,* **expressionism**,* and **fauvism**.

PROFUMO AFFAIR One of the great twentieth-century scandals. In 1963 it was discovered that the secretary of state for war, **John Profumo**, had been having an affair with **Christine Keeler**, a call-girl who was at the same time involved with a Soviet naval attaché. Profumo was forced to resign after lying about it to Parliament. The affair fatally damaged **Harold Macmillan's** premiership and fueled an increasing cynicism, particularly among the young, about the British establishment.

SPANISH CIVIL WAR (1936–9) The civil war in Spain that overthrew the Republican government and established the dictatorship of the Nationalist General **Francisco Franco** (1892–1975). Supported by Italy and Germany, Franco's military revolt gradually overwhelmed the Republicans, in spite of help they received from Russia and the **International Brigade**. For many Europeans the war crystallized the ideological conflicts of the 1930s, offering a focus for liberal and left-wing idealism. Among the horrors it added to modern warfare was the use of indiscriminate air raids on a civilian population, initiated by the German destruction of the town of **Guernica** on April 26, 1937.

SUEZ CRISIS In 1956 Egypt nationalized the **Suez Canal**, thereby taking control of a vital supply line (notably for petrol from the Persian Gulf) which had previously been in the hands of the British and French. Supported by the Israelis, Britain and France launched a joint invasion of the canal zone but were quickly

228

forced into a humiliating withdrawal by international opposition. The episode was a stark indication of Britain's waning international power.

SUFFRAGETTES Term coined by the *Daily Mail* in 1906 for British women campaigning for the right to vote. In 1903 **Emmeline Pankhurst**, with the support of her daughter **Christabel**, had founded the Women's Social and Political Union, which favored direct action – "deeds not words" – in pursuit of its goal. For the next 11 years, until the campaign was called off at the start of World War I, the movement engaged in various forms of civil disobedience and disruption that were frequently punished by terms of harsh imprisonment. Women won a limited franchise in 1918, but it was not until 1928 that the vote was extended to all women over 21.

SURREALISM A movement in art and literature led by the poet **André Breton**, who published the Surrealist Manifesto in Paris in 1924. Influenced by Freud, the surrealists emphasized above all the importance of the subconscious. Dream, instinct, and unexplained juxtaposition could offer routes to a new kind of awareness. Though a number of other writers were associated with the movement, including **Paul Eluard** and **Louis Aragon**, it was the painters who exploited this insight most successfully, among them **Salvador Dali**, **René Magritte**, **Paul Delvaux**, **Max Ernst**, and **Yves Tanguy**.

TELEVISION The first practical television system was demonstrated by **John Logie Baird** in 1926. From 1936 the BBC operated a regular television service which was suspended during World War II and resumed in 1946. The first commercial channel in Britain opened in 1955.

VIETNAM WAR (1954–75) Following the surrender of the French army to nationalist forces at **Dien Bien Phu** in 1954, French Indochina was divided into two separate states, communist North Vietnam and non-communist South Vietnam. The ensuing civil war pitted the communist **Viet Cong**, supported by the Chinese and Russians, against the South Vietnamese government forces, supported by the USA. From 1961 the United States, anxious to check the spread of communism in South East Asia, increased its involvement in the war until, by 1969, there were over half a million American troops in Vietnam. It became a deeply unpopular war, causing waves of protest in America and Europe. In the end it proved unwinnable by the Americans, who began to withdraw their forces in 1973. An invasion of South Vietnam by the North in 1975 led in the following year to the unification of the two countries as the Socialist Republic of Vietnam.

VORTICISM A movement in art and literature that was founded by **Wyndham Lewis** in 1913 and petered out with the onset of World War I. Influenced by cubism and futurism, it sought to reflect the forms and feeling of a mechanical age.

WAR ON TERROR A concept developed in the wake of the terrorist attacks that destroyed New York's **World Trade Center** (the "Twin Towers") on September 11, 2001. Its initial focus was the Islamic fundamentalist **al-Qaida** group responsible for the attacks, to whom a variety of terrorist acts have since been attributed. The loosely defined "war on terror" went on to become an umbrella for a wide range of military campaigns and security legislation, including the wars in **Afghanistan** and **Iraq**,* Israeli action against the Palestinians, Russian action against the Chechens, and numerous legal and administrative measures claimed as necessary to guard against terrorist attack.

WARSAW PACT A military treaty between the USSR and the communist states of Eastern Europe. It was signed in 1955, following West Germany's admission to **NATO**, in order to counteract the western alliance. The pact dissolved in 1991.

WITTGENSTEIN, LUDWIG (1889–1951) Austrian philosopher whose thinking, particularly about the nature and limits of language, has had enormous influence on modern British philosophy and related disciplines. His major work was the *Tractatus Logico-Philosophicus* (1921).

WORLD WAR I (1914–18) War between the **Allied Powers** and the **Central Powers**. The Allies included Britain and its empire, France and Russia (the Triple Entente), and, from 1917, the USA; the Central Powers were Germany and Austria-Hungary, joined soon after the outbreak of war by Turkey. Sometimes referred to as the **Great War**, it was sparked by the assassination of the Archduke Franz-Ferdinand of Austria in Sarajevo, but its underlying causes reached back into the nineteenth century. There was fighting on a number of fronts, notably in the Balkans and the Middle East, including a disastrous allied landing on the **Gallipoli** peninsula. The main focus of the war, however, was the **western front**, where opposing forces were locked in the murderous stale-

230

mate of trench warfare along lines that ran from the Channel coast to Switzerland. Sites where the great battles took place such as Verdun, the Somme, Ypres, and Passchendaele have entered modern consciousness as symbols of four years of futile carnage. The war ended with Germany defeated, some 10 million dead, and both sides exhausted. The **treaty of Versailles** in 1919 imposed the kind of victors' justice that guaranteed a future renewal of hostilities.

WORLD WAR II (1939–45) War between the **Allied Powers** and the **Axis Powers**. The Allies included Britain and the Commonwealth, France and the Free French, Russia (from June 1941) and the United States (from December 1941); the main Axis Powers were Germany, Italy, and (from December 1941) Japan. The immediate cause of war, rooted in resentment at the peace terms imposed after World War I, was the aggressive expansion of Germany under **Adolf Hitler**, which the **Munich Agreement** in 1938 had failed to check. Among the episodes that most deeply impressed themselves on British folk memory were the evacuation of the British Expeditionary Force from **Dunkirk** in a flotilla of small boats (1940); the **Battle of Britain** (1940), in which RAF fighter command drove off the Luftwaffe, whose aerial bombardment of London (the **Blitz**) and air bases in the southeast had been intended to pave the way for an invasion; the fall of **Hong Kong** and **Singapore** to the Japanese (December 1941 and February 1942); the **battle of the Atlantic** to protect sea-routes against the threat of German battleships and U-Boats; the defeat of General Rommel's *panzer* (armored) divisions in North Africa at the **battle of El Alamein** (1942); the allied landings on the beaches of Normandy on **D-Day** (June 6, 1944) that led to victory in Europe; and the virtual obliteration of **Dresden** by massive bombing raids in the closing months of the war. Britain's war leader was **Winston Churchill** (1874–1965), whose personal bearing, and speeches in the House of Commons, established him as a symbol of indomitable resistance to Hitler's Germany. See also HIROSHIMA.

This is a spine of dates that lays out in chronological order some of the principal events glossed in the foregoing entries.

55 and 54 BC	**Julius Caesar** invades Britain but leaves no occupying force.
AD 43	The **Roman conquest** of Britain begins.
410	The Roman legions **leave Britain**.
ca. 450	The **Jutes, Angles, and Saxons** begin their invasion of Britain.
455	**Rome* is sacked** by the Vandals.
597	**St. Augustine's*** landing in Kent heralds the conversion of Britain to Christianity.
793	**Lindisfarne Abbey** is destroyed by the **Vikings,*** whose raids cause widespread terror and devastation for much of the next century.
878	**King Alfred's*** defeat of the Vikings at the **battle of Edington** checks their expansion, forcing them to remain within the boundaries of the **Danelaw**.
1066	The **Norman Conquest.*** Duke William of Normandy defeats King Harold Godwinson at the battle of Hastings and becomes King William I of England.
1086	William I orders the **Domesday*** survey to be made.
1215	King John is forced by his barons to sign the **Magna Carta.***
1337–1453	The **Hundred Years War.***
1348	The **Black Death*** reaches England.
1381	Wat Tyler leads the **Peasants' Revolt.***
1453	The **sack of Constantinople** by the Turks marks the last gasp of the Byzantine empire and gives an oblique stimulus to the **Renaissance*** by releasing numerous classical texts into the west.
1485	The defeat and death of Richard III at the battle of Bosworth Field ends the **Wars of the Roses*** (1455–85) and establishes the Tudor dynasty. Henry Tudor becomes King Henry VII.
1517	Martin Luther's 95 theses set in train the **Reformation.***
1588	The **Spanish Armada*** is defeated.
1600	The **East India Company*** is established.
1605	The **Gunpowder Plot.***
1620	The **Pilgrim Fathers*** set sail in the *Mayflower* and found a colony in what becomes New England.

1649	Following his defeat by Parliament in the **English Civil War**,* King Charles I is executed. The **Commonwealth** is declared.
1660	The **Restoration*** of the monarchy brings Charles II to the throne.
1665	The **Great Plague of London**.*
1666	The **Great Fire of London**.*
1688	The **Glorious Revolution**.*
1701	The **Act of Settlement*** ensures the Hanoverian succession. The **War of the Spanish Succession*** (1701–14) begins.
1746	The battle of **Culloden** marks the end of **Jacobite*** hopes.
1757	The victory of Clive at the **battle of Plassey** in the **Seven Years War*** (1756–63) establishes the basis of British India.
1775	The start of the **American Revolution**.*
1789	The start of the **French Revolution**.*
1805	The battle of **Trafalgar**. **Nelson's*** victory puts an end to Napoleon's hopes of invading Britain.
1815	The battle of **Waterloo** marks the final defeat of **Napoleon**.
1845–9	**Famine in Ireland**.
1848	A year of **European revolutions**, affecting France, Germany, Italy, and Austria.
1854–6	The **Crimean War**.*
1857	The **Indian Mutiny**.*
1899–1901	The Second **Boer War**.*
1914–18	**World War I**.*
1917	The **Russian Revolution** brings the Bolsheviks to power.
1936–9	The **Spanish Civil War**.*
1939–45	**World War II**.*
1945	The dropping of atomic bombs on **Hiroshima*** (August 6) and **Nagasaki** (August 9) brings World War II to an end.
1950–3	The **Korean War**.*
1954–75	The **Vietnam War**.*
1956	The **Suez Crisis**.*
1963	American President **John F. Kennedy is assassinated**.
1982	The **Falklands War**.*
1991	The **Gulf War**.*
2001	The **destruction of New York's World Trade Center** on September 11 provokes the beginning of what the USA calls the **War on Terror**.*

Since historical periods often take their name from the reigning monarch, it might be helpful to have a list of them for reference.

NORMANS

1066 William I
1087 William II
1100 Henry I
1135 Stephen

PLANTAGENETS

1154 Henry II
1189 Richard I
1199 John
1216 Henry III
1272 Edward I
1307 Edward II
1327 Edward III
1377 Richard II

LANCASTRIANS

1399 Henry IV
1413 Henry V
1422 Henry VI

YORKISTS

1461 Edward IV
1483 Edward V
1483 Richard III

TUDORS

1485 Henry VII
1509 Henry VIII
1547 Edward VI
1553 Mary
1558 Elizabeth I

STUARTS

1603 James I
1625 Charles I
1649 *Commonwealth*
1653 *Protectorate*
1660 Charles II
1685 James II
1689 William of Orange and Mary
1702 Anne

HANOVERIANS

1714 George I
1727 George II
1760 George III
1820 George IV
1830 William IV
1837 Victoria

SAXE-COBURG-GOTHA/WINDSORS

The dynastic name of Edward VII was Saxe-Coburg-Gotha, but in 1917 George V changed it to Windsor in an effort to play down the family's German ancestry.

1901 Edward VII
1910 George V
1936 Edward VIII
1936 George VI
1952 Elizabeth II

234

Part 4

Surviving the Academy

The aim here is to summarize basic elements of the critical vocabulary – the sort of things a literature student might be expected to know already but sometimes doesn't. Primed to explain more complex issues, your tutors may well glide past terms such as "Georgian poetry" or "pathetic fallacy" without a backward glance. If you happen to be unsure what they mean, they can be a source of embarrassment and confusion. To be told that a poem is written in iambic pentameters is helpful only if you know what an iambic pentameter is. For convenience I've put some of the entries relating to poetry in a separate group at the end, together with basic information about rhyme and meter. More comprehensive explanations of the literary terms discussed here can be found in a number of frequently reissued books, including Chris Baldick's *Concise Dictionary of Literary Terms* (Oxford University Press, 2004), M. H. Abrams's *Glossary of Literary Terms* (Heinle & Heinle, 2005), and *The Penguin Dictionary of Literary Terms and Literary Theory* (Penguin, 2004) by J. A. Cuddon and C. E. Preston.

Developments in literary criticism since the beginning of the last century now receive a good deal of attention in university courses, as well as in schools and Sixth Form colleges. The earlier critical background is less often considered. For this reason, I've ended the section with a few details about the most influential figures in pre-twentieth-century literary criticism. Like the brief guide to Roman numerals, they're intended to offer no more than a preliminary framework.

ABSURD, THEATER OF THE Term applied to the work of a number of playwrights in the 1950s whose plays reflected a sense that life was without ultimate significance and that meaningful communication was impossible. The philosophical basis of Absurdist drama was developed by **Albert Camus** (1913–60), though its theatrical roots go back to works such as **Alfred Jarry's** *Ubu roi* (1896) and **Guillaume Apollinaire's** *Les mamelles de Tirésias* (*The Breasts of Tiresias*, completed 1917). The main writers associated with the theater of the Absurd are **Arthur Adamov**, **Samuel Beckett**, **Eugene Ionesco** and, later, **Harold Pinter**.

AESTHETICISM The doctrine that art is its own justification and owes allegiance to beauty rather than to moral or social concerns. Emerging from **Romanticism*** (see p. 214) and mediated by French writers such as **Théophile Gautier**, it developed in opposition to the utilitarian philosophies and materialist preoccupations of the nineteenth century. In Britain it was reflected in the views of the **Pre-Raphaelites*** (see p. 213) and reached its peak towards the end of the century in the work of, among others, **Swinburne**, **Walter Pater**, **Oscar Wilde**, and **Aubrey Beardsley**. Its most complete expression in literature is perhaps the French novel *A Rebours* (1884) by **J.-K. Huysmans**.

From **Walter Pater, *Studies in the History of the Renaissance* (1873), Conclusion**

Every moment some form grows perfect in hand or face; some tone on the hills or sea is choicer than the rest; some mood of passion or insight or intellectual excitement is irresistibly real and attractive for us, – for that moment only. Not the fruit of experience, but experience itself is the end. A counted number of pulses only is given to us of a variegated, dramatic life. How may we see in them all that is to be seen in them by the finest senses? . . .

To burn always with this hard gem-like flame, to maintain this ecstasy, is success in life.

ALLEGORY A work whose surface narrative corresponds to a secondary level of meaning – religious, moral, political – that is the real point of the story. Spenser's *Faerie Queene* and Bunyan's *Pilgrim's Progress* are both examples.

ALLITERATION The repetition of initial consonants for literary effect – for example, Bolingbroke's reference to *"Eating the bitter bread of banishment"* in Shakespeare's *Richard II*.

ANGRY YOUNG MEN A group of young writers in the 1950s, often from lower-middle or working-class backgrounds, whose works expressed powerful disenchantment with the attitudes and institutions of the British establishment. The most prominent of them was **John Osborne**, whose play *Look Back in Anger* appeared in 1956. Among others more or less accurately identified with the group were the novelists **Kingsley Amis**, **John Braine**, and **Alan Sillitoe**, and the dramatist **Arnold Wesker**.

ASSONANCE The repetition of vowel sounds for literary effect – for example, Keats's *"Life is the rose's hope while yet unblown."*

AUGUSTAN A term applied to the literature of the late seventeenth and early eighteenth centuries. The aim is to suggest qualities of classical elegance, harmony, and restraint by analogy with the Latin writers – among them, Virgil, Horace, and Ovid – alive at the time of the Roman Emperor Augustus (r. 27 BC–AD 14).

BATHOS An abrupt descent from the high, serious, or sublime to the low, trivial, or commonplace, producing an effect of absurdity. This is sometimes unintentional but can be used as a poetic device: *"there is a tide in the affairs of women, / Which, taken at the flood, leads – God knows where"* (Byron, *Don Juan*, canto 6, stanza 2).

BILDUNGSROMAN (German = *education novel*) A novel about the education and development of the young hero. Well-known examples are Goethe's *Wilhelm Meisters Lehrjahre* (1795–6) and Flaubert's *L'Éducation sentimentale* (1869).

BLOOMSBURY GROUP A group of writers, artists, and intellectuals who were centered on the Bloomsbury area of London, primarily in the 1910s and 1920s. Among them were **Virginia** and **Leonard Woolf**, **Lytton Strachey**, **E. M. Forster**, the art critics **Clive Bell** and **Roger Fry**, the artists **Vanessa Bell** and **Duncan Grant**, and the economist **John Maynard Keynes**.

BURLESQUE Comic send-up of a serious literary or artistic genre, author, or work. It can range from slapstick parody to delicate mock-heroic. *The Beggar's*

Opera (1728) by John Gay is a famous example, as is Pope's *Rape of the Lock* (1714). In the US the term came to refer to music-hall variety acts.

CANON A list of books accepted as authoritative. The books included in the Bible are thus part of the biblical canon. In English studies, the term has come to refer to those texts and authors generally regarded as central to the history of English literature, though the question of what should be included in the canon is much disputed. The term can also be used of texts known to have been written by a particular author. *King Lear*, for example, is part of the Shakespeare canon.

CAROLINE PERIOD (Latin *Carolus* = Charles) The period of Charles I (1625–49). Among writers active at the time were the **Cavalier poets,*** most of the **metaphysical poets,*** **John Milton**, and **Sir Thomas Browne**.

CAVALIER POETS A group of witty, graceful lyric poets who wrote during the reign of Charles I. They included **Thomas Carew**, **Richard Lovelace**, **Sir John Suckling**, **Edmund Waller**, and, at a slight remove, **Robert Herrick**. Most of them – Herrick is an exception – were associated with the court.

CELTIC TWILIGHT Name for the Irish literary revival movement in the late nineteenth century. The phrase was used as the title of a book of Irish tales that W. B. Yeats published in 1893.

CHORUS A group whose original function was to dance and sing at religious festivals in honor of **Dionysus*** (see p. 82). Their performances were the basis from which **Greek tragedy** developed. In time, the Chorus was displaced from center stage by actors, and its role became that of describing and commenting on the action.

CONCEIT An ingenious metaphor, simile, or other **figurative*** device of the kind particularly associated with the **metaphysical poets.*** A classic example is Donne's comparison of parting lovers to a pair of mathematical compasses in "A Valediction: Forbidding Mourning."

CONDITION OF ENGLAND NOVEL Term referring to a number of mid-nineteenth-century novels that focused on the social effects of the Industrial Revolution, particularly in the Midlands and the North. **Disraeli**, **Gaskell**,

Dickens, and **Kingsley** were among those who wrote "condition of England" novels.

> **From** Benjamin Disraeli, *Sybil: or, the Two Nations*, Bk. II, Chapter 5
>
> "Well, society may be in its infancy," said Egremont, slightly smiling; "but, say what you like, our Queen reigns over the greatest nation that ever existed."
>
> "Which nation?" asked the younger stranger, "for she reigns over two."
>
> The stranger paused; Egremont was silent, but looked enquiringly.
>
> "Yes," resumed the younger stranger after a moment's interval. "Two nations; between whom there is no intercourse and no sympathy; who are as ignorant of each other's habits, thoughts, and feelings, as if they were dwellers in different zones, or inhabitants of different planets; who are formed by a different breeding, are fed by a different food, are ordered by different manners, and are not governed by the same laws."
>
> "You speak of – " said Egremont, hesitatingly.
>
> "THE RICH AND THE POOR."

COURTLY LOVE A form of idealized romantic love, governed by an agreed code of behavior, that originated in twelfth-century Provence. It reversed the accepted medieval hierarchy, setting the lady on a pedestal and casting the lovesick (and adulterous) lord as her humble vassal who must sue for mercy and do her bidding. Though the troubadour culture that elaborated this code came to an end in the thirteenth century, the ideals of courtly love have had an incalculable influence on both the literature and social life of the western world.

CRUELTY, THEATER OF A concept of theater developed by the French actor and dramatist **Antonin Artaud** in the 1930s. Its aim was to use strident theatrical effects to break through the conventional veneer of civilization and shock spectators into an instinctual response. Artaud's call for a liberating assault on the audience's sensibilities influenced, among others, **Arthur Adamov** and **Jean Genet**.

CYCLE A group of plays, poems, songs, stories, or operas that are linked by a central theme.

DENOUEMENT (French = *unknotting*) The point in a literary work at which the complexities of the plot are resolved. In a murder mystery, for example, the denouement is the stage at which the identity, methods, motives, etc. of the murderer are revealed.

DEUS EX MACHINA (Latin = *god from the machine*) Someone or something introduced out of the blue to resolve a critical situation in a work of literature. (The phrase refers to the practice in Greek drama of resolving crises through the intervention of a god who would be lowered on to the stage from a contraption suspended above it.)

DIDACTIC LITERATURE (Greek *didaskein* = teach) A work written with the aim of giving the reader instruction, usually moral but sometimes also practical. Virgil's *Georgics*, for example, combines advice on husbandry with moral precepts.

DRAWING-ROOM COMEDIES Plays of upper-middle-class social comedy that brought success to writers such as **Noel Coward** and **Somerset Maugham** in the early twentieth century.

EDWARDIAN AGE Strictly, the reign of Edward VII (r. 1901–10), though used loosely of the years leading up to the outbreak of World War I in 1914. It was a period of reaction against certain aspects of the Victorian age, but it was also, in retrospect, the last, extravagant parade of a social world that was about to be engulfed.

EPISTOLARY NOVEL (Latin *epistola* = letter) A novel presented in the form of letters written by characters in the story. Popular in the eighteenth century, it was a form used by, among others, **Richardson** and **Smollett**.

EUPHEMISM The substitution of a term considered inoffensive for one that might bring the reader or listener too close to an uncomfortable reality. Euphemisms for death and disability abound; warfare has spawned a whole vocabulary of them. The words Tacitus puts into the mouth of a rebellious Briton – *Ubi solitudinem faciunt, pacem appellant* ("Where they create desolation, they call it peace") – have not lost their sting. Today we reduce cities to rubble and speak of liberating them.

FIGURATIVE LANGUAGE Language that uses figures of speech such as metaphors and similes (*he clawed his way up the wall*), as opposed to language that is literal (*he climbed the wall with difficulty*).

GEORGIAN The term can be confusing. In architecture and the decorative arts it refers to the period of the first four Hanoverian kings – George I, II, III, and IV – from 1714 to 1830. Any reference to the **Georgian age** is likely to be to this period. In literature, however, the term **Georgian poetry** refers to the early years of George V's reign, specifically to the five anthologies of Georgian poetry edited by Edward Marsh between 1912 and 1922 and containing works by **Rupert Brooke**, **Edward Thomas**, **W. H. Davies**, **Walter de la Mare**, and others.

GOTHIC NOVEL A type of novel that revelled in sensational horrors with a supernatural flavor and, often, a medieval setting. Popular in the second half of the eighteenth and the early nineteenth centuries, the genre was launched by Horace Walpole's ***The Castle of Otranto*** (1764) and includes such novels as William Beckford's ***Vathek*** (1786), Ann Radcliffe's ***Mysteries of Udolpho*** (1794), M. G. Lewis's ***The Monk*** (1796), and Mary Shelley's ***Frankenstein*** (1818).

***From* Jane Austen, *Northanger Abbey*, Chapter 25**

Charming as were all Mrs. Radcliffe's works, and charming even as were the works of all her imitators, it was not in them perhaps that human nature, at least in the midland counties of England, was to be looked for. Of the Alps and Pyrenees, with their pine forests and their vices, they might give a faithful delineation; and Italy, Switzerland, and the South of France, might be as fruitful in horrors as they were there represented. Catherine dared not doubt beyond her own country, and even of that, if hard pressed, would have yielded the northern and western extremities. But in the central part of England there was surely some security for the existence even of a wife not beloved, in the laws of the land, and the manners of the age.

HYPERBOLE Calculated exaggeration for emphasis or other literary effect.

IMAGISM A movement of English and American poets that flourished just before and during World War I. Influenced by the philosophy of **T. E. Hulme**, it rejected romantic vagueness and the constraints of "poetic" subject matter, emphasizing spareness, clarity, and the precision of concrete images. Among its leaders were **Ezra Pound**, **Richard Aldington**, **H.D.** (Hilda Doolittle), **William Carlos Williams**, and **Amy Lowell**.

Ezra Pound, "In a Station of the Metro"

The apparition of these faces in the crowd;
Petals on a wet, black bough.

INKHORN TERMS Extravagantly difficult words coined mainly from Greek and Latin, fashionable among pedants in the sixteenth century.

IN MEDIAS RES (Latin = *into the middle of things*) The phrase refers to the common practice of opening a story in the middle of the action. It was a convention of the **epic*** that it should begin *in medias res* and then go back at a later stage to reveal what had happened before.

INTERLUDE A short dramatic entertainment usually performed at court or in a great house to enliven a banquet or provide amusement between the acts of a play. The fashion for interludes was at its height during the fifteenth and sixteenth centuries.

JACOBEAN (*Jacobus* = James) Relating to the reign of James I (1603–25). Among writers active at the time were Shakespeare, Jonson, Webster, Middleton, Donne, Bacon, and Burton. Avoid confusing the term with **Jacobin** (see p. 209) and **Jacobite** (see p. 189).

KENNING A literary device much used in Old English poetry whereby something is referred to by a metaphorical compound – for example, *hronrade* (whale-road = sea).

LEITMOTIF A term borrowed from music – where it is particularly associated with the operas of Wagner – to describe a recurring thematic element in a literary work or group of works. ("Thematic element" because a full-blown theme is something more substantial than a leitmotif.)

MAGIC REALISM A term borrowed from art criticism and applied to a kind of fiction that mixes realism with flights of myth and fantasy. It is associated preeminently with Latin American novelists such as **Gabriel García Márquez** and **Alejo Carpentier**, but its techniques can also be seen in the work of a number of British writers, including Angela Carter and Salman Rushdie.

MASQUE Aristocratic theatrical entertainment, with elaborate costumes and sets, in which a brief poetic drama provides the vehicle for music, song, and dance. It was popular with the court and nobility in the sixteenth and seventeenth centuries, and reached its height in masques by **Ben Jonson** (1572–1637), who collaborated on them for a time with the architect and designer **Inigo Jones***

(p. 172). It was Jonson who introduced the **anti-masque** as a farcical prelude to, or interlude in, the masque itself.

METAPHOR Figure of speech in which a comparison or analogy is suggested by describing one thing in terms of another (*All the world's a stage . . .*). In the case of a **simile** the comparison is made explicit by the use of "like" or "as" (*. . . as chaste as unsunn'd snow . . .*). A **mixed metaphor** occurs when two incompatible metaphors are used together (*The Fascist octopus has sung its swan song*, to borrow one of George Orwell's examples).

METAPHYSICAL POETRY Name given to the work of a number of seventeenth-century poets, including **John Donne**, **George Herbert**, **Richard Crashaw**, **Henry Vaughan**, and **Andrew Marvell**, whose poems were notable for their intellectual complexity, metrical ingenuity, and fondness for witty conceits and paradoxes. **Dryden** first accused Donne of affecting "the metaphysics," but it was **Samuel Johnson** in his *Lives of the Poets* who coined the label "metaphysical poets."

> *From* **Samuel Johnson, "The Life of Cowley" (1779) (The Metaphysical Poets)**
>
> But Wit, abstracted from its effects upon the hearer, may be more rigorously and philosophically considered as a kind of *discordia concors*; a combination of dissimilar images, or discovery of occult resemblances in things apparently unlike. Of wit, thus defined, they have more than enough. The most heterogeneous ideas are yoked by violence together; nature and art are ransacked for illustrations, comparisons, and allusions; their learning instructs, and their subtlety surprises; but the reader commonly thinks his improvement dearly bought, and, though he sometimes admires, is seldom pleased.

METONYMY Figure of speech in which something is referred to by one of its attributes (e.g., *crown* for monarchy). It tends to overlap with **synecdoche**, which is the use of a part to refer to the whole (e.g., *sail* for sailing vessel).

MOCK HEROIC Form of writing that applies a high-flown epic style to trivial subject matter for the purposes of satire. Pope's *Rape of the Lock* (1714) is an outstanding example.

MODERNISM An early twentieth-century movement in literature and the arts that broke with traditional forms, conventions, and expectations, challenging accepted notions of the relationship between art and everyday life, and experimenting with new techniques and new modes of representing reality. It was at its peak in the first three decades of the century. In literature the term is associated with **free verse** (see p. 253) and **stream-of-consciousness**,* and, more broadly, with the work of writers such as **Conrad**, **Pound**, **Eliot**, **Woolf**, and **Joyce**.

MOVEMENT, THE Label attached to a group of British poets in the 1950s, including **Philip Larkin**, **Kingsley Amis**, **Elizabeth Jennings**, **Thom Gunn**, and **Donald Davie**, whose work seemed to exhibit a postwar shift towards more traditional and more personal concerns than had attracted poets in the first half of the century.

MYSTERY PLAYS Medieval dramas, originally performed in church, which took biblical stories such as the Fall and the crucifixion as their subject. Later, the productions moved into the market place and became increasingly elaborate before being suppressed in the wake of the **Reformation**.* The four main cycles in England were those of Chester, Coventry, Wakefield (also called the Towneley cycle), and York. They are sometimes also referred to as **Miracle plays**, though the latter tended to focus on the Virgin Mary or specific saints. A slightly later development were the **Morality plays**, popular in the fifteenth and early sixteenth centuries, in which allegorical characters were used to dramatize moral lessons.

NATURALISM In literature this refers to the scientific realism pioneered in late nineteenth-century France by the **Goncourt brothers** and **Emile Zola**. Influenced by Darwin's work on evolution and the historical determinism of the historian **Hippolyte Taine**, these writers set out to describe reality with a clinical precision that would reveal the hereditary and environmental factors governing human behavior. The impact of naturalism can be seen in the work of **George Moore** and **George Gissing**, or, in the US, in that of **Theodore Dreiser** and **Stephen Crane**.

ONOMATOPOEIA The use of words whose sound imitates what they refer to – for example, *buzz*, *splash*, *pop*. A kind of onomatopoeia can sometimes be used for more subtle and extended effects, as when W. H. Auden suggests the train's movement over the rails in "Night Mail": "*this is the Night Mail crossing the border, / Bringing the cheque and the postal order . . .*"

OXYMORON A combination of words that appear to contradict each other – e.g., *a wise fool*.

PANEGYRIC A speech or piece of writing in effusive praise of someone or something.

PARODY Satirical imitation of the style of a particular author, work, or literary genre. By exaggerating certain aspects, the parodist points up its inherent potential for absurdity.

PASTICHE A piece of writing that closely imitates the style of an earlier work. It differs from parody in that the imitation is usually a form of tribute, conscious or unconscious. (The terms *parody* and *pastiche* are not confined to literature.)

PATHETIC FALLACY A term coined by **Ruskin*** (pp. 214–15) for the poetic tendency to attribute human characteristics (emotions, thoughts, actions) to natural objects – *dancing leaves*, *angry waves* etc.

From **John Ruskin, *Modern Painters* (1856), Vol. 3, Pt. 4**

... I want to examine the nature of the other error, that which the mind admits when affected strongly by emotion. Thus, for instance, in *Alton Locke*, –

They rowed her in across the rolling foam –
The cruel, crawling foam.

The foam is not cruel, neither does it crawl. The state of mind which attributes to it these characters of a living creature is one in which the reason is unhinged by grief. All violent feelings have the same effect. They produce in us a falseness in all our impressions of external things, which I would generally characterize as the "pathetic fallacy."

PERIPHRASIS A roundabout way of saying something.

PHILISTINE The poet and critic **Matthew Arnold*** (p. 258) gave the word currency as a label for people, particularly those from the prosperous middle classes, who have little feeling for culture and who measure value in purely material terms. See also p. 48.

PICARESQUE NOVEL (Spanish *picaro* = rogue) A type of episodic novel, originating in mid-sixteenth-century Spain, which follows the career of a knavish central character whose adventures cast a satirical light on contemporary society. In the eighteenth century **Defoe**, **Fielding**, and **Smollett** all wrote picaresque novels.

PLOT A mechanism by which a narrative sequence of events (story) is structured and organized. This will normally, as E. M. Forster pointed out in *Aspects of the Novel* (1927), introduce an element of causality; it may also reflect the desire to produce particular effects (of shock, suspense, amusement, etc.) on the reader or spectator.

POET LAUREATE Title given by the monarch to an eminent contemporary poet, who becomes an officer of the royal household. The post has no specific duties but the laureate is expected from time to time to produce poems marking notable public occasions, especially ones which concern the royal family. The first officially appointed poet laureate was **Dryden** in 1668.

POSTMODERNISM A vague term used to cover a number of cultural phenomena in the second half of the twentieth century. Its specific reference to literary and artistic developments in the wake of modernism has been overlaid by a more general application to the products and attitudes of a hi-tech culture that is characteristically ironic, fragmented, suspicious of coherence or closure, and glibly self-aware about its own transient enthusiasms.

PROSODY The study of versification, particularly its metrical aspects. (The word is pronounced with a short first "o.")

PROTAGONIST The main character in a work of literature or film.

ROMAN À CLEF (French = *novel with a key*) A novel in which real people are represented in the guise of fictional characters.

ROMANCE A form of literature, primarily concerned with deeds of chivalry, that enjoyed its heyday in France and Germany between the mid-twelfth and mid-thirteenth centuries. The treatments of Arthurian legend by **Chrétien de Troyes** were particularly influential. *Sir Gawain and the Green Knight* (late fourteenth century) and **Sir Thomas Malory's** *Le Morte Darthur* (ca. 1470) both belong to the romance tradition. The term later came to be applied to a wide range of more or less escapist literature.

ROMAN-FLEUVE (French = *novel-river*). A series of novels which stand on their own but are related to one another by recurring characters whose destinies unfold across the series. A modern example is Anthony Powell's 12-volume *A Dance to the Music of Time* (1951–75).

SATIRE Writing that mocks the follies and vices of society with the aim of reforming behavior. For English literature, the late seventeenth and early eighteenth centuries – the period of **Dryden**, **Pope**, and **Swift** – were particularly rich in satire.

SENTIMENTAL NOVEL Term applied to a kind of fiction popular in the mid-eighteenth century which laid great emphasis on displays of feeling and sensibility, tending to present them as a sign of moral worth. Samuel Richardson's *Pamela* (1740), Oliver Goldsmith's *The Vicar of Wakefield* (1766), and Henry Mackenzie's *Man of Feeling* (1771) are well-known examples.

SOLILOQUY A dramatic device that allows characters, alone on stage or out of contact with the other actors, to speak their thoughts or feelings as though to themselves, giving the audience an insight into their motivation and state of mind.

STREAM OF CONSCIOUSNESS (also referred to as "**interior monologue**") A technique used in some twentieth-century fiction to convey the complex flow of unorganized impressions, thoughts, and feelings that make up the individual's awareness of and response to the surrounding world. James Joyce's *Ulysses* (1922) provides some celebrated examples of its use. In essence, the writer attempts to represent the free swirl of the mind's activity rather than a rationally edited version of it. The term was first used by William James in *Principles of Psychology* (1890).

SUBLIME An aesthetic concept that was first addressed in a treatise *On the Sublime*, traditionally attributed to the first-century Greek philosopher **Longinus*** (p. 256). It was later discussed by **Edmund Burke*** (p. 183) in *A Philosophical Enquiry into the Origin of our Ideas of the Sublime and the Beautiful* (1757). The notion of a transcendent quality located in awe-inspiring grandeur of thought, feeling, or appearance greatly influenced Romantic attitudes, particularly to landscape but also more generally.

SYMBOL An object that can stand for something else by virtue of the qualities and associations it suggests. It is distinct from an image in that it has a "real" existence and what it symbolizes is a matter of inference. To talk of the "fog of battle" is to use fog as an image of confusion and uncertainty, but when Dickens describes the pervasive fog at the start of *Bleak House* (1852–3) he is using it symbolically to suggest, among other things, the obscurities and obfuscations of the legal system.

TROPE A **figurative*** use of language.

UNITIES The classical unities of time, space, and action were extrapolated by **Aristotle*** (see p. 256) from contemporary drama. They required, with a small amount of room for maneuver, that the action should take place within a single day, that it should be confined to one location, and that it should be unadulterated by detachable subplots. Most English dramatists disregarded the classical unities, but in modified form they were of central importance to the development of French drama.

VERISIMILITUDE The appearance of truth to reality. If a work has verisimilitude, the reader will be convinced of its realism, even if the author's world is one of fantasy or science fiction.

WELTANSCHAUUNG (German = *world view*) Term used for a writer's outlook on life, or, more generally, for the assumptions and attitudes of a particular period.

WELTSCHMERZ (German = *world pain*) Sense of melancholy attributable to the dismal nature of the world and of human existence.

ZEITGEIST (German = *spirit of the time*) The prevailing currents of thought and feeling at a particular time.

Schools and colleges spend less time on poetry than they used to, so fairly basic words and concepts can sometimes cause a problem. Here's the survival-level information.

Poetic Forms

BALLAD Originally a song to accompany a dance. The ballad tells a story, usually in 4-line stanzas with a simple rhyme scheme. Common subjects include love, battle, personal tragedy, and the adventures of folk heroes like Robin Hood. Many of the most famous ballads date back to the fifteenth century. Border ballads are a particular group concerned with the border country between England and Scotland, and the conflicts that arose there. The term "broadside ballad" refers to the practice, from the sixteenth century onwards, of printing ballads on one side of a single sheet of paper.

BLANK VERSE Unrhymed verse in iambic pentameters, i.e., 10-syllable lines containing five feet, each with a short stress followed by a long stress – though the form is flexible enough to allow considerable variation. Introduced by the **earl of Surrey** in the mid-sixteenth century, it is one of the most common verse forms in English, used, for example, in Shakespeare's plays, Milton's *Paradise Lost*, and Wordsworth's *Prelude*.

CANTO A subdivision sometimes used in long narrative poems – for example, Spenser's *Faerie Queene* and Byron's *Don Juan*.

CONCRETE POETRY Poetry that uses typographical layout to create a visual image or impression. It's a modern version of what George Herbert (1593–1633) did when he laid out his poem "Easter Wings" in the shape of a pair of butterfly wings.

COUPLET A pair of rhyming lines. A **heroic couplet** is a pair of ten-syllable rhyming lines, usually iambic pentameters. Spenser, Shakespeare, and Donne all use the heroic couplet, but its full possibilities were realized in the work of Dryden and Pope. A **triplet** is a group of three successive rhyming lines.

ECLOGUE A short poem, usually a pastoral in the form of a dialogue that illustrates the virtues of the rural life. The most notable examples in classical literature were the bucolic poems of Theocritus and, later, Virgil's *Eclogues*. The form was revived in the Renaissance.

ELEGY Since about the seventeenth century the term has narrowed in meaning to refer to a poem reflecting on death, usually the death of a friend of the poet. Examples in English literature are Milton's *Lycidas,* Shelley's *Adonais,* and Tennyson's *In Memoriam*.

EPIC A long narrative poem that recounts the deeds of a hero or group of heroes – often in the context of events that shaped a nation's history. Among the most celebrated epics in western literature are Homer's *Iliad* and *Odyssey* (eighth century BC), Virgil's *Aeneid* (first century BC), the *Chanson de Roland* (ca. 1100), Ariosto's *Orlando Furioso* (1532), Tasso's *Gerusalemme Liberata* (1575), and Milton's *Paradise Lost* (1667).

EPITHALAMION A song or poem written to celebrate a marriage, traditionally sung outside the bride's door on her wedding night.

FABLIAU A short, often ribald, comic tale in verse, usually in octosyllabic couplets. It was common in medieval French poetry. The tales told by the Miller and the Reeve in Chaucer's *Canterbury Tales* are examples from English literature.

GEORGIC A semi-didactic poem on practical aspects of farming. Virgil's *Georgics* is the most famous example.

LYRIC Originally a song to be accompanied on the lyre, the term is now used for any short poem that expresses the poet's thoughts, feelings, or responses to personal experience.

NONSENSE VERSE Comic verse that is deliberately absurd and irrational. It is a genre particularly associated with **Edward Lear** (whose *Book of Nonsense* was published in 1846) and **Lewis Carroll**, but it has a distinguished line of twentieth-century practitioners, including Hilaire Belloc, G. K. Chesterton, T. S. Eliot, Ogden Nash, and Stevie Smith.

OCCASIONAL VERSE Verse written for a particular occasion, usually to mark some event of public or, less often, private significance.

ODE A lyric poem, usually of some length and technical variety, which tends to be elevated in tone and addressed to a specific person, object, or abstraction.

OTTAVA RIMA A stanza of eight lines rhyming *abababcc*. Introduced into English by **Sir Thomas Wyatt** in the early sixteenth century, it was used to brilliant effect by Byron in *Don Juan*.

PASTORAL (Latin *pastor* = shepherd) Literature that deals with the life of shepherds, contrasting an idealized vision of its rural simplicity with the complexity and corruption of city life. The pastoral mode has its origins in classical literature, going back to the works of the Greek poet **Theocritus** (third century BC).

QUATRAIN A stanza of four lines.

SONNET A poem of 14 lines, usually in iambic pentameters, with a set rhyme scheme. It was introduced into English poetry in the first half of the sixteenth century by **Sir Thomas Wyatt** and the **earl of Surrey**. The two major sonnet forms are the Italian, or Petrarchan, and the English, or Shakespearean. The **Petrarchan** is arranged as an octave (or octet) rhyming *abbaabba* and a sestet commonly rhyming *cdecde*. The **Shakespearean** sonnet is arranged as three quatrains and a couplet, rhyming *abab cdcd efef gg*. (A variant of this is the **Spenserian** sonnet, which rhymes *abab bcbc cdcd ee*.)

STANZA A group of lines that form a separate unit within a poem. It's the term used in literary criticism for what is commonly called a verse.

VERSE PARAGRAPH The term is most often used to refer to a unit of blank verse within a long poem.

Rhyme

A poem's **rhyme scheme** is the pattern in which its rhymes are arranged, usually expressed alphabetically. For example, the rhyme scheme of the **Spenserian stanza** (a nine-line stanza invented by Edmund Spenser for *The Faerie Queene*, consisting of eight iambic pentameters and a final iambic hexameter) is *ababbcbcc*.

These are the terms you're most likely to come across in connection with rhyme:

strong (masculine) rhyme: the rhyme in the last syllable is stressed (*tent/spent, contain/abstain*).

weak (feminine) rhyme: an unstressed rhyming syllable follows the stressed rhyming syllable (*torpid/morbid*).

half rhyme: the same consonant sound follows different vowel sounds (*kind/ wand*).

eye (sight) rhyme: the words have similar spelling but different pronunciation (*rough/cough*).

internal rhyme: the rhyme occurs within a line.

Meter

The meter of a line of poetry is the pattern of stressed and unstressed syllables. You need to know the five or six most common meters in English poetry. Of these much the most important is the **iambic (⌣—)**, an unstressed syllable followed by a stressed syllable: "Let **spades** be **trumps**! she **said**, and **trumps** they **were**." Each unit is called a **foot**, so in this ten-syllable line we have five feet, each of them an iamb. It is therefore an **iambic pentameter**.

Within the basic iambic meter, poets will often introduce variations – for example, by reversing one of the feet – to achieve particular effects of emphasis: "The **stalk** is **with**er'd **dry**, my **love**, / **So** will our **hearts** de**cay**."

Apart from the **iambic**, these are other meters you should be able to recognize:

anapaestic (⌣⌣—) Two unstressed followed by a stressed: "The As**syr**ian came **down** like the **wolf** on the **fold**."

dactylic (—⌣⌣) One stressed followed by two unstressed: "**Can**non to **right** of them / **Can**non to **left** of them."

spondaic (— —) Two stressed. The spondee is sometimes used with powerful effect to interrupt a dominant iambic rhythm: "The **world's whole sap** is **sunk**."

trochaic (—⌣) One stressed followed by one unstressed: "**By** the **shore** of **Git**che **Gu**mee, / **By** the **shi**ning **Big**-Sea-**Wat**er."

This extract from Coleridge's poem "Metrical Feet" may help you to remember the basic meters:

> Trochee trips from long to short;
> From long to long in solemn sort
> Slow Spondee stalks, strong foot! yet ill able
> Ever to come up with Dactyl's trisyllable.
> Iambics march from short to long.
> With a leap and a bound the swift Anapaests throng.

The following are a few terms commonly used in talking about meter:

ALEXANDRINE A term, borrowed from French, for an iambic hexameter.

CAESURA (Latin = *cutting*) Most lines of poetry offer a natural pause for breath somewhere near the middle. This is referred to as the caesura.

ENJAMBEMENT The term used when the sense of one line or couplet runs over into the next without any intervening punctuation, e.g., *"Flutt'ring his pennons vain plumb down he drops / Ten thousand fadom deep . . ."*

FREE VERSE Poetry without any regular meter.

HEXAMETER A line of verse with six feet.

PENTAMETER A line of verse with five feet.

TETRAMETER A line of verse with four feet.

TRIMETER A line of verse with three feet.

The process of analyzing the metrical pattern in a piece of poetry is referred to as **scansion**. It's not always easy to identify the meter of a poem, partly because poets often introduce variations in the dominant pattern. If you read a few lines aloud, paying attention to their meaning, you should be able to answer the relevant questions: (1) How many syllables are there in a line? (2) Which are stressed and which are unstressed? (3) Does the rhythm break them most naturally into groups of two or three? This last question might not be as straightforward as it sounds, but if you're in doubt it's likely to be an iambic meter with variations rather than something more exotic.

Examining a poem's metrical pattern can help you to understand how it achieves its effects. (Pope's famous couplet about the Alexandrine neatly exemplifies the point: *"A needless Alexandrine ends the song, / That, like a wounded snake, drags its slow length along."*) That said, there's no point in fretting about it too much. If you're losing sleep over whether to call something a trochee or a reversed iamb, it's probably time to move on.

These aren't much used today, but it's worth knowing them because they still crop up in various contexts – clocks, dates, chapter numbers, and the like. A bibliography that recommends, for example, Vol. XLVI of a particular journal can cause frustration if you don't know how to read Roman numerals. They are easily learnt:

1–10: **I, II, III, IV, V, VI, VII, VIII, IX, X**

11–20 are written simply by taking **X** and adding the numerals from 1–10:

XI, XII, XIII, XIV, XV, XVI, XVII, XVIII, XIX, XX

Thereafter you can work out most numbers if you know that 50 is **L**, 100 is **C**, 500 is **D**, and 1,000 is **M**. The general principle is that a lower numeral placed in front of a higher is deducted from it (e.g., **IX** = 9), a lower numeral placed after a higher is added to it (e.g., **XI** = 11).

Here are a few more examples to clarify how the system works:

XXX = 30, **XL** = 40, **LX** = 60, **LXIX** = 69, **LXX** = 70, **LXXX** = 80, **XC** = 90, **CI** = 101, **CC** = 200, and so on.

With the exception of **D** and **M**, the numbers can be written in upper or lower case, so 7 could be **VII** or **vii**.

There are variant forms, but this should be enough to enable you to make sense of whatever numbers you come across.

English found its way on to the university syllabus at Oxford in 1893, but it took another quarter of a century to shift the focus of the curriculum from language to literature. Even then, literary criticism remained something of a minority pastime. It was the work of the Cambridge don I. A. Richards, with his *Principles of Literary Criticism* in 1925 and *Practical Criticism* in 1929, that marked the true beginning of modern academic literary criticism. Until the second half of the twentieth century the volume of books, essays, articles, and papers was fairly manageable. Since then, the trickle has become a torrent. Every university in America and the UK now has a cohort of harassed literature teachers for whom publication is the only way to be sure of tenure, promotion, pay rises, and blessed leaves of absence. How much of it do you really want to read? You will have to rely on the discretion of your tutor to guide you through the flood waters.

It may be helpful, however, to know something about the antecedents of this phenomenon. There are fewer than a dozen names that you're likely to come across with any frequency. In classical times, Plato, Aristotle, and Longinus made the most enduring contributions to literary criticism; in Renaissance England, Sir Philip Sidney; in the seventeenth and eighteenth centuries, Dryden and Johnson; in the Romantic period, Wordsworth, Coleridge, and Shelley; and among the Victorians, Matthew Arnold – who died just five years before English became part of the university curriculum. There were many others, from Horace to Hazlitt, whose writings on literature are still worth reading today, but their names do not loom quite so large in the history of literary criticism. Below, I've given brief details about the major figures, in historical rather than alphabetical order.

PLATO (ca. 428–ca. 347 BC) Greek philosopher (see p. 104). Plato touches on imaginative literature in both the *Phaedrus* and the *Ion*, but it is his skeptical analysis of it in the *Republic* that has had the greatest impact. If the concrete world is no more than an imperfect reflection of the ideal forms that lie behind it, then poetic imitations of that world are at an even further remove from true reality. Moreover, Plato is suspicious of poetry's appeal to emotions that should properly be controlled by reason. The case against literature can be summed up thus: it offers a third-hand version of reality; it is created by tricksters; and it has dangerous side-effects.

ARISTOTLE (384–322 BC) Greek philosopher (see p. 73). His *Poetics* was the first and most influential work of literary criticism written in the classical age. It suggests that literature, rather than simply imitating reality, can shape it in ways that give access to a deeper truth. Aristotle's analysis focuses on the contruction and constituents of tragedy, introducing a number of terms that became part of critical vocabulary:

catharsis (Greek = *cleansing*): The therapeutic release of emotion that Aristotle took to be a central effect of tragedy. He argued that the play excited emotions of pity and fear, which were then purged by the tragic resolution.

hamartia (Greek = *error*): The tragic error that, according to Aristotle, is the cause of the hero's downfall. This notion was misleadingly applied to Shakespeare by the critic A. C. Bradley in his highly influential *Shakespearean Tragedy* (1904), which presented the tragedies as consequent on a fatal flaw in the hero's character.

hubris (Greek = *insolence*): Overweening pride that offends the gods and provokes retribution.

mimesis (Greek = *imitation*): The representation of reality. In Aristotle's use of it, the term implies selection and organization rather than slavish imitation.

peripeteia (Greek = *change suddenly*): The sudden reversal of fortune that plunges the tragic hero from triumph to tragedy. It is often prompted by what Aristotle refers to as the ***anagnorisis*** (Greek = *recognition, discovery*), the moment at which a vital piece of information is revealed that dramatically changes the protagonist's understanding of events.

LONGINUS Traditionally identified as the author of a Greek treatise from the first century AD, *On the Sublime* (see p. 248). In considering the qualities that impart nobility to a work of literature, Longinus gives new importance to the response of the reader. The writer's success in achieving sublimity is dependent on grandeur of thought and emotion, on technical mastery, and not least on inspiration, but it is measured on the reader's pulse.

SIDNEY, SIR PHILIP (1554–86) Elizabethan courtier, soldier, and poet, celebrated for his gallant death at the battle of Zutphen. (Mortally wounded, he is said to have passed his water bottle to another dying soldier with the words, "*thy necessity is yet greater than mine*"). His importance in the history of literary criticism is due to his *Defence of Poesie* (also called *An Apologie for*

Poetrie), published posthumously in 1595 but written some fifteen years earlier. The *Defence* examines the literature of the day and makes an eloquent case, in response to contemporary Puritan attacks, for imaginative literature as a moral force. The poet, Sidney insists, can be a better teacher than the philosopher or historian.

From Philip Sidney, "The Defence of Poesie" (written, 1580)

For [the Poet] doth not only shew the way, but giveth so sweet a prospect into the way, as will entice any man to enter into it. Nay, he doth, as if your journey should lye through a faire vineyard, at the very first give you a cluster of grapes, that full of the taste, you may long to pass further. Hee beginneth not with obscure definitions, which must blur the margent with interpretations, and load the memory with doubtfulnesse: but he cometh to you with words set in delightful proportion, either accompanied with, or prepared for, the well enchanting skill of music, and with a tale forsooth he cometh unto you, with a tale, which holdeth children from play, and olde men from the Chimney corner; and pretending no more, doth intend the winning of the mind from wickednesse to vertue; even as the child is often brought to take most wholesome things by hiding them in such other as have a pleasaunt taste . . .

DRYDEN, JOHN (1631–1700) Poet and dramatist whose main work of literary criticism was his *Essay of Dramatic Poesie* (1668), written in the form of a dialogue. Containing a notable appreciation of Shakespeare, it is primarily a discussion of drama, and particularly the use of rhyme in drama. Dryden argues the superiority of English over French drama in fulfilling the true function of a play (and by extension of imaginative literature in general) as *"a just and lively image of human nature, representing its passions and humours, and the changes of fortune to which it is subject, for the delight and instruction of mankind."*

JOHNSON, SAMUEL (1709–84) Lexicographer, scholar, and poet, Johnson was the dominant critical presence in the second half of the eighteenth century. The preface to his eight-volume edition of *The Plays of William Shakespeare* (1765) and his *Lives of the Poets* (1781), containing biographical studies of 52 poets, are landmarks in a wide-ranging body of literary criticism. His huge influence was due less to any change he effected in ways of thinking about literature than to the intellectual and stylistic force of his judgments.

WORDSWORTH, WILLIAM (1770–1850) Wordsworth's central contribution to the history of literary criticism was his preface to the second edition of *Lyrical Ballads* (1800). In its emphasis on poetry as *"the spontaneous overflow of powerful feelings,"* in its championship of *"common life"* and the *"language really used by men,"* and in its hostility to the effects of industrialization, it became, along with Coleridge's *Biographia Literaria* and Shelley's *Defence of Poetry*, one of the three great manifestos of English Romantic poetry.

COLERIDGE, SAMUEL TAYLOR (1772–1834) Coleridge brought to English literary criticism a philosophical bent influenced by the work of German thinkers and writers such as Kant, Fichte, and Schlegel. At the heart of the *Biographia Literaria* (1817), his most important critical work, is the role he attributes to the Imagination. Its unifying power is what he takes to be the basis of human creativity, seen at its peak in the work of the poet.

SHELLEY, PERCY BYSSHE (1792–1822) Shelley's *Defence of Poetry*, written in 1821 but not published until 1840, is the supreme expression of a Romantic ideal of the poet's role. Writing in response to his friend Thomas Love Peacock's *The Four Ages of Poetry* (1820), which argued that poetry's day as a social force was over, Shelley mounts a passionate defense of literature as the *"very image of life expressed in its eternal truth."* Poetry is seen as a powerful force for social good, and poets as *"the unacknowledged legislators of the world."*

ARNOLD, MATTHEW (1822–88) A poet who was also an inspector of schools, Arnold was keenly aware of the social and cultural context from which literature emerged. His main collections of criticism, *Essays in Criticism* (1865 and 1888), *Culture and Anarchy* (1869), and *Literature and Dogma* (1873) share an emphasis on wider cultural issues that has made him the starting point for many strands of later work in literary and cultural studies. It was his contention that the dominant cultural force of Hebraism, which stressed the moral at the expense of the aesthetic, needed to be balanced by Hellenism's celebration of art, beauty, and intellect – what he called "sweetness and light." One of Arnold's most famous pronouncements was his characterization of the British upper classes as Barbarians, and the money-obsessed middle classes as Philistines (see p. 245). In a world where beliefs were collapsing, he argued that literature would increasingly take on the guiding and consolatory functions of religion.

From Matthew Arnold, *Culture and Anarchy* (1882), Chapter 1, "Sweetness and Light"

But the point of view of culture . . . is best given by these words of Epictetus: – "It is a sign of αφυια," says he, – that is, of a nature not finely tempered, – "to give yourselves up to things which relate to the body; to make, for instance, a great fuss about exercise, a great fuss about eating, a great fuss about drinking, a great fuss about walking, a great fuss about riding. All these things ought to be done merely by the way: the formation of the spirit and character must be our real concern." This is admirable; and, indeed, the Greek word ευφυια, a finely tempered nature, gives exactly the notion of perfection as culture brings us to conceive it: a harmonious perfection, a perfection in which the characters of beauty and intelligence are both present, which unites "the two noblest of things," – as Swift, who of one of the two, at any rate, had himself all too little, most happily calls them in his *Battle of the Books*, – "the two noblest of things, sweetness and light." The ευφυης is the man who tends towards sweetness and light; the αφυης, on the other hand, is our Philistine. The immense spiritual significance of the Greeks is due to their having been inspired with this central and happy idea of the essential character of human perfection.

This section picks out some of the errors that recur most often in vocabulary, spelling, and punctuation. There are, in addition, a few generally accepted academic conventions that you need to be aware of. If the more tendentious advice about essay writing and exams is unwelcome, it's easy to ignore.

Forced to justify their existence, university departments make ever-more extravagant claims for the learning outcomes, transferable skills, and magic powers associated with studying literature. Employers of English graduates know well enough that this is a political game. They nonetheless keep alive the hope of finding applicants who can write a coherent sentence. In most contexts, what matters more than anything else is clarity. With this in mind, you could do worse than pin above your computer the six rules formulated by George Orwell in his essay "Politics and the English Language":

1 **Never use a metaphor, simile, or other figure of speech which you are used to seeing in print.**
2 **Never use a long word where a short one will do.**
3 **If it is possible to cut a word out, always cut it out.**
4 **Never use the passive where you can use the active.**
5 **Never use a foreign phrase, a scientific word, or a jargon word if you can think of an everyday English equivalent.**
6 **Break any of these rules sooner than say anything outright barbarous.**

A SURVIVOR'S GUIDE TO PUNCTUATION

The quotations in this section are from Max Beerbohm, Conan Doyle, Dickens (Mrs. Gamp in *Martin Chuzzlewit*), and Sydney Smith.

APOSTROPHE Don't neglect apostrophes. They do a valuable job, whether by indicating an omitted letter (*What's in a name?*) or identifying possessives. Their absence is likely to be taken as a sign of indifference or illiteracy, neither of which will endear you to your reader. In the case of words ending in "s," be guided by educated habits of speech. If you'd say *St. James's Park*, then that's probably how you should write it. If you'd say *Procrustes' bed*, the same holds true. It's not infallible, but it won't lead you into any particularly outrageous errors. Note that possessive pronouns do **not** have an apostrophe. *The book is yours, hers, ours, theirs. Its price is on the cover.*

260

COLON Introduces an explanation or elaboration of what immediately precedes it. *"Mankind is divisible into two great classes: hosts and guests."* Don't put a dash after the colon, and don't staple a colon into the middle of a sentence that would get on well enough without it. *The Seven Deadly Sins are:* ... A colon here is unnecessary.

COMMA (1) Again, rely on the rhythms of educated speech. This works reasonably well, but only if you take the trouble to read your sentences through carefully, thinking about them as you go. Read them aloud, if possible.

(2) Be alert to the difference between a clause that defines what has gone before, and one that comments on it. Consider these two sentences, and take your pick: *Politicians who lie should be mistrusted.* OR, *Politicians, who lie, should be mistrusted.*

(3) Make sure you don't overload your commas. If the rhythm of the sentence demands more than a light pause, you'll need something stronger – a semicolon or a full stop. A comma should not be used to separate what are really distinct sentences.

DASH A delightful punctuation mark that often gets a bad press – probably because it makes life too easy. It charms by its versatility and should be used with discretion.

EXCLAMATION MARK *"Mr. Holmes, they were the footprints of a gigantic hound!"* Unless you have something similarly sensational to say, the exclamation mark is best avoided. (A direct admonition to your tutor – *"No, Betsey! Drink fair wotever you do!"* – might be an exception, but the case is unlikely to arise in an academic essay.)

FULL STOP The most reliable aid to clarity. When in doubt, put a full stop and begin a new sentence.

HYPHEN If you're unsure whether a compound word needs a hyphen, look in a dictionary. Centuries require a hyphen when used adjectivally, not otherwise: *nineteenth-century novelists,* but *novelists writing in the nineteenth century.*

QUESTION MARK Indirect questions are not followed by a question mark. *She asked what I wanted.* But, *She said, What do you want?* A question mark is normally followed by a capital letter.

SEMICOLON (1) It functions as a heavier stop than the comma to mark the pause between two statements that are sufficiently connected not to require separate sentences. "*I have no relish for the country; it is a kind of healthy grave.*"

(2) It can also be useful in listing a series of items that might become confused if separated only by commas. See, for example, the entry in Part 3 on the Royal Society (p. 197).

A SURVIVOR'S GUIDE TO GRAMMATICAL TERMS

The quotations in this section are from Swift, Dickens, Shakespeare (Sir Andrew Aguecheek in *Twelfth Night* and Cleopatra in *Antony and Cleopatra*), and Bacon.

The terminology used by grammarians has grown increasingly complex, but it's well to know what is meant by the standard terms for parts of speech:

Adjective: A word that qualifies a noun or pronoun by adding a descriptive element.

Adverb: A word that modifies another word (not a noun) or group of words to give supplementary information. Since most adverbs end -*ly*, they are fairly easy to recognize. (In the previous sentence, the adverb *fairly* is used to modify the adjective *easy*.)

Article: The **definite article** is *the*; the **indefinite article** is *a* or *an*.

Conjunction: A word that connects phrases, sentences, or other words. *And, but, or* are common conjunctions, called **coordinating conjunctions** because they join main clauses. Words like *although, if, when, because* are called **subordinating conjunctions** because they join a subordinate clause (see below) to a main clause. Note that the **main clause** is the part of a complex sentence that contains the main verb and can stand on its own; the **subordinate clause** supplements what is in the main clause and cannot stand on its own. "*Satire is a sort of glass* [main clause], *wherein beholders do generally discover everybody's face but their own* [subordinate clause]."

Noun: A word used to name or identify. **Proper nouns** name specific places, people, etc. (*Venice, Mozart*) and should be written with an initial capital letter; the rest are referred to either as **common nouns** or, if they name a group (e.g., *flock, swarm*), **collective nouns**.

Preposition: A word expressing a spatial or temporal relation to the word it governs. Words like *to, on, under, into, above, behind, between, before, after* are, or can be, prepositions. (Don't worry too much about the sort of unhelpful rules that tell you never to start a sentence with a conjunction, never to end one with a preposition, never to split an infinitive. Use your sense. Sometimes it will sound too casual to end a sentence with a preposition, sometimes not. Sometimes it will sound clumsy to split an infinitive; sometimes it will sound even clumsier not to.)

Pronoun: A word that stands in for a noun or noun phrase. **Personal pronouns**: I, me; you; he, him, etc. **Reflexive pronouns**: myself, yourself, himself, etc. **Possessive pronouns**: my, mine; your, yours; her, hers, etc. **Demonstrative pronouns**: this, that; these, those. **Indefinite pronouns**: all, any, either, everyone, no one, etc. **Relative pronouns**: that, which, who, whom, whose. **Interrogative pronouns**: what, which, who, whom, whose.

Verb: A word that expresses some form of action or mode of existence. Verbs are **active** when the subject does the action (*"I positively adore Miss Dombey"*); they are **passive** when the action is done to the subject (*"I was adored once, too"*).

The **mood** of a verb is either **indicative** (normal statements or enquiries), **subjunctive** (where what is expressed is hypothetical or conditional), or **imperative** (commands): "*If it be love indeed* [subjunctive], *tell me how much* [imperative]." The vast majority of verbs in both speech and writing are in the indicative.

A **transitive verb** is one that takes a direct object; an **intransitive verb** is one that doesn't. Many verbs can of course be used transitively or intransitively: "*Men fear* [transitive] *death, as children fear* [intransitive] *to go in the dark.*"

A **finite verb** is one used with a subject; a **non-finite verb**, such as an infinitive or a participle, is one used without a subject. In the example above, from Bacon's essay "Of Death," *fear* is finite, *to go* is non-finite.

An **auxiliary verb** is one that is used with another verb to express tense (past/present/future), voice (active/passive), or mood (indicative/subjunctive) (*be, have, may, might, will, shall, would, should, must, can, could*).

Computer spell-checks have made spelling less of a problem than it used to be, but they're not an infallible guide and they don't help with handwritten exams. I've included in the list below some of the spelling errors that recur most often.

accommodation: Note spelling: 2 Cs, 2 Ms.

affect, effect: *Affect* is normally a verb, *effect* a noun. (In other words, if you can put *an* or *the* in front of the word, it should probably be *effect*.) Alcohol can *affect* one's balance; it can also have an *effect* on one's speech. When used as a verb, *effect* means "bring about": *his campaign effected a change in the law*.

amend: Note spelling: only one *m*. It means "to make a small change or revision." The term *emend* refers specifically to making textual corrections and is used mainly in scholarly contexts.

beg the question: Best avoided. If you use it in the sense of "invite the question", it will grate on the nerves of educated readers. If you use it in its original sense, to refer to a circular argument that is premised on the truth of its own conclusion, you are quite likely to be misunderstood. You run a similar risk if you use the phrase in its more recent sense of "to evade the question."

behalf: Note the difference between *on behalf of* and *on the part of*. The following sentence is wrong: *If there has been any delinquency on his behalf, he should be brought before a court*. What the writer means is *on his part*; delinquency on his behalf would have been an act by someone else for his benefit.

born, borne: To be *born* is to be given birth to; to be *borne* is to be carried. You are *born* into the world but *borne* to your grave.

cannon, canon: A *cannon* is a large gun, or a shot in billiards, snooker, etc.; *canon* refers most commonly to a clergyman, or to a list of books or authors that enjoy authoritative status (see p. 237).

classic, classical: *Classical* refers to the civilization of ancient Greece and Rome (e.g., *classical drama*), or to serious, as opposed to popular, music. *Classic* refers either to something recognized as enduringly good (e.g., *a classic production of* King Lear) or to something notably typical (e.g., *a classic case of government incompetence*).

complement, compliment: To *complement* is to complete something or enhance it. To *compliment* is to express praise or admiration.

correspondence: Note the spelling: *-ence*.

commitment: Note the spelling: only one *t* in the middle.

comprise: Frequently misused, and probably best avoided. If you can substitute *consist of*, you're probably OK – e.g., *the property comprises* [i.e., consists of] *a house and two outbuildings* – but in that case, why not use the more familiar phrase? *Comprise of* is always wrong.

council, counsel: Note the difference. A *council* is an administrative body, *counsel* is advice. *Counsel* can also be used as a verb, meaning "to give advice."

criteria: This is a plural noun; you cannot have *a criteria*. The singular form is *criterion*. The same goes for **phenomenon/phenomena**.

dependant, dependent: *Dependant* is the noun – your *dependants* are those who are *dependent* on you. (Note that **independent** is always so spelt.)

devil's advocate: This is not someone who speaks in favor of an evil person or cause. It is someone who puts the contrary side of an argument in order to test its validity. Originally, the devil's advocate was the person charged with making the case against a candidate for sainthood.

disinterested: The difference between *disinterested* (= impartial) and *uninterested* (= indifferent to) is worth preserving.

e.g.: From the Latin *exempli gratia*, it means "for example." Avoid confusing it with **i.e.** (Latin *id est* = that is). *i.e.* introduces some sort of definition or alernative formulation of what has gone before; *e.g.* introduces an example of what has gone before. If you can substitute *for example*, you should be using *e.g.* If you can substitute *that is to say*, you should be using *i.e.*

embarrass: Note the spelling: 2 Rs, 2 Ss.

equally as: Avoid. In the sentence, *He is 6 foot, and his brother is equally as tall*, either the *as* or the *equally* is redundant and should be omitted.

flaunt, flout: To *flaunt* something is to make an ostentatious display of it. Avoid confusing this with *flout*, which is normally used of rules or conventions. To *flout* them is to show contemptuous disregard for them.

forty: Note the spelling: no *u* – don't be misled by *four* and *fourteen*.

Frankenstein: Not the name of the monster but of the man who created him.

grievous: Note the spelling: **not** *grievious*. The same should be noted of **mischievous**.

historic, historical: A *historical* event is something that happened in the past, i.e., that is part of history. To be *historic*, the event must have particular significance.

ingenious, ingenuous: *Ingenuous* means "open, innocent, frank" and should not be confused with *ingenious*.

its, it's: In spite of the apostrophe's natural association with possessives, *it's* = it is. The possessive is *its*. This is worth getting right, if only because so many people get it wrong.

-ise, -ize: In many cases the spelling is a matter of choice, though Americans tend to favor *-ize* and the British *-ise*. The main thing is to be consistent. Since a number of words (for example, *advertise, advise, arise, compromise, despise, exercise, revise, supervise, surprise, televise*) have to be spelt *-ise*, this is probably the safer option.

judicial, judicious: *Judicial* relates to the work of judges, as in "a judicial enquiry"; *judicious* means sound in judgment. A *judicial* decision would be one made by a judge or court of law; a *judicious* decision would be one that was wise and well considered.

luxuriant, luxurious: *Luxuriant* means "abundant, lush," as in "luxuriant vegetation"; *luxurious* has to do with the trappings of wealth and comfort, and relates to the common meaning of luxury.

militate, mitigate: *Militate* comes from the same root as military and is normally used in the phrase *militate against*, meaning to "tell against" or "weigh against" something (*His grinding poverty militates against his chances of happiness*). *Mitigate* means to moderate, temper, lessen the severity of something (*The occasional day of sunshine mitigates the gloom of the English winter*).

minuscule: Note the middle U – **not** *miniscule*.

media: This is a plural noun and should be followed by a plural form of the verb – *the media have . . ., the media are . . .* etc.

parallel, paralleled: Note the spelling: one R, two Ls in the middle, no doubling of the final L in the past tense.

passed, past: We *passed* the winning post at a run; we ran *past* the winning post. We *passed* the time; we talked of *past* times.

practice, practise: In general, the British use "c" for the noun and "s" for the verb, the Americans use "c" for both.

precipitate, precipitous: *Precipitate* (adj.) means over-hasty, headlong; *precipitous* means steep, having the characteristics of a precipice. The two are often confused, even by otherwise competent writers.

prescribe, proscribe: *Prescribe* is what doctors do; *proscribe* means to outlaw or prohibit.

principal, principle: The *principal* is the chief person or thing; a *principle* is a general truth, a moral standard, or a basis on which something operates.

quotation, quote: *Quote* is a verb. If you want to avoid raising any hackles, you should refer to what is quoted as a *quotation* not as a *quote*.

refute: To rebut something by proving it to be false. Avoid *refute* when all you mean is *deny* or *repudiate*. Politicians use it to give spurious authority to their denials.

seize, siege: Note the spellings. The rule that *i* goes before *e* except after *c* is out of favor now, but if you bear in mind that it applies to words pronounced *-ee-* (*believe, receive*, etc.) rather than *-ay-* (*rein, neighbor, beige*, etc.), it's still likely to prevent more mistakes than it causes. *Seize* is one of the exceptions.

separate: Note the spelling: two Es sep**ara**ted by two As.

substitute: To put one thing (or person) in the place of another. If A is substituted for B, then it's B that is taken away.

supersede: Note the spelling: **not** supercede.

their, there, they're: *Their* is the possessive, *there* = in that place, *they're* = they are.

tortuous, torturous: Avoid confusing the two. The word you want is almost certainly *tortuous*, meaning "twisty, circuitous." *Torturous* is a little-used adjective from torture.

transpire: If used at all, it should be used to mean "come to light, become apparent." The sense of "happen, occur" has been on the sidelines for a couple of centuries but is not generally accepted.

unique: Avoid using this with words (*fairly, very, rather, more*, etc.) that contradict its basic meaning. There cannot logically be degrees of uniqueness.

venal, venial: *Venal* means open to bribery and corruption; *venial* – generally used of sins – means pardonable.

People handing out good advice tend to proffer rather more of it than one actually wants, so here are just ten points that might be worth bearing in mind:

1 **Make an argument that interests you**. If essay-writing is just a task to keep your teachers happy, the result will bore them as much as it does you. Literature takes in pretty well every aspect of human life. If you've got even a passing interest in sex, death, politics, or crossword puzzles, you should be able to find something that sparks a line of thought, whether you're looking at a medieval lyric or an eighteenth-century novel. It helps if you have an argument to make. Find something you want to say, and then set out to persuade people it's true. Tone, structure, choice of words, presentation of evidence will all need to play their part. You already know how to do it. Most of us start learning the devious skills of argument as soon as we can speak – how else to prove to the world that we're right? Consider opposing evidence, modify your argument if necessary, close any loopholes. It's a dynamic process that should have its own momentum, like a case in a court of law. Unless the argument moves on from stage to stage, overcoming obstacles along the way, it will be lifeless and repetitive, so think carefully about how you structure it. (If you run into an objection that's strong enough, you might have to rethink your argument altogether, in which case you could perhaps restructure it in terms of thesis-antithesis-synthesis.) This is only one kind of essay, but a useful one.

2 **Avoid surveys**. There are interesting things to be said about mirrors in nineteenth-century fiction, but if you start with the title "Mirrors in the Victorian novel" you probably won't say them. You're much more likely to slide towards a series of banal and directionless comments on a dozen different books. Work on the novels, see if your comments add up to anything you want to say (and that anyone else might want to read), then start thinking about your title. Once you've got it, you can use it to keep both yourself and the reader in mind of where the essay is going.

3 **Organize your material before starting to write**. It can be helpful to jot down in a haphazard way as many points as you can think of about the topic – whatever ideas, perceptions, textual insights occur to you. You

can then shuffle them around, looking for connections, contradictions, threads of argument. It is out of this process that the shape of what you want to say emerges. When you come to put it all together, some points will inevitably have to be left out – they'll be part of a different argument, a different essay. Let them go.

4   **Avoid plagiarism**. Work for the essay will probably involve reading not just primary texts but also background and critical material. Unconscious plagiarism comes about quite easily from the sort of slipshod preliminary work we all do from time to time. Keep notes on what you read, and references for the notes you take. Conscious plagiarism is a different matter. If it really seems like a good idea to copy other people's writing and pass it off as your own, you'd almost certainly be happier in another subject, probably in another walk of life altogether.

5   **Don't rehash every twist in the plot**. For the most part your treatment of texts should be analytical rather than descriptive. Nothing identifies a mediocre student more quickly than a tedious enthusiasm for synopsising plots. Of course, you'll need to refer to specific passages in order to anchor your argument in the text, and you'll need quotations to provide textual evidence. But make use of what you quote. There's no virtue in clogging your essay with inert slabs of quotation when the point could have been made just as forcefully with a couple of lines or even a couple of words.

6   **Get things right** – names, dates, spellings, meanings, quotations, references. If you're unsure about anything, look it up. Errors are inevitable but they should at least be a source of shame.

7   **Use literary criticism skeptically**. Don't spend too much time doffing your cap to other critics – *As X has rightly said . . ., As Y perceptively remarks* . . . Apart from sounding creepy, you risk edging yourself out of your own essay. Better to take a critical position you disagree with and then use it as a springboard for making the contrary argument.

8   **Don't let yourself be paralyzed by the prospect of writing**. It can be as big a mistake to delay too long as to start too soon. Once you've gathered your material and worked out the structure of your argument, start writing, even if the result seems embarrassingly bad. The first draft is for your eyes only, so save your perfectionism for later. In general, it's easier to rewrite than to write.

9 **Know the basic conventions for presenting your work**. For detailed guidelines on presenting academic work, you should refer to one of the standard handbooks such as the *MLA Style Manual and Guide to Scholarly Publishing*. The conventions can look complicated when they're written down in the form of a series of instructions, but the essentials are easy enough to learn. It helps if you take note of how things are set out in the books of literary criticism you read. There are one or two basic points to keep in mind:

(a) **Layout**. Best to double-space your work and use a 12-point font size. Leave serviceable margins, particularly on the left.

(b) **Titles**. Use italics for the titles of books, journals, and longer poems; use inverted commas for shorter poems, short stories, and components of longer works (articles, chapters, etc.). If your work is handwritten, underline rather than trying to use italics. The Bible is one title that is not italicized, and books of the Bible are not given inverted commas.

(c) **Quotations**. Make sure they fit grammatically into your sentence. If you're quoting more than three or four lines of prose, the quotation should be separated from your text, left-indented and not enclosed by quotation marks. Line endings in poetry should be marked by / ("*Me only cruel immortality / Consumes: . . .*") unless you're quoting more than a couple of lines, in which case they should be set out separately, as they appear in the text you're quoting from. Use square brackets to enclose any material that is not part of the quotation (e.g., the name of a character).

(d) **References and bibliography**. Practice varies in small ways, but the principle remains the same: you're providing an author and/or editor, a title, a place of publication, a publisher, a date of publication and, where necessary, a page number. A footnote or endnote could be presented as follows: **Paul Fussell, *Abroad: British Literary Traveling Between the Wars* (New York: Oxford University Press, 1980), 49–50**. If the name had already been given in the text, it would be unnecessary to repeat it in the note. A later reference to the same book could be noted simply as **Fussell, 63** or, if other works by Fussell have been quoted, **Fussell, *Abroad* 63**. For a bibliography, the entry would be as follows: **Fussell, Paul. *Abroad: British Literary Traveling Between the Wars*. New York: Oxford University Press, 1980**. This is the basic format. Details of how to deal with the possible ramifications – books with two, three, or more authors, books with no identified author, books in translation, books with one or more editors, etc. – can be found in the *MLA Style Manual*. In the case of articles, a footnote or endnote could be presented as follows: **Mark Schorer, "Pride Unprejudiced," *Kenyon Review* 18 (1956): 83**. For a bibliography, the entry would be as follows: **Schorer, Mark. "Pride Unprejudiced." *Kenyon Review* 18 (1956): 72–91**.

10 **Read through what you've written.** Look for error, awkwardness, obscurity, and unintentional ambiguity. You're trying to find things that are wrong with the essay, so cast yourself in the role of hostile critic: try to pick holes. What are the weaknesses in the argument? Are any of your assertions unsupported by evidence? Where are you waffling? Where are you being pretentious or boring? Where are you trotting out half-baked arguments from other people? Where have you let yourself settle for a cliché? If possible, get someone else to read it through and point out anything that jars or confuses. Finally, if you can bear to, read it aloud. This is the only way you can really pay attention to the sound of words and the rhythm of sentences.

There can be several reasons for writing an essay, but the only point of taking an exam is to get as high a mark as possible. I hope this will excuse any taint of cynicism in what follows. Normally it would seem foolish to repeat advice that's been given thousands of times before, but with heroic persistence people go on making exactly the same mistakes. So here again are five basic points:

1 **Read the rubrics**. This sounds obvious but in the heat of the moment it's easy to dive past them straight into the questions. If the paper tells you to answer one question from each Section, and you do two from A and none from C, it's probable that one of your answers will get 0. If you're asked for three answers, do not persuade yourself that it will be better to concentrate on doing two well and ignoring the third. It won't. However poor your third answer, make sure you do it. Even a dismal attempt will almost certainly get you another 30 or 40 marks – far more than you would have collected by improving your other two answers.

2 **Read the questions**. They'll probably look as though they've come from a parallel universe, but don't panic. Setting exams is largely a matter of thinking up new ways to ask old questions. If you take a breath and look again, the horrifying sense of unfamiliarity will begin to fade. Undo the packaging, and you'll almost certainly find that the questions are much the same as usual. But make sure: give yourself time to read them carefully and understand them.

3 **Study past papers**. For the reason above, this is probably the most effective form of preparation. Get a sense of how the questions are framed and try to work out what they're after. Think of it as an exercise in literary criticism, if you like. What you're looking for are themes, patterns, recurrent lines of enquiry. Not many of us can keep a whole field of knowledge in our heads, process it at a moment's notice, and spit out a 50-minute essay that isn't rubbish. By looking intelligently at past papers, you can give yourself a chance to do some provisional groundwork. When you go into the exam, you should have at least a rough sense of what you might write about and the material you might need. Don't take this too far, though. There may be room for maneuver – finding a favorable angle of entry into the question is one of the skills of taking exams – but in the end you have to answer the question that's been asked, not the one you think should have been asked.

4 **Get basic details into your head**. Is it Elizabeth Bennet or Bennett? George Eliot or Elliot? The heavens won't fall if you get this sort of thing wrong, but getting it right will improve your confidence and give new heart to your examiner. For obvious reasons, exam essays tend to be light on detail, and it's not difficult to make your answer stand out. Don't try to memorize acres of text, but do make sure you can refer accurately to specific passages in support of the arguments you want to make. Sometimes a couple of words are enough to give a pleasant illusion of familiarity with the text. Instead of talking about Marlow's (Marlowe's?) concern in *Heart of Darkness* with the details of everyday reality, you might, for example, refer to his focus on "the redeeming facts of life." Any drop of water is welcome in the desert, and examiners of unseen papers tend to be easily pleased.

5 **Keep a sense of perspective**. Exam hysteria has its enjoyable side, but don't let it get out of hand. There's a temptation to believe that one's whole future hangs in the balance at the exam-room door. It's unlikely. Exams matter, but not that much. The odds are that you'll end up with a 2:1 or a 2:2, that in retrospect you won't care which, and that whatever determines the quality of your future life will be quite different.

It seems a pity to end on exams. They're the one aspect of a literature degree that doesn't afford much scope for pleasure. The rest of it should be fun – that's its justification.

Index

Eglon   21

Egypt, Flight into   25

Egypt, Plagues of   24, 49

Ehud   21

El Alamein, battle of   231

Elaine   151

Eldorado   177

Eleanor of Aquitaine   122

Electra   83

elegy   250

Eli   21

Elijah   21–2, 42, 63

Eliot, T. S.   104

Elisha   22, 26, 42

elixir of life   164

Elizabeth (mother of John the Baptist)
   39, 64

Elizabeth I   164

Elysium (Elysian Fields)   83

Emmanuel   22

Emmaus   22

Empedocles   83

empiricism   186

enclosure   186

Encyclopédie   186

Endor, witch of   22

Endymion   83

enjambement   253

Enlightenment   186

Enoch   23

EOKA   219

Eos   106, 116

Ephesians, Epistle to the   23

Ephesus   74

epic   250

Epictetus   112

Epicurus   83

Epimetheus   101

Epiphany   23

epistolary novel   240

epithalamion   250

Erasmus, Desiderius   169

Erastianism   169

Erinyes   84

Eris   101

Eros   83, 106

Erymanthian Boar   88

Esau   10, 23

essay writing   268–71

Essex, Robert Devereux, 2nd earl of
   169

Esther   23–4

Et in Arcadia ego   72

Eteocles   71, 99

Ethelbert, King   151

Ethelred the Unready, King   155

Etna, Mount   83, 84

Eumenides   84

euphemism   240

Euphrates, river   24

Euripides   84, 100

Europa   84

European Economic Community   219

Euryalus   98

Eurydice   100

Eurystheus   88

Evangelicals   205, 212

Eve   24–5

evolution   205, 209

exams   272–3

Excalibur   150

existentialism   223

Exodus   7, 24, 26

Expressionism   224

Fabian Society   205–6

Fabius Maximus, Q. (Cunctator)   86,
   205–6

fabliau   250

Factory Acts   206

Fairfax, Thomas   169

Falklands War   224

Fall, the   24–5

fasces   84

Gog and Magog   27
Golden Age   69, 109
Golden Apples   74
Golden Bough   78, 110
Golden Calf   27
Golden Fleece   85
Golden Hind   168
Golgotha   16
Goliath   27
Gomorrah   49, 59
Goncourt, Edmond and Jules de   244
Good Friday Agreement   225
Gorbachev, Mikhail   222
Gordian Knot   85
Gordon riots   187
Gordon, Charles George   207
Gorgons   85
Goshen   36
Gothic novel   241
Gothic Revival architecture   214
Graces, the Three   85
grammar   262–3
Grand Remonstrance   173
Grand Tour   187
Great Exhibition   207
Great Game   208
Great War   230–1
Gregory XIII, Pope   151, 183
Grey Friars   156
Grey, Lady Jane   170
Griselda   153
Grub Street   188
Guelphs   155
Guercino   72
Guernica   228
Guimard, Hector   203
Guinevere   150
Gulf War   225
Gunpowder Plot   170
Gustavus Adolphus   171
Gutenberg, Johannes   138
Gyges   85–6

Hades   86, 100, 102, 110
Hadrian   71, 86
Haemon   71
Hagar   27, 29
Halcyone   70
Ham   44
hamadryads   82
Haman   24
hamartia   256
Hamilton, Emma   212
Hampton Court Conference   8
Hananiah   57
Hanging Gardens of Babylon   43
Hannibal   86, 109
Hanoverians   188
Hargreaves, James   189
Harpies   86
Harvey, William   171
Hastings, battle of   159
hearth tax   188
Hebe   86
Hebraism   258
Hecate   86
Hector   71, 86, 87
Hecuba   87
Hegel, Georg Wilhelm Friedrich   208,
   210
Helen of Troy   87, 94
Helicon, Mount   97, 102
Helios   87
Helle   85
Hellen   82
Hellenism   258
Hellespont   85, 89, 118
Hellfire club   200
helots   111–12
Hengist   157
Henry III, King   155
Henry Tudor *see* Henry VII
Henry V, King   158
Henry VII, King   161
Henry VIII, King   163, 168, 169, 179

Imagism   241

Immaculate Conception   40

impotent man, healing of the   15

Impressionism   208

in medias res   242

Incitatus   77

Indian Mutiny   208–9

Indulgences   173

Industrial Revolution   189

inkhorn terms   146, 242

Innocents, Murder of the   28

Inquisition   172

INRI   28

interior monologue   247

interlude   242

International Brigade   228

Interregnum   172

Io   73

Iole   81

Iona   158

Iphigenia   91–2, 100

IRA *see* Irish Republican Army

Iraq War   226

Iris   92

Irish Republican Army (IRA)   219

iron curtain   222

Ironsides   166

Isaac   7, 23, 28

Isaiah   29

Isandlwana   218

Ishbosheth   29

Ishmael   29

Isis   92

Ismene   99

Israel   7, 18, 52

Israel, Twelve Tribes of   7, 29, 52

Israelites   24, 48

Ithaca   99

Ixion   92

Jack the Ripper   209

Jacob   7, 23, 24, 29–30

Jacobean   242

Jacobins   209

Jacobite   189

Jael   30

Jairus   30

James I of England   163, 170, 174

James I of Scotland   158

James II of England   187, 189, 192

James, William   248

Jameson Raid   203

Janus   92

Japheth   44

Jarrow   158

Jarry, Alfred   236

Jason   92, 95

Jazz age   226

Jeffreys, Judge George   183

Jehoram (Joram)   7, 31

Jehoshaphat   30

Jehovah   64

Jehu   7, 31, 32

Jenkins' Ear, War of   189–91

Jenner, Edward   209

Jephthah   31, 57

Jeremiah   28, 31

Jericho   31, 51

Jeroboam   7, 31

Jerome, Saint   8

Jerusalem   8, 13, 32, 58

Jesse   32

Jesuits   167, 172

Jesus   15, 16, 22, 25–6, 30, 32, 34,
  40, 47–8, 58, 63

Jezebel   32, 42

Joab   10, 33

Joan of Arc   158

Job   33

Jocasta   99

John the Apostle (evangelist)   3, 17,
  33–4

John the Baptist   28, 34, 37, 53

John, King   122, 158

Pericles   74, 75, 102

Peripatetic (school of philosophy)   73

peripeteia   256

periphrasis   245

Perrault, Charles   194–5

Persepholis   70

Persephone   68, 89, 109

Perseus   71, 75, 81, 95, 103

Persians   75

Peter (apostle)   47–8, 60

Peterloo Massacre   212

Petrarch (Francesco Petrarca)   160

Petronius Arbiter, Gaius   110

Phaedra   103

Phaeton   103

Phalaris   103

Phaon   108

Pharaoh   48

Pharisee   48, 54

Pharsalus, battle of   77, 105

Phidias   75

Philby, Kim   221–2

Philemon   76

Philip (apostle)   58

Philip II of Macedon   70, 73, 81

Philippe le Bel   161

Philippi, battle of   72

Philistines   18, 19, 48, 53–4, 245

Phillip II of Spain   164

Philoctetes   99, 104

Philomela   104

philosopher's stone   163–4

philosophes   186

Phlegethon   104

Phoebus *see* Apollo

Phoenix   104

Phoenix Park murders   212

Phrixus   85

phylacteries   48

picaresque novel   246

Pierus, Mount   97

Pilate, Pontius   14, 28, 48–9

Pilgrim Fathers   176

Pilgrimage of Grace   176

pillory   160

Pindar   104

Pirithous   78, 88, 114

Pisgah   49

Piso's conspiracy   109

Pitman, Isaac   147

Pitt the elder, William   195

Pitt the younger, William   195

Plague, Great   188

Plagues of Egypt *see* Egypt

Plain, Cities of the   49

Plassey, battle of   185

Plato   85, 104, 111, 255

Plautus, Titus Maccius   105

Pleiades   105

plot   246

Plutarch   105

Pluto *see* Hades

Plymouth Brethren   193

pocket boroughs   196

poet laureate   246

Poitiers, battle of   158

police force   212

poll tax   160, 228

Pollux   73, 78, 94

Polynices   71, 83–4, 99

Polyphemus   84, 105

Pompey the Great (Gnaeus Pompeius)
   8, 39, 97, 105

Poor Laws   212–13

Pope, Alexander   77, 100, 187

Popish plot   195

Porteous riots   195

Poseidon   71, 74, 93, 97, 103, 105

postage   213

postimpressionism   228

postmodernism   246

Potiphar   35–6, 49

Potter's Field   49

Pound, Ezra   241

steam engine   140

Stentor   112

Stephen (martyr)   60

Stephenson, George   214

stocks   161

Stoics   112

Stopes, Marie   143

Strafford, Thomas Wentworth, 1st earl
    of   178

stream-of-consciousness   247

Stymphalian Birds   88

Styx   66, 78, 112

sublime, the   248

Suez canal   127, 228–9

Suez crisis   228–9

suffragettes   229

Sulla, Lucius Cornelius   108

Supremacy, Acts of   175, 178

Surrealism   229

Surrey, earl of see Howard, Henry, earl
    of Surrey

Susanna   60

Swift, Jonathan   146

Sybaris   112

Sycophants   113

symbol   248

Symplegades   73

symposium   113

synecdoche   243

Synod of Whitby see Whitby, synod of

synoptic gospels   6

Syrinx   113

tabernacle   60

Tabitha   60

Tabor, Mount   60

Tacitus, Gaius Cornelius   12, 113,
    240

Taine, Hippolyte   244

Taiping rebellion   207

Tamar   45, 61

Tantalus   98, 113

Tarpeian rock   113

Tarquin II   110

Tarquinius Collatinus   94

Tarquinius Superbus   93, 94, 113

Tarsus   61

Tartarus   86

Tauris   92

Telamon   69

Telemachus   113

Telephus   68

television   229

Telford, Thomas   210

Templars   161

Temple of Jerusalem   7, 12, 59,
    61

Temptations in the Wilderness   61

Ten Commandments   12, 19, 62

Tennyson, Alfred   99, 151

Terence (Publius Terentius Afer)
    113–14

Tereus   104

Terpsichore   97

Test Acts   198

tetrameter   253

tetrarch   62

Thackeray, W. M.   211

Thais   70

Thatcher, Margaret   129, 224, 228

Thea see Ge

Thebes   76, 83–4, 99

Themistocles   114

Theocritus   114, 251

Theophilus   62

Thermopylae   114

Thersites   114

Theseus   73, 88, 103, 106, 114–15

Thespis   115

Thetis   115

Thirty-Eighth Parallel   226

Thirty-Nine Articles   178

Thirty Years War   178

Thisbe   107

INDEX

villeins 162

Villiers, George, 1st duke of Buckingham 178–9

Virgil (Publius Vergilius Maro) 68–9, 118

Virgin Birth 64

Visigoths 108

Visitation 64

Vitruvius 175

Voltaire (François-Marie Arouet) 197, 199–200

Vorticism 230

Vulcan *see* Hephaestus

Vulgate 8

Wall Street stock market crash 223

Walpole, Robert 191, 200

Walsingham, Sir Francis 179

Wandering Jew 162

War on Terror 230

Warbeck, Perkin 161

Warsaw Pact 230

water into wine, miracle of the 16

Waterloo, battle of 207

Watling Street 162

Watt, James 189, 200

Webster, Noah 147

Wedgwood, Josiah 200

Wellington, Arthur Wellesley, 1st duke of 207

weltanschauung 248

weltschmerz 248

Wesley, Charles 193

Wesley, John 193

Whig Interpretation of History 209–10

Whigs 200

Whitby, synod of 152

White Friars 156

Whitefield, George 193

Whitsun *see* Pentecost

Wilberforce, Bishop Samuel 205

Wilberforce, William 218

Wilkes, John 200

William I (the Conqueror), King 156, 157, 159

William (III) of Orange, King 187

Window Tax 200–1

Winstanley, Gerard 168

Wittgenstein, Ludwig 230

Wolfe, James 201

Wollstonecraft, Mary 218

Wolsey, Cardinal Thomas 168, 178, 179

Worcester, battle of 166

Wordsworth, William 258

World War I 230–1

World War II 231

Wren, Christopher 197

writing on the wall 15

Wyatt, Sir Thomas 251

Wycliffe, John 8, 158, 162

Xanthippe 111

Xenophon 118

Xerxes I 10, 23, 64, 118

Yahweh 64

Yeats, W. B. 94

yeoman 162

Yorktown, surrender at 181

Young, Brigham 217

Young England Group 295

Young Pretender (Bonnie Prince Charlie) 185, 195–6

Zacchaeus 64

Zadok 64

Zama, battle of 86

Zealots 64

Zebedee 12

Zedekiah 64

zeitgeist 248

Zeno of Citium 112

Zenobia 118

Zephyrus 91

Zeus 8, 70, 73, 74, 76, 77, 79, 81,
     92, 94, 95, 103, 109, 115, 118

Zeuxis 119

ziggurat 64

Zimri 32

Zipporah 42, 64

Zola, Emile 244

Zulu War 218

Zutphen, battle of 256